A Clash of Color

The marginalization of Black Americans due to White supremacy and the oppression of Indians under British colonialism featured inescapable similarities. At the turn of the twentieth century, these parallels led Indian and Black nationalists, intellectuals, and activists to share their experiences and engage in dialogues toward improving the social status of their people. Specifically, Black internationalists such as W. E. B. Du Bois, Walter White, and Paul Robeson studied the Indian independence movement, and came to regard India as a template in the fight against White supremacy in the United States. Similarly, various Indians including Rabindranath Tagore, Lala Lajpat Rai, B. R. Ambedkar, and Taraknath Das theorized crucial parallels between race, colonialism, and caste when studying the experiences of Black Americans. This book analyzes how they came together in their desire to overthrow the structures that subjugated them.

Avinash Hingorani is an Indian American transnational historian and Assistant Professor of History at Newberry College, Newberry, South Carolina. He is also currently a postdoctoral fellow at the Center for African American Urban Studies and the Economy at Carnegie Mellon University, Pittsburgh.

GLOBAL SOUTH ASIANS

Throughout the modern era, South Asia and South Asians have been entangled with global flows of goods, people and ideas. In the context of these globalised conditions, migrants from the subcontinent of India created some of the world's most extensive and influential transnational networks. While operating within the constraints of imperial systems, they nevertheless made distinctive and important contributions to international trade, global cultures and transnational circuits of knowledge. This series seeks to explore these phenomena, placing labourers, traders, thinkers and activists at the centre of the analysis. Beginning with volumes that seek to radically reappraise indenture, the series will continue with books on the mobility of elite actors, including intellectuals, and their contributions to the global circulation of ideas and the evolution of political practice. It will highlight the creativity and agency of diasporic South Asians and illuminate the crucial role they played in the making of global histories. As such it sets out to challenge popular misconceptions and established scholarly narratives that too often cast South Asians as passive observers.

A Clash of Color

Dialogues on Race, Caste, and Solidarity in the United States and India

(1900–1954)

Avinash Hingorani

CAMBRIDGE
UNIVERSITY PRESS

Shaftesbury Road, Cambridge CB2 8EA, United Kingdom

One Liberty Plaza, 20th Floor, New York, NY 10006, USA

477 Williamstown Road, Port Melbourne, VIC 3207, Australia

314–321, 3rd Floor, Plot 3, Splendor Forum, Jasola District Centre, New Delhi – 110025, India

103 Penang Road, #05–06/07, Visioncrest Commercial, Singapore 238467

Cambridge University Press is part of Cambridge University Press & Assessment, a department of the University of Cambridge.

We share the University's mission to contribute to society through the pursuit of education, learning and research at the highest international levels of excellence.

www.cambridge.org
Information on this title: www.cambridge.org/9781009526784

First published 2024

Printed in India by Avantika Printers Pvt. Ltd.

A catalogue record for this publication is available from the British Library

ISBN 978-1-009-52678-4 Hardback

As Dalit activists and intellectuals have pointed out, the history of making connections between our two communities stretches back to the 19th century when most U.S. black people were enslaved. We deeply appreciate the solidarity that has been generated on so many occasions by Dalit activists. However, we must also be critical, self-critical, of our own failure to produce meaningful and transformative solidarity with Dalit people. Most recently, Dalit feminists have on several occasions made passionate calls for solidarity, especially with their efforts to resist the interminable assaults, particularly assaults involving sexual violence, against Dalit women. And so, we salute those who are standing up to resist casteism, patriarchy, and capitalism. As we here in the United States attempt to move forward in our struggles against structural racism, and state and vigilante violence, we thank you for your solidarity and recognize that it is our responsibility to join you. We need to express our rage against racial, sexual and caste-based violence in India, and we need to demand justice for the victims, the survivors, and their families. This is a time when the world is beginning to rise together to demand justice for those who are targeted by white supremacists and casteists. Therefore, we stand with those who are issuing a global cry for an end to racism and who not only say black lives matter but also Dalit lives matter and Muslim lives matter.

—Angela Davis[*]

* International Dalit Solidarity Network, 2020, https://idsn.org/angela-davis-speaks-up-about-dalitlivesmatter/, accessed May 8, 2024.

Contents

Acknowledgments

The writing of this book has been a long journey. It has taken me on many exciting adventures. I would like to take this opportunity to thank family and colleagues for support.

I would particularly like to thank my Ph.D. supervisors, Christopher Harding and Mark Newman, for their guidance and their useful constructive criticism. Additionally, I would like to thank Crispin Bates and David Silkenat for their recommendations at my annual reviews. Lastly, I would like to credit my M.A. thesis advisor, Darryl Barthé, for encouraging me to pursue a Ph.D. on this topic.

I am also grateful to many archivists at Vanderbilt University, Nashville, Swarthmore College, the New York Public Library, the National Library of Scotland, Edinburgh, and the Nehru Memorial Library, New Delhi. Additionally, I would like to thank my parents for supporting my decision to pursue a career as a historian.

Finally, I would like to thank Talat Ahmed, Andrew Jolivétte, and Nico Slate for offering constructive feedback. I value their expertise tremendously.

Prologue

I have chosen to connect the unique histories of both India and the United States (US) for a multitude of reasons. My grandfather, Lakhan H. Massand, was an activist and a freedom fighter during British rule in India. He had an idealistic vision of a free and secular India where there was no oppression, and everyone was equal. To achieve this lofty goal, he was willing to make supreme sacrifices and even withstand the tortures of imprisonment. In fact, when India finally achieved independence in 1947, my grandfather was in jail and was released only in 1948. Unfortunately, my research and visits to India have impressed upon me that my grandfather's vision for an egalitarian Indian society never truly came to fruition. I noticed that many low-caste Indians in Rajasthan, Punjab, Haryana, and New Delhi lived in dilapidated homes in a hyper-segregated region with a history of especially pernicious race and caste prejudice. Likewise, while I studied at Tulane University, I came to understand that a similar form of class and social stratification existed in New Orleans, which consistently disadvantaged local Black Americans. This situation became clearest to me when a fellow academic and friend was racially profiled by the New Orleans Police Department. When he was eighteen, he was picked up at random, physically assaulted by the police, and driven to meet a White woman who had been mugged near Tulane and Loyola University. The police tried to get her to name my friend as the perpetrator. The woman refused and insisted that the man who mugged her was someone else. Yet the police persevered with the false charges until he revealed that one of his relatives was the Deputy Superintendent of Police in New Orleans.

Inspired by my friend's story, and countless others who have experienced discrimination based on their racial background, I have chosen to write a book which further disseminates the realities of the lived experiences of low-caste Indians and Black Americans. Defenders of the American Dream preach that one of the core American values is equality for all, regardless of age, color, disability, gender, national origin, race, religion, creed, sexual orientation, or social status.

However, my research has served to emphasize that this optimistic ideology has not always been readily applied in American society. It is my ambition that my work should contribute toward the social advancement of both racial minorities in the US and low-caste Indians in India.

In the twenty-first century, some Dalit (low-caste Indians) and Black intellectuals have called for increased solidarity between their two groups. Among these voices are Black feminist activist Angela Davis and Dalit activist Ruth Manorama, who is the President of the National Federation of Dalit Women in India. In October 2020, Davis filmed a video statement for India Civil Watch International, a membership-based civil rights monitoring and campaign group based out of North America in which she decried the structural violence against and marginalization of Black Americans and Indian Dalits in their respective societies. Davis's statement was a response to two crucial historical events that had occurred earlier in the year: the murder of George Floyd by a White police officer in Minneapolis and the brutal gang rape and murder of a nineteen-year-old Dalit woman by four upper-caste men in Hathras, India. Both tragedies galvanized tens of thousands of protestors across the world to rise up against the vicious injustices perpetrated against Black Americans and Indian Dalits. Protesters used the phrases "Black Lives Matter" and "Dalit Lives Matter" to highlight the fact that the lives of these two groups have too often been devalued and ignored. Although these unifying slogans shared by Black American and Dalit struggles have only recently appeared, there is a long history of interaction between Black Americans and marginalized Indians. As Davis accurately noted in her statement, "the history of making connections between our two communities stretches back to the nineteenth century when most US Black people were enslaved."

Caste is a form of social differentiation widely understood as being based upon hereditary customs and habits. It enforces a fixed lifestyle which commonly includes an individual's occupation, status in a hierarchy, and customary social interactions and exclusions. Caste in India is perpetuated by societal pressures, employment practices, state policies, and – most importantly – endogamous marriage practices. Essentially, caste allocates or withholds privileges based upon birth.[1] In the classic structuralist interpretation of the French sociologist Louis Dumont, caste hierarchy was determined by a religious ideology of purity and pollution. This religious ideology was legitimized by higher-caste informants through references to ancient Sanskrit texts, most importantly the *Manusmriti*, an ancient Hindu legal code.[2] Contemporary sociologists have tended to regard caste as political, as well as a changeable social and economic form of hierarchy, sustained by diverse local customs, practices, and beliefs.[3] Historians have equally argued that castes are similar to tribes in India, which perform important political functions that have changed over time in response to exogenous political, economic, or environmental pressure.[4] Whatever interpretation is offered for its origins and development, caste is unequivocally the foundational element of a powerful, non-voluntarist, and hierarchal social system that has suppressed social mobility right across the Indian subcontinent, influencing social hierarchies even in non-Hindu neighboring societies.

Just as activists like Angela Davis have attempted to connect the struggles of Black Americans and Indian Dalits, linking together White supremacy and caste discrimination, others have made far bolder connections between race in the US and caste in India even to the point of describing White supremacy in the US as a "caste system." These conversations have been ignited in both academic and popular culture discourse by Isabel Wilkerson's controversial book, *Caste: The Origins of Our Discontents*. In her book, Wilkerson argues that "caste" in the US was a historical racial hierarchy that persists to the contemporary age.[5] Wilkerson's book has been praised by popular culture figures such as Oprah Winfrey, Barack Obama, and Fatima Bhutto. Suraj Yengde, a first-generation Dalit scholar, commended Wilkerson's work for demonstrating that caste "needs a renewed focus, for it has the potential to subvert hegemonic tropes across the world." Yengde asserts that caste "is not a foreign, old, traditional Indian problem; it is as American as white supremacy" because White supremacy is a "fixated, theoretical, and pervasive system that reproduces for new eras the same channels of oppression" that Dalits experience under the Hindu caste system. Yengde, like Wilkerson, theorizes that White supremacy is a "caste system" because, like caste in India, it is a "rigid, unbreakable hierarchy" that derives "immobility from one's birth rank."[6]

While celebrated by Yengde, Wilkerson's book has been criticized by anthropologist Arjun Appadurai. Although Appadurai praises Wilkerson's work for reaching the "mass liberal reading public of the US," he notes that direct analogies between the Indian caste system and American racism could be problematic. The Indian caste system, according to Appadurai, was a highly religious system that idealized purity and pollution as the primary cause of caste. Additionally, Appadurai claims that the Indian caste system was not a racialized system (amongst Indians themselves), even though some British ethnologists might have interpreted endogamous castes as being comparable to racial groups.[7] Furthermore, social mobility in the Indian caste system could occur (with difficulty) through marriage, while in the US binary racial classifications greatly limited social mobility.[8]

While caste was an integral element of orthodox Hinduism, Appadurai's argument that caste is essentially incomparable to American racism because caste was connected to religion is disputable. The Hindu religion primarily legitimized social and gender discrimination rooted in material conditions, power relations, and politics. Race and caste are both systems of endogamous hierarchical subdivisions whose membership was permanent as well as hereditary.[9]

Indian scholars have equally noted that race and caste often overlapped in Indian society. Projit Bihari Mukharji argues that after World War I, "discussion about races [in India] came to intersect, overlap and dominate discussions about the nature, origin and mutual relationship of different castes."[10] The ideology that there were racial differences between castes remained popular throughout the twentieth century, particularly amongst north Indian Brahmins, and the Anthropological Survey of India passionately believed that there were specific physical differences between the various castes and tribes of India.[11]

Because some Indians saw caste groups as different races, there is a rationale to study the links between race and caste. Although race and caste shared similar qualities and that there are clear intersections between the two, it does not necessarily mean that the two terms can be used interchangeably, which she commonly does.[12] The original anthropological use of caste was associated with class. Caste in colonial societies evolved and (according to some) became more rigid in the modern era, especially during colonial rule. Caste is a form of class discrimination at a primitive level. As historian Talat Ahmed notes, although "caste does not equate to class," caste is not "totally unconnected from [class]. It is the interaction between [caste and class] that helps to further our understanding of how caste evolved."[13] By ignoring class in the US and utilizing a simplistic argument that rich and poor Black Americans have the same caste experience, Wilkerson is unable to dissect fully how race in the US relates to caste in India. Caste in India was tied to class. It reserved professions with high wealth and income opportunities for the upper castes.[14] It is crucial to study caste in a way that incorporates class divisions and its origins rather than simply investigating caste from a racial perspective.

Caste in India was not a colonial invention. It largely reflected the worldview of Indian elites; hence the end of British colonialism in 1947 did not result in the annihilation of the institution. Caste-related structures persisted after Indian independence. Gyanendra Pandey argues that in both contemporary American and Indian society, groups such as Native Americans, Black Americans, and Dalits are stereotyped as being "inherently poor, disorganized, and lazy" and thus "culturally unsuited to middle-class modernity."[15] Pandey notes that the "privileged" members of both contemporary American and Indian societies use similar tropes which justify the lowered socioeconomic status of the marginalized groups of their respective societies and argue that those who fail to arise out of a lower-class status are simply not "determined or talented enough."[16] However, the reality of the situation in both India and the US is that the privileged are motivated to keep the underclass from achieving class mobility. As Pandey states,

"[B]ecause ruling and dominant groups and classes across the globe believe it is their inherited right to rule and to live in special comfort and prosperity," they perpetuate a culture of "racism, because that is a way of keeping subordinated and marginalized groups – sometimes called minorities – 'in their place.'"[17]

While the Black middle class and Black upper class have expanded, and a Black president has been elected since the culmination of the civil rights movement, there are staggering racial disparities when assessing wealth distribution in the US. At USD 171,000, the net worth of a typical White family is nearly ten times greater than that of a Black family (USD 17,150) in 2016. Researchers at the Brookings Institute have asserted that the historical marginalization of Black Americans impacts "contemporary inequality in part because its legacy is passed down generation-to-generation through unequal monetary inheritances which make up a great deal of current wealth."[18] Particularly in capitalist nations such as the US, wealth impacts class in many ways; it determines access to housing in safe neighborhoods with good schools, and hence it enhances and determines the prospects of Black children.[19] Therefore, understanding the historical legacy of American racism and how it relates to contemporary race and class issues is a vital part of understanding how the opportunity for Black social mobility after the civil rights movement did not simply create equality between Black and White Americans.

Contemporary American and Indian societies provide clear examples of class and caste inequality. Isabel Wilkerson's research has shown how the power relations and political motivations between the Indian caste system and racial hierarchies in the US are similar to one another, with an emphasis on the experience of Black Americans. Yet the modern manifestations of caste in India are perhaps more pressing than her work conveys. According to Dalit writer Yashica Dutt, "Dalits in India are routinely abused and subjected to violence and even murder" for challenging the upper castes. Dutt notes that Wilkerson gives in to the "idea of American exceptionalism and centers [on] Western narratives while failing to dig into the continued brutalization of Dalits who largely reside in India – in the global south." Hence, there remains a need for additional intellectual dialogue regarding the connections between the Black American and Indian Dalit experiences which gives equal weight to both.[20]

Caste violence in India often includes gendered violence. As upper-caste men seek to maintain caste privilege, they often use violence against women to punish them for choosing a partner from a lower caste. This brutal punishment is often exercised by the woman's own family members and these women are often murdered by their male family members in the form of "honor killings." These honor killings are motivated by the perpetrators' belief that the victim has brought shame or dishonor upon the family, or has violated the principles of a community or a religion. These abhorrent forms of killing often occur when a member of a family refuses an arranged marriage, has sexual relations outside a marriage, or even when a family member is raped.[21] Honor killings serve as a clear example that women from even privileged castes only have value to male caste supremacists if they help them retain the status quo and defend patriarchal caste purity. Many honor killings have occurred in response to the growing economic opportunities for young people and lower castes (although still limited) in contemporary India which has in turn made "love marriages" more common.

Another way in which patriarchal caste elites have continued to enforce inter-caste marriage restrictions are through child marriages. Historically, upper-caste Indians saw unmarried adult women with a free sexual agency as a threat to caste purity as they feared that these women would copulate and reproduce with lower-caste men. Child marriage prevented the possibility of girls breaking caste norms because marriage prevented them from having sexual relations outside of caste lines.[22] Although child marriage in now illegal in Indian society, many marriages are often "arranged" at an early age to prevent women from choosing their own partners who may be from a different caste or ethnic group. The United Nations reports that over 1.5 million girls under the age of eighteen are forced into marriage. In some cases, parents of low-caste women plan early marriages for their daughters in order to protect them from violence from other men in the community who sometimes feel entitled to the bodies of single low-caste women due to their higher caste status.[23] The violent and exclusionary repression of women and low-caste Indians seeking to choose their own partner has risen in tandem with upper-caste men fighting to hold on to power, status, and property in the face of a modern India which is moving toward rewarding its citizens based on merit rather than birth privilege.

Just as increased economic opportunities do not shield low-caste Indians from caste discrimination, in the US a higher socioeconomic status does not offer Black Americans protection from some social aspects, such as racial profiling. In July 2009, Harvard professor Henry Louis Gates Jr. was arrested at his home in Cambridge, Massachusetts, by local police officer Sergeant James Crowley after Lucia Whalen, a White neighbor, called the police believing that Gates was a burglar. President Barack Obama condemned the Gates arrest as an example of racial profiling and noted accurately that it was a continuation of the "long history in [the US] of African Americans and Latinos being stopped by law enforcement disproportionately."[24] Just as low-caste Indians often do not "belong" in romantic relationships with upper-caste women in the eyes of upper-caste men, in the US some White Americans continue to question whether Black Americans belong in wealthy historically White neighbourhoods. Hence, we as a society need to make a conscientious effort to understand the different lived experiences of low-caste and high-caste Indians, and White and Black Americans. There are those in the US and India who deny that "White supremacy" or "caste supremacy" exist in modern society. However, this is naïve and it minimizes the work we still have to do to achieve a fully egalitarian society. Understanding the history behind these issues is an important step toward understanding how they exist in contemporary times.

While I have addressed the ways in which the Indian caste system indiscriminately punishes women through honor killings and child marriage, gender distinctions are not a central part of my analysis of caste. My reason for this is best described by Suraj Yengde who notes that "woke politics" or liberal politics in India often "draws on oppression paralympics," and "rests on finding identities (gender and sexuality)" that some deem to be more "devastating [than caste] as a precursor to granting Dalits their legitimacy." He notes that gender is the most common identity used to separate the identities of Dalit men and women, framing the struggle of Dalit women as separate and oftentimes in opposition to that of Dalit men. The struggles of Dalit women are often tied to the greater struggle of women as a group rather than as part of a larger caste struggle that includes all Dalits. As a result, as Yengde accurately notes, "class gets the least, if not the last attention." This is not to invalidate the legitimacy of a feminist movement that combines the struggles of Dalit and upper-caste women to overthrow oppressive patriarchal structures which are sometimes endorsed and utilized by Dalit men as well. Dalit patriarchy is an issue and Dalit men are not immune from letting it govern their treatment of women. However, as Yengde astutely argues, "the charge of Dalit patriarchy is now being used to put down any assertion of being Dalit. Both Dalit males and females are reduced to defining their identities in opposition to the other, rather than through their own autonomous selves."[25]

The brutal Hathras rape case has brought more attention to increased violence that Dalit women experience due to their disadvantaged background. Caste is the strongest factor which causes Dalit women to experience sexual violence at a disproportionate rate. As political scientist Ajay Kumar notes, "the caste hierarchy provides legitimacy to the men from higher castes to embolden them with impunity even after they commit heinous atrocities like sexual violence, sexual assault, rape, and murder." The "low" and "impure" status of Dalit women makes them "available for any kind of exploitation and violence" by upper-caste men.[26] Hence, the struggle of Dalit women is unique from that of upper-caste women. The Hathras rape case is a clear example of this. However, as Yengde warns, when assessing and critiquing sexual violence in India, "the layering of caste has completely been ignored or sidelined, even by the progressive circles, let alone the world media." Due to the undervaluing of caste, my aim in this book is to accentuate the common shared identity and struggles of Dalit men and women together and I explore their marginalization as an oppressed caste and class first and foremost as Dalits. I use this same philosophy for analyzing the Black American struggle and I investigate the struggle of Black Americans without gender distinctions even though Black men, like Dalit men, endorse and practice many of the same patriarchal elements that White and upper-caste men do.

The turn of the twentieth century provided opportunities for Indian intellectuals to travel to the US and engage in conversations with African Americans and White liberals to discuss ideas about colonial exploitation and emancipatory concepts such as nationalism, self-determination, and economic liberation. Indians like Rabindranath Tagore, the first Indian Nobel Prize laureate, regarded nationalism as a hinderance to cosmopolitanism and peace due to the divisions it created based on racial, ethnic, and class lines. Furthermore, Indians in particular began to see their anti-colonial struggle against the British as a similar racial struggle to that which African Americans faced in the US. By the end of the twentieth century, Indians and Black Americans had amassed an invaluable amount of knowledge about each other's struggles and low-caste Indians began to theorize their own struggle against caste as one that could be tied to racial discrimination. This culminated in 2001 when Dalit activists traveled to Durban, South Africa, to inform the international community about their fight against caste oppression at the United Nations World Conference against Racism, Racial Discrimination, Xenophobia, and Related Intolerance. However, the Indian government did not see the anti-caste movement as a racial struggle and the efforts of Dalit activists had little tangible impact.

Although low-caste Indians did not succeed in convincing the United Nations and the Indian government that caste marginalization was a form of racial discrimination, African Americans have remained a source of inspiration for some low-caste Indians. This is exemplified by the fact that nearly "half the books" at a museum library dedicated to B. R. Ambedkar in Aurangabad, Maharashtra, focused upon the American Black Panthers.[27] Thus, artifacts affiliated with the Indian caste struggle are directly related to the Black American struggle against White supremacy. The battle against caste and racial discrimination is invariably linked together. To solve these issues in the modern era, it is imperative for us to understand the historical dialogues that set up a basis for interactions and solidarity between Indians and African Americans in their quest for liberation, freedom, and civil rights.

Notes

1. Gordon Marshall, "Caste," in *A Dictionary of Sociology*, ed. John Scott (Oxford, UK; New York, NY: Oxford University Press, 2005), 66; Robert H. Winthrop, *Dictionary of Concepts in Cultural Anthropology* (Santa Barbara: ABC-CLIO, 1991), 27–30.

2. Louis Dumont, *Homo Hierarchicus: The Caste System and Its Implications* (Chicago: Chicago University Press, 1970).

3. Andre Beteille, *Caste, Class and Power: Changing Patterns of Stratification in a Tanjore Village* (Berkeley: University of California Press, 1965); Dipankar Gupta, *Interrogating Caste: Understanding Hierarchy and Difference in Indian Society* (New Delhi: Penguin, 2000).

4. Nicholas Dirks, *Castes of Mind: Colonialism and the Making of Modern India* (Princeton: Princeton University Press, 2001); Sumit Guha, *Beyond Caste: Identity and Power in South Asia, Past and Present* (Leiden: Brill, 2013). Guha builds upon the classic political historical interpretation of tribes and caste offered by Richard G. Fox in *Kin, Clan, Raja and Rule! State–Hinterland Relations in Pre-industrial India* (Berkeley: University of California Press, 1971).

5. Isabel Wilkerson, *Caste: The Origins of Our Discontents* (New York: Random House, 2020).

6. Suraj Yengde, "Castes of Mind: On the Intersection of Race and Caste," review of *Caste: The Origins of Our Discontents*, by Isabel Wilkerson, *The Baffler* no. 56, March 24, 2021.

7. Crispin Bates, "Race, Caste and Tribe in Central India: The Early Origins of Indian Anthropometry," in *The Concept of Race in South Asia*, ed. P. Robb, 219–259 (New Delhi: Oxford University Press, 1995), 14. Bates notes that Indian Brahmins, especially north Indian Brahmins, believed that racial differences existed "between northern Indians and southern Indians and between high castes and low castes." Hence, race and caste hierarchies overlapped in India and some Indians saw caste as a racial hierarchy.

8. Arjun Appadurai, "Comparing Race to Caste Is an Interesting Idea, but There Are Crucial Differences Between Both," review of *Caste: The Origins of Our Discontents*, by Isabel Wilkerson, *The Wire*, September 12, 2020.

9. Gerald D. Berreman, "Caste in India and the United States," *The American Journal of Sociology* 66, no. 2 (1960): 120–127.

10. Projit Bihari Mukharji, "From Serosocial to Sanguinary Identities: Caste, Transnational Race Science and the Shifting Metonymies of Blood Group B, India c. 1918–1960," *Indian Economic and Social History Review* 51, no.2 (2014): 143–176, 145.

11. Bates, "Race, Caste and Tribe in Central India," 4.

12. Wilkerson, *Caste*, 53.

13. Ahmed, *Mohandas Gandhi*, 66.

14. Hazel V. Carby, "The Limits of Caste," review of *Caste: The Origins of Our Discontents* by Isabel Wilkerson, *London Review of Books* 43, no. 2, January 21, 2021.

15. Gyanendra Pandey, *A History of Prejudice: Race, Caste, and Difference in India and the United States* (New Delhi: University of Cambridge Press, 2013), 20.

16. Ibid.

17. Gyanendra Pandey, "Racialization of Subaltern Populations across the Globe: The Politics of Difference," *Review of Black Political Economy* 43, no. 2 (January 2016): 87–99, 98.

18. Kriston McIntosh, Emily Moss, Ryan Nunn, and Jay Shambaugh, "Examining the Black–White Wealth Gap," *Brookings Institute* (February 27, 2020), https://www.brookings.edu/blog/up-front/2020/02/27/examining-the-Black-white-wealth-gap/, accessed May 31, 2021.

19. Ta-Nehisi Coates, "The Case for Reparations," *The Atlantic*, June 2014. Coates notes that due to both wealth disparities and housing discrimination, Black families earning USD 100,000 typically live in the kinds of neighborhoods inhabited by White families making USD 30,000, leading to different economic outcomes for Black and White children.

20. Yashica Dutt, "Feeling Like an Outcast," *Foreign Policy*, September 17, 2020.

21. Dietrich Oberwittler and Julia Kasselt, "Honor Killings," in *The Oxford Handbook of Gender, Sex, and Crime*, ed. Rosemary Gartner and Bill McCarthy, 652–670 (New York: Oxford University Press, 2014).

22. Durba Mitra, "'Surplus Woman': Female Sexuality and the Concept of Endogamy," *The Journal of Asian Studies* 80, no. 1 (2021): 3–26, 15–18.

23. Sushmita Pathak and Lauren Frayer, "Child Marriages Are Up in the Pandemic. Here's How India Tries to Stop Them," *National Public Radio*, November 5, 2020, https://www.npr.org/sections/goatsandsoda/2020/11/05/931274119/child-marriages-are-up-in-the-pandemic-heres-how-india-tries-to-stop-them, accessed March 1, 2022.

24. Michelle McPhee, "Obama Called Cop Who Arrested Gates, Still Sees 'Overreaction' in Gates' Arrest," ABC News, July 24, 2009.

25. Suraj Yengde, "Charge of Dalit Patriarchy Is Now Being Used to Put Down Any Assertion of Being Dalit," *Indian Express*, December 13, 2020, https://indianexpress.com/article/opinion/columns/dalits-and-the-oppressions-within-suraj-yengde-7102507/, accessed March 1, 2022.

26. Ajay Kumar, "Sexual Violence against Dalit Women: An Analytical Study of Intersectionality of Gender, Caste, and Class in India," *Journal of International Women's Studies* 22, no. 10 (2021): 131–132.

27. Nico Slate, "Translating Race and Caste," *Journal of Historical Sociology* 24, no. 1 (March 2011): 75–76.

Introduction

The marginalization of Black Americans due to White supremacy and the oppression of Indians under British colonialism featured inescapable similarities. At the turn of the twentieth century, these parallels led Indian and Black nationalists, intellectuals, and activists to share their experiences and engage in dialogues toward improving the social status of their people. Specifically, Black internationalists such as W. E. B. Du Bois, Walter White, and Paul Robeson studied the Indian independence movement and came to regard India as a template in the fight against White supremacy in the United States (US). Ultimately, they came together in their desire to overthrow the structures that subjugated them. Throughout the late nineteenth and early twentieth centuries, some Indians and Americans exchanged ideas about race, caste, and class, creating lasting cultural connections.

In this book, I explore the foundational cultural and political connections between India and the US between the late nineteenth and mid-twentieth centuries by focusing on a small select group of Indians and Americans and their ideas on race, caste, and class. Several key figures of the time, on both sides, attempted to assess whether the Black experience in the US mirrored caste, colonialism, or racial discrimination in India. Both Indians and Americans studied race, caste, and class dynamics outside their own countries in order to learn what they could apply to their own struggles. This study spans from the start of the twentieth century when W. E. B. Du Bois notably declared at the first Pan African Conference in 1900 that "the problem of the twentieth century is the problem of the color line" until the immediate aftermath of the 1954 *Brown v. Board of Education* Supreme Court case, in which the US Supreme Court ruled that racial segregation in public schools was unconstitutional.

In a June 2021 seminar, historian Dwaipayan Sen noted that although alliances between oppressed groups are interesting and worthy of discussion, he queried whether any meaningful social change can be accomplished by race and caste solidarities between Americans and Indians. Sen argued that since Black American and Dalit struggles are local issues that exist within separate nation states, it is doubtful that that Black and Dalit alliances possess a transnational impact. Sen frames his concerns in a contemporary context, examining what mark Indians can make in the fight against racist police brutality in the US, or what influence Black Americans can have in challenging privileged Indians to prevent the lynching and flogging of Dalits by upper-caste Hindu cow vigilantes.[1] In this study, I evaluate the same issues in a historical context. My claim is that Indians and Black Americans did learn about each other's struggles and used that knowledge to modify their aspirations for their respective societies. While the direct transnational impact of Black American and Indian exchanges during the early and mid-twentieth century was limited, solidarity between the two groups achieved a meaningful social impact, particularly in the US.

Each of the six chapters of this book focuses on key Indian or Black American thinkers or activists. They analyze the ideas and impact of these individuals and the ways they relationally theorize intersections of race, caste, class, and colonialism across the two contexts. The first chapter centers on Indian poet and Nobel Prize winner Rabindranath Tagore and compares his ideas to Indian mystic Swami Vivekananda. The second chapter chronicles the efforts of the Ghadar Party and particularly focuses on Indian independence activist Taraknath Das. Chapter three turns to Black sociologist W. E. B. Du Bois and Indian independence leader Lala Lajpat Rai, analyzing the alliances these two men built with each other to challenge British colonialism and racism in the US. The fourth chapter considers Rai's activism against caste, colonialism, and White supremacy in India. In the fifth chapter, I explore Du Bois's use of journalism during the 1920s and the early 1930s to convey the racial significance of the Indian independence struggle and the Gandhian movement to American supporters of the National Association for the Advancement of Colored People (NAACP) along with his evaluation of caste. The sixth and final chapter looks at how Black Americans such as Du Bois, White, and Robeson sought to draw upon India as a form of inspiration to advance civil rights for Black Americans after Indian independence. Additionally, it examines and focuses on Indian caste reformer B. R. Ambedkar.

Historians such as Nico Slate, Daniel Immerwahr, Gerald Horne, and Gyanendra Pandey have written about the transnational histories of anti-colonialism and connections between race, caste, and class in the US and India. Nico Slate surveys different theories regarding the racial classifications that White Europeans used to differentiate high-caste Indians from those of lower caste within the Hindu *varna* and *jati* system of social stratification. He further explains how in some instances racial classifications such as "Aryan" and "non-Aryan" hindered solidarity among Indian intellectuals who racially classified themselves as "Aryan" and Black Americans who were deemed by racial theorists as being "non-Aryan" and an inferior race.[2] While Slate documents the shortcomings of Black and Indian solidarities, he displays multiple examples of the transnational impact of Black Americans on prominent Indians. For example, he analyzes how Booker T. Washington shaped Gandhi's outlook on African Americans. Slate also investigates the influence Gandhi had on Martin Luther King Jr.'s civil rights activism.

Like Slate, Gerald Horne analyzes the various ways in which Indians and Black Americans worked together to fight against colonialism in India and to advance civil rights for Black Americans, Indians, and other marginalized groups in the US. Horne presents the early twentieth century as a time when Black Americans and Indians had a shared affinity for each other, which made alliances between the two groups easier to build. While some Black and Indian relationships were built through shared affinity such as Rai and Du Bois's, other Indian figures believed that Blacks were indeed an inferior race to both Whites and Indians. Notable Indian figures such as Mohandas Gandhi, while in South Africa from 1893 to 1914, believed that Black Africans were inferior to Indians and shunned building alliances with Black activists.[3]

Transnational Black and Indian relationships have generated a debate of whether being Black in the US was more comparable to being a colonized Indian or being a low-caste member in a caste system such as an untouchable in India. Daniel Immerwahr concludes that Black internationalists more commonly saw the Black experience in the US as being comparable to an Indian living under British colonialism and they rarely compared the Black experience to an Indian "untouchable."[4] Immerwahr examines Black internationalism, B. R. Ambedkar's anti-caste movement, and the changing significance of India to Black civil rights activists such as Martin Luther King Jr. He concludes that Indian figures had more of an interest in the US than Black internationalists had in India. Additionally, he observes that Dalit activists made a "concerted bid to establish casteism as equivalent to racism" more so than Black activists tried to equate racism to caste.[5]

Throughout the early part of the twentieth century, Indians and African Americans negotiated the complexity of the race and caste question in an attempt to establish political solidarity. Black internationalists understood that caste in many ways contradicted Indian anti-colonial claims and as a result Black Americans favored looking at the Indian population as being marginalized by British White supremacy rather than focusing on the exclusion of Indian Dalits by Hindu Brahmins. The purpose of this book is to highlight the cosmopolitanism of colonial Indian figures and how race and caste fit into this. Black figures such as W. E. B. Du Bois broadened the concept of caste to include all colonized subjects. Du Bois saw all Africans, Black Americans, Indians, and East Asians as being part of a marginalized "color caste" and called upon them to unite on a common basis of racial solidarity, or "colored cosmopolitanism," to challenge White supremacy and colonialism. Du Bois called upon both Black Americans and Indians to put aside their notions of internal color prejudice or any caste hierarchies and stand together as "representatives of the coloured races" and fight against the "insistent problem of the assumption of the white peoples of Europe that they have a right to dominate the world and especially so to organize it politically and industrially as to make most men their slaves and servants."[6]

Du Bois's conception of caste mirrored that of contemporary South Asian scholars such as Vijay Prashad. Like Du Bois, Prashad argues that the "European 'white' labourer by the nineteenth century was seen as a juridical citizen who could formally bargain for his (and occasionally her) rights as a seller of labour power, while the non-European 'darker' labourer was seen as racially suited to various forms of hard labour in tropical conditions." Under these circumstances "caste" and "race" became linked together and regardless of an Indian's class background they were similarly disadvantaged in the labor market as a Black American in the US. Therefore, Indians of all caste and class backgrounds had an incentive to achieve solidarity with African Americans to challenge White supremacy.[7] Prashad contends that this form of "color caste" that devalues the labor of people in developing countries is still prevalent in contemporary society and that this is practiced through the income deflation of laborers in Africa, Asia, and Latin America.[8]

Black and Indian solidarity aided the fight for Black civil rights in many ways. After Indians achieved independence, Du Bois, Robeson, and William Patterson identified India as a source of sympathy for the Black American cause and successfully igniting outrage there regarding American racism through their "We Charge Genocide" petition. The negative press the petition drew concerning America's international reputation pressured Americans, such as Supreme Court Justices William O. Douglas and Earl Warren, into making a strong statement in support of civil rights and to endorse the landmark *Brown v. Board of Education* decision in favor of desegregating public schools. The Indian impact on the *Brown* decision was meaningful; it proved that more power could be found in transnational relationships between Indians and Black Americans than in both groups working independently to achieve social change in their own societies. The *Brown* decision offers a historical response to Dwaipayan Sen's question as to what transnational solidarities could actually accomplish locally in terms of human civil rights.

It is important to note that the Indian figures in this book, with the exception of B. R. Ambedkar, were not caste activists. I primarily selected upper-caste Indian individuals to analyze how the Indian caste system contradicted the anti-colonial claims by Indians. Caste in some ways hindered racial solidarity between Indians and Black Americans rather than providing ground for unity. The concept of race was more useful for Indians and Black American political figures when understanding oppression, and the concept of race was what enabled solidarity and inspired reflections on caste by Indian thinkers.

There are limitations inherent in concentrating upon a small group of elite individuals in leadership roles, including a potential undervaluing of the subaltern elements of race, caste, and class. The activities of a set of individuals does not necessarily reflect the thoughts of the Black and Indian masses, nor how the common Black American and Indian saw each other's struggles. Sources that reflect historic Dalit agency are thin on the ground. With the exception of B. R. Ambedkar, the marginalization of Dalits has historically deprived them of education and a literary voice. Hence, the majority of Indians in leadership positions were those who had not directly suffered under the caste system. Additionally, most Dalits, aside from Ambedkar, did not have the opportunity to travel to the US like Tagore and Rai. Therefore, relationships between Americans and low-caste Indians were far rarer than those between Americans and high-caste Indians.

There were several reasons why interactions between Americans and Indians did not contribute much toward achieving caste reform in India. One of the reasons why Americans did not garner a proper understanding of caste issues in India was because most American exchanges with Indians were with Indians from privileged castes such as Tagore and Lajpat Rai.

Additionally, Black leaders such as Du Bois and Walter White did not engage regularly with the anti-caste viewpoint of Indians such as B. R. Ambedkar. Ambedkar's communication with Du Bois was brief. Both men expressed mutual admiration for each other's efforts to uplift Dalits and Black Americans, but the two men never collaborated to attain their goals. Ambedkar and Du Bois's lack of active and continued cooperation exposed the shortcomings of trying to achieve social change through an isolationist lens, instead of trying to place the Dalit struggle within a transnational context. Finally, Black Americans like Du Bois believed that Indian independence could serve as a powerful force to pressure the US to adopt Black civil rights. Hence, he unconditionally supported the Indian movement and believed that India would be better able to solve its caste issues after independence was achieved.

Hurdles which hindered Black American and Indian solidarity included the identification of Indians as "Aryan" and, therefore, racially more European. This distanced the Indians that endorsed it from the Black American struggle. However, Lala Lajpat Rai challenged the worldview that Indians were racially distinct to Black Americans. He recognized the relationship between racism and colonialism and used his relative privilege to fight against both. As a result, Rai sought to build bridges with Black Americans in order to advocate for meaningful reform. This was shown by his reliance on Du Bois to inform Indians about the Black American struggle. Furthermore, the efforts of Du Bois and other Black leaders rallied Indian youth to express solidarity with Black Americans, proving how many Indians saw themselves as people of color similarly subjugated by White supremacy. This kinship encouraged the US Supreme Court to issue the *Brown v. Board of Education* resolution.

Finally, It is important to reach an understanding of why many Americans misunderstood the internal issues of India such as caste, and why the Black and Indian masses were mostly incognizant of each other's struggles during the early twentieth century. American audiences at Tagore's lectures did not properly understand the Indian struggle against British colonialism, perhaps because he was careful with his words, being aware that the British government in India was closely monitoring his movements. Additionally, as Du Bois correctly noted, Americans were not taught Indian history in American schools from an Indian viewpoint. They learned about India through British textbooks and the works of British colonial sympathizers such as Rudyard Kipling, so had little awareness of the fact that there was a vibrant anti-colonial movement within the subcontinent.

Caste in the United States

Racial discrimination in the US was a caste system, particularly in the Jim Crow South, because race determined the birthright privileges of individuals and created a hereditary system of marginalization. While Europeans, as well as the Indian populace, primarily used caste to describe India's social structure, the US was a caste society during both the antebellum and Jim Crow eras, especially in states that practiced de jure segregation. According to Daniel Immerwahr, although caste was "never central to abolitionist analysis" of slavery, many anti-slavery activists such as Frederick Douglass, William Lloyd Garrison, Horace Greeley, Harriet Beecher Stowe, William Seward, Gerrit Smith, Charles Sumner, Theodore Parker, and Cassius Clay used the term "caste" to describe the institution.[9] Comparisons of American race relations to caste persisted after the abolition of slavery. After the 1896 *Plessy v. Ferguson* decision, a case which ruled that Jim Crow segregation was legal, Justice John Marshall Harlan (the lone dissenter) argued that a race-based administration of segregation constituted a caste society. He condemned the verdict in explicit terms stating, "[I]n the eye of the law, there is in this country no superior, dominant, ruling class of citizens. There is no caste here. Our constitution is color-blind, and neither knows nor tolerates classes among citizens. In respect of civil rights, all citizens are equal before the law."[10]

During the early and mid-twentieth century, there was an active debate whether American race relations could best be described as a system of caste or class. In 1936, sociologist William Lloyd Warner argued that while the socioeconomic hierarchy of the US South was intended to be a merit-based class system, in reality, Jim Crow had transformed class into caste, because occupational, social, and educational opportunities for Black Americans were so scarce that middle-class Whites enjoyed greater social advantages than Black elites.[11] In 1943, Swedish sociologist Gunnar Myrdal similarly argued that caste was far more applicable to American society because "group prejudices against particular persons or types of people (Black Americans and other non-white groups) dominate[d]" the outlook of the "average [White] American" more so than any Marxist type class struggle.[12] Nevertheless, some sociologists such as Oliver C. Cox, E. Franklin Frazier, and Charles S. Johnson disagreed with Warner and Myrdal. They did not believe that caste was applicable to race relations in the US. Frazier argued that caste was "essentially static" and American race relations were fluid.[13] However, Frazier did not properly understand that caste in India was a fluid and dynamic system, which, as Susan Bayly notes, was never a "fixed fact of Indian life."[14]

Black American intellectuals such as W. E. B. Du Bois referred to race relations in the US during the first half of the twentieth century as a form of "color-caste" or "caste of color." He noted that although legal chattel slavery had ended in 1865, "color caste" in the US metaphorically enslaved "Black men who were not slaves."[15] Historian Gyanendra Pandey notes that like Du Bois, caste reformers B. R. Ambedkar and Jyotirao Phule described racial segregation as a system of caste. Ambedkar "transcoded racial segregation in the United States" to be a direct parallel to the experience of Dalits in India.[16] Various high-caste Indians, including Rabindranath Tagore, Lala Lajpat Rai, and Taraknath Das, similarly made this crucial race and caste parallel when studying the experiences of Black Americans. The race and caste parallel as propounded by these men demonstrated that multiple Indian intellectuals saw the Black American struggle as a useful analogue to untouchability. Tagore theorized that caste in India was an endogamous system based on racial and physical differences, and he surmised it to be akin to American racism directed at Black and Indigenous Americans. Thereupon, he tried to use caste division in India to urge American audiences not to make the same mistakes as India and to have an internationalist and egalitarian outlook to achieve racial harmony. Rai and Das also saw American racism, particularly the marginalization of Black Americans, to be a cogent parallel to the lived experiences of untouchables in India, showcasing the intersection of caste and racial science.

The Intersection of Caste and Racial Science

Like race in American society, caste was a fluid concept in India. Prior to British rule, caste in India was a Hindu system that kept castes separate through endogamy. However, British ethnographers such as Herbert Hope Risley asserted that Indians practiced endogamy based upon their self-description and the differences in skin color or bone structure between various Indian castes. These differences, he argued, made high-caste Indians "distinct in race and blood from the scavengers who swept the road."[17] Hence, Risley presented a racialized explanation for the Indian caste system to assert that Vedic Indian society, including the caste system, was created by Aryan invaders from central Asia who conquered the Indigenous people of the Indian subcontinent circa 1500 BCE. Aryan invaders created a caste system that differentiated the social status of the Aryan conquerors from the Indigenous conquered Indians.

Aryan invasion theories advanced a narrative that ancient Indian society was akin to the early-twentieth-century societies in British India and

America in which fair skin signified the ruling class, whereas darker skin signified the lower-class subjects. Risley aggressively encouraged racialized caste theories by dividing Indians into seven racial types, with fair "Indo-Aryans" the most "advanced," and dark-skinned Dravidians the most "primitive." The Dravidian, Risley claimed, was "recognizable at a glance by his Black skin, his squat figure and the negro-like proportions of his nose." British historian William Wilson Hunter encouraged a racially hierarchical classification of Indians. In his 1882 book *Indian Empire*, he asserted that "India [formed] a great museum of races, in which we can study man from his lowest to his highest stages of culture."[18] Hunter's book was widely circulated in Indian schools and used as a template by Risley who had been hired by Hunter as a research assistant in the 1870s.[19] The nature of colonial administration was materially influenced by Risley and Hunter and through their ideology, the British understood caste in India as a racialized system that prioritized Indo-Aryans.

It is important to note that "caste" in ancient India intertwined with the idea of "color." Varna was the Brahminic ideology of hierarchizing society into classes (Brahmins, Kshatriya, Vaishya, and Shudras). Dalits were excluded from the four-fold varna system of Hinduism and were seen as forming a fifth varna, also known by the name of Panchama. In contemporary India, "Scheduled Castes" is the official term for Dalits as per the Constitution of India. "Varna" translates directly to the term "color" which "has played a consistent role in racialized conceptions of caste."[20] At times, Indians like Tagore offered a "racialized" conception of caste in India, stating in 1910, "It has never been India's lot to accept alien races as factors in her civilization. You know very well how the caste that proceeds from colour takes elsewhere a most virulent form." Caste in India, according to Tagore, historically was a system of racial segregation designed around endogamy even before the British arrived to the subcontinent.

Tagore's racialized conception of the Hindu caste system was supported by B. R. Ambedkar. Ambedkar noted, "The Aryans cherished color prejudice and thereby formed the Chaturvarnya [the caste system], whereby they separated the white race from the black race."[21] The rigidity of the caste system was ultimately defined by "the difference in color between the upper and lower castes."[22] The Brahmins were portrayed as representing the color "white" while the Shudras were the color "black."[23] "White" represented purity and nobility, and "black" represented the enslaved and disenfranchised. These representations based on color are significant because they show how high-caste Indians cherished color prejudice, and the fact that the Brahmins were represented by the color white shows that there was a priority on "whiteness" in the Indian caste system even if this did not necessarily equate to having "white skin." Indians like Lala Lajpat Rai also transferred terminology from the Indian caste system to describe American racism referring to "white Americans" as "white Brahmins," noting that "the discrimination against people of different color (between the Varnas of the Hindus)"were "manifested in almost identical ways"in the US. [24]

There is a scholarly debate regarding just how much European racial science and "Aryan racial theories" influenced caste categorizations, or if the British primarily adopted a racialized explanation for caste to satisfy the self-image of high-caste Hindus. While European theories of race certainly influenced how the British saw the Indian population, some historians such as Christopher Bayly argue that Brahmin informants, who saw themselves as racially superior to lower castes, played a significant role toward racializing the caste system, and the British largely adopted racialized caste categories to appease them.[25] Additionally, other contemporary scholars refute Aryan invasions of the Indian subcontinent, and many historians such as Edwin Bryant and Laurie L. Patton dispute the migrations themselves and their impact on caste. Philologist and Indologist Michael Witzel argues that the theory of the immigration of Indo-Aryan-speaking Arya ("Aryan invasion") was simply utilized as a means of British policy to justify their own intrusion into India and their subsequent colonial rule: in both cases (the Aryan invasion of India and British colonialism), a "white race" subdued the local darker colored population.[26] This argument is supported by Vijay Prashad who notes that "caste, unlike race, predates the colonial era" and "British imperialists tied together the concepts of race and caste to justify colonizing India." Hence, "caste," in Prashad's view, was "not *manufactured* by colonialism," but it was "reshaped and strengthened by it to the interests and fantasies of European colonisers."[27] Historian Nicholas Dirks similarly notes that by the middle of the twentieth century, Indians such as B. R. Ambedkar aggressively challenged the Indo-Aryan migration theories.[28]

Debate regarding the validity of the Indo-migration theories and the racial origins of the ethnic groups that inhabit India continues today, proving that such narratives remain a live and controversial issue in the twenty-first century. In terms of modern genetics, the distribution of some haplogroups such as haplogroup R1a, more specifically R1a1a1b, that are found in high frequencies in Eastern Europe and South Asia, may serve as loose evidence of the Indo-European migrations.[29] The place of origin of this haplogroup may give an indication of the "homeland" of the Indo-Europeans, and the direction of the first migrations.[30] Nevertheless, since research on haplogroups and the genetic origins of Indian ethnic groups is ongoing, it is difficult to offer a definitive stance on the accuracy of the Indo-European migrations.

It is important to note that although the concepts of caste such as the avoidance of inter-marriage, inter-mixing, and inter-dining were already practiced by Indians before European arrival upon the subcontinent, the term "caste" was a European term that was imported into India and the Americas by the Portuguese. "Casta" (the Spanish and Portuguese term) translates to "lineage," and it has historically been used as a racial and social identifier in post-Columbus colonial societies such as the Americas and India. The Portuguese imported the term "caste" to Asia in the sixteenth century, and then to the Iberian empires of the Americas. Hence, when Indians such as Rabindranath Tagore and Lala Lajpat Rai used the term "caste," it was an anglicized version of the Portuguese term "casta." The Hindu caste divisions were historically known by Indians as "varna" which as explained earlier directly translates to "color" but can also mean type, order, or class.[31]

According to anthropologist Susan Bayly, the Hindu caste system was a flexible system. She argues, "Caste is not and never has been a fixed fact of Indian life." During the eighteenth century, she notes, post-Mughal elites associated themselves with kings, priests, and ascetics, and they utilized caste to divide their populace and consolidate their power. In addition, in this fluid, stateless environment, some of the previously casteless segments of society assembled themselves into caste groups. Indians did not treat caste norms as given absolutes, but they challenged, negotiated, and adapted these norms to their circumstances.[32] When the British East India Company arrived in India during the seventeenth century, it adopted constitutional laws and segregated Indians by religion and caste to appease the Indian people.[33] Nicholas Dirks suggests that it is difficult to assess the true nature of caste before British rule because eighteenth-century British writings on India say little about the caste system in India, and predominantly discuss territorial conquest, alliances, warfare, and diplomacy.[34] Dirks cites the work of social historian Colin Mackenzie who collected vast numbers of texts on Indian religions, culture, traditions, and local histories from south India and the Deccan region. However, Dirks claims that Mackenzie's collection and writings provide little information on the caste system in eighteenth-century India, making it difficult for contemporary historians to give an objective account of how caste was used prior to British rule.[35]

Just as low-caste Indians experienced life in India as second-class citizens, Black Americans were victimized by a similar "caste system" in the US. However, unlike Indians, Black Americans did not have a caste system which they practiced amongst themselves; they suffered under a racialized "caste system" created by White supremacists. Even though the Black American experience could be compared to that of a low-caste Indian, and Indians such as Rai and Das commonly made these connections in their writings, Black Americans and White liberals often ignored India's caste problems. They did not regularly employ a race and caste parallel between the Hindu caste system and the Black American experience. Black Americans and White liberals primarily spoke with Indians of high-caste status such as Tagore and Rai who often did not present caste in India as a central issue. Hence, many Americans misunderstood the internal issues of Indian caste. While Tagore, Rai, and Taraknath Das saw caste in India and racism in the US as sharing clear similarities, solidarities were more commonly built upon a comparison between the Black American experience and that of Indians under British colonialism rather than that of low-caste Indians under high-caste oppressors. Black Americans often ignored India's caste problems, failing to engage with a race/caste parallel between the Hindu caste system and the Black American experience because they saw British colonialism as a clear example of White supremacy. This outlook allowed them to connect their plight to other colonized Asian and African groups and took precedence over analogies between American racism and the Hindu caste system.

Because caste was an undervalued theme in the discussions between Black American and Indian activists, they united over a shared struggle against White supremacy and connected their plight to other colonized Asian and African groups. The outlook of connecting White supremacy to colonialism took precedence over analogies between American racism and the Hindu caste system. Since Black Americans saw their struggle as being more relatable to the experience of Indians under British colonialism, interactions between the two groups did not have a strong impact toward achieving caste reform in India. Tagore and Rai did not reveal the true pervasiveness of the issue to their American audiences because they feared that exposing India's internal caste issues could cost them support from American sympathizers of Indian independence. However, despite their limitations in informing the American community about the toxicity of Hindu caste, Tagore and Rai acknowledged and tried to modify caste prejudice amongst the Hindu community and they saw caste as a central issue that prevented Indian unity.

One of the limitations of early Indian travelers to the US such as Vivekananda and Rabindranath Tagore was their lack of interaction with Black Americans. Their reach was mostly limited to educated and upper-class White Americans. Consequently, direct solidarity and alliances between Indians and Black Americans were not a feature of Vivekananda and Tagore's tours of the US. The most notable relationship between an Indian and Black American was that between Lala Lajpat Rai and W. E. B. Du Bois. Both identified with each other's struggles and had several exchanges which modified each other's goals. Using Du Bois as an influence, Rai tied the Indian independence movement to a larger global struggle against White supremacy and aligned his aspirations with those of the Black American struggle. Du Bois, for his part, influenced by Rai's death during a peaceful protest in 1928, saw Indian independence as an urgent necessity for the Indian people and for racial equality.

Rai did not actively bring caste to the forefront of his dialogue with Americans because he wanted to forge alliances against British colonialism and sway American opinion to make India appear fit for self-rule. Tagore also occasionally used American racism as a shield against caste criticism, to justify the competency of the social order of Indian society and to convince American audiences to donate money for his university. Rai and Tagore understood that negative press about the Hindu caste system would bolster British rule and provide a negative impression of Hindus to Americans. However, while speaking to other Indians, Vivekananda, Tagore, and Rai consistently criticized India's caste problem and tried to challenge caste discrimination. They all blamed privileged Hindus for perpetuating an oppressive caste culture.

Even though Vivekananda, Tagore, and Rai were prominent and influential Indian figures, they could not produce much meaningful change toward erasing caste discrimination in India and they could not end the stigma of caste hierarchies in the Hindu society. Caste in India was an integral part of the Hindu social order and upper-caste Hindus were not convinced enough by Tagore and Rai to challenge the system, especially when they wanted to retain their privilege. Gandhi, a powerful and central figure in the Indian independence movement, condemned untouchability but did not support the complete annihilation of the caste system or prioritize caste as an urgent concern in the Indian independence movement.

Nevertheless, Indians like Lala Lajpat Rai related social classes in the US to caste in India. Rai believed that race, caste, and class overlapped, and there was a relationship between them in both American and Indian society. Because of the similar race, caste, and class dynamics in India and the US, some Indians and Black Americans claimed solidarity with one another, such as Lala Lajpat Rai and W. E. B. Du Bois. They exemplified their solidarity in exchanged letters and a variety of other sources such as newspaper articles, monologues, speeches, and interviews. In a few of these more public sources, Indian intellectuals such as Rabindranath Tagore softened some of their criticisms of American race relations as well as British colonialism to avoid scrutiny from both the US and British governments. Additionally, some American internationalists such as Du Bois, Walter White, and Oswald Garrison Villard ignored some of the internal caste issues amongst Indians, especially in newspapers, because they wanted to rally support for the Indian independence movement amongst their readers. They thus avoided any controversy that could lead to negative press about Indian culture and Indian leaders such as Gandhi. These factors contribute to the difficulty in exploring the parallels and differences between American and Indian political thinking on the issue of caste.

Just as the Hindu caste system was not a central theme during Black and American exchanges during the early twentieth century, even in modern-day discourse African American activists rarely engage with Dalit issues in India. It is possible that the lack of engagement from African American activists regarding the plight of Dalits stems from Black activists from the early twentieth century such as Du Bois and Walter White framing the Indian struggle as primarily a colonial struggle against White supremacy and not placing enough focus upon the internal issues of caste. Conversely, as Dwaipayan Sen notes, in contemporary society Dalits have had a greater interest in the plight of African Americans, and Dalits commonly compare their plight to the Black experience in the US.[36] Dalit awareness of the issues of Black Americans is due in part to B. R. Ambedkar reading the works of W. E. B. Du Bois and comparing the issues of Dalits to those of Black Americans, and in turn projecting the Dalit struggle as being analogous to the apartheid faced by Black Americans in the Jim Crow era. However, in recent years we have seen some shared dialogue between individuals like Suraj Yengde and Cornel West, noting how we must listen to individuals like Du Bois and Ambedkar and bring the African American and Dalit struggles closer together as both a "fight against white supremacy and Brahmin supremacy" and that the "prophetic spirits of Ambedkar and Du Bois must come alive as never before."[37]

Notes

1. Dwaipayan Sen, "Uncanny Juxtapositions: Conditions of Possibility for the Comparison of Race and Caste," lecture, *Race and Racism in the Global South* from King's College London, June 1, 2021.
2. Nico Slate, *Colored Cosmopolitanism: The Shared Struggle for Freedom in the United States and India* (Cambridge: Harvard University Press, 2013); Daniel Immerwahr, "Review of Colored Cosmopolitanism: The Shared Struggle for Freedom in the United States and India by Nico Slate," *Journal of Social History* 47, no. 2 (2013): 547–549.
3. Gerald Horne, *End of Empires: African Americans and India* (Philadelphia: Temple University Press, 2008); Talat Ahmed, *Mohandas Gandhi: Experiments in Civil Disobedience* (London: Pluto Press, 2019), 55–57.
4. Daniel Immerwahr, "Caste or Colony? Indianizing Race in the United States," *Modern Intellectual History* 4, no.2 (2007): 275–301.
5. Ibid., 300–301.
6. Ibid.
7. Vijay Prashad, "The Wretchedness of Caste – Ambedkar, Fanon, and the Blocked Indian Revolution," *Leftword*, https://mayday.leftword.com/blog/post/the-wretchedness-of-caste-part-one, accessed October 2023.
8. Ibid.
9. Immerwahr, "Caste or Colony?" 277.
10. *Plessy v. Ferguson*, 163 U.S. 559 (1896).
11. Immerwahr, "Caste or Colony?" 280; W. Lloyd Warner, "American Caste and Class," *American Journal of Sociology* 42, no.2 (1936): 234–237.
12. Gunnar Myrdal, *An American Dilemma*, Volume I: *The Negro in a White Nation* (1944; reprint in New York: McGraw Hill, 1964), lxx–lxxi; Gyanendra Pandey, *A History of Prejudice: Race, Caste, and Difference in India and the United States* (New Delhi: University of Cambridge Press, 2013), 22–23; Immerwahr, "Caste or Colony?" 281.
13. Immerwahr, "Caste or Colony?" 281.
14. Susan Bayly, *Caste, Society and Politics in India from the Eighteenth Century to the Modern Age* (New York: Cambridge University Press, 1996). 25–28.
15. Pandey, *Race, Caste, and Difference in India and the United States*, 6.
16. Ibid.
17. Crispin Bates, "Race, Caste and Tribe in Central India: The Early Origins of Indian Anthropometry," *Edinburgh Papers in South Asian Studies* no. 3 (1995): 1–35, 12, 22; Thomas R. Trautmann, *Aryans and British India* (New Delhi: Vistaar Publications, 1997), 183; H. H. Risley, "The Study of Ethnology in India," *Journal of the Anthropological Institute of Great Britain and Ireland* 20 (1891): 235–263, 253.
18. Slate, *Colored Cosmopolitanism*, 11.
19. "Sir Herbert Hope Risley," *Oxford Dictionary of National Biography* (Oxford: Oxford University Press, 2004).

20. Nico Slate, "Translating Race and Caste," *Journal of Historical Sociology* 24, no. 1 (March 2011): 62–79, 63–64.
21. B. R. Ambedkar, *Who Were the Shudras? How They Came to Be the Fourth Varna in the Indo-Aryan Society.* (Bombay: Thackers, 1970), 76.
22. Arthur Anthony Macdonell and Arthur Barriedale Keith, *Vedic Index of Names and Subjects, Vol. 2* (London: John Murray, 1912), 267. See also Trautmann, *Aryans and British India*, 206–211; G. S. Ghurye, *Caste and Race in India* (Bombay: Popular Prakashan, 1969), 163.
23. Linda Edwards, *A Brief Guide to Beliefs: Ideas, Theologies, Mysteries, and Movements* (Louisville: Westminster John Knox Press, 2001), 139.
24. Slate, "Translating Race and Caste," 64.
25. C. A. Bayly, *Empire and Information: Intelligence Gathering and Social Communication in India, 1780–1870* (New York: Cambridge University Press, 1996), 7, 25, 29, 68, 310, 371.
26. Michael Witzel, "Indocentrism: Autochthonous Visions of Ancient India," in *The Indo-Aryan Controversy: Evidence and Inference in Indian History*, ed. Edwin Bryant and Laurie L. Patton, 341–401 (London: Routledge, 2005), 348.
27. Prashad, "The Wretchedness of Caste."
28. Nicholas Dirks, *Castes of Mind: Colonialism and the Making of Modern India* (Princeton, NJ: Princeton University Press, 2001), 267; Arvind Sharma, "Dr. B.R. Ambedkar on the Aryan Invasion and the Emergence of the Caste System in India," *Journal of the American Academy of Religion* 73, no.3 (2005): 843–870, 844.
29. A haplotype is a group of alleles (variant forms of a gene) in an organism that are inherited together from a single parent, and a haplogroup is a group of similar haplotypes that share a common ancestor with a single-nucleotide polymorphism mutation (the most common type of genetic variation).
30. Peter A. Underhill, "The Phylogenetic and Geographic Structure of Y-chromosome Haplogroup R1a," *European Journal of Human Genetics* 23, no. 1 (2015): 124–131; Sanghamitra Sahoo, "A Prehistory of Indian Y Chromosomes: Evaluating Demic Diffusion Scenarios," *Proceedings of the National Academy of Sciences of the United States of America* 103, no. 4 (2006): 843–848.
31. Andrea Stanton, *An Encyclopedia of Cultural Sociology of the Middle East, Asia, and Africa* (New York: Sage Publications, 2012), 12–13.
32. S. Bayly, *Caste, Society and Politics in India* , 25–31.
33. Douglas Peers, *India and the British Empire* (New York: Oxford University Press, 2012), 104–108.
34. Dirks, *Castes of Mind*, 28.
35. Ibid., 29–30.
36. Sen, "Uncanny Juxtapositions."
37. Cornel West and Suraj Yengde, "A Shared History of Struggle Should Unite India's Dalits and African Americans in the Shared Struggle for Equality," *The Root* (June 12, 2017).

1

Rabindranath Tagore in America
Ideas and impact

There is only one history – the history of man and I am not against one nation in particular, but against the general idea of all nations.

—Rabindranath Tagore

During the early twentieth century, Rabindranath Tagore sought to spread his intellectual ideas in a fight against a scientific racist ideology which presented non-White or non-European individuals as downtrodden and in need of European colonialism to civilize them. Tagore was born in 1861 into a prominent Bengali Brahmin family as the youngest of thirteen children. His family was extremely wealthy, mainly due to the success of his grandfather Dwarkanath who had amassed a fortune through his firm, Carr, Tagore and Co. Dwarkanath had earned a great deal of respect from the British for his business accomplishments. From an early age, Tagore was an avid reader. Heavily influenced by the Upanishads, he was inspired to become a writer himself. In his works, Tagore set out to find unity and "a stability of belief and moral principal to give meaning and order to everything he did."[1] He looked for harmony in all things while paying attention to the deep religious beliefs of ancient India. Tagore believed the "unity of God and his creation was the unity of a creative personality."[2] He expressed his creative passions by writing poetry that had strong spiritual messages. His writings referred heavily to the landscape of eastern India where he described the flowers, forests, birds, and the sacred Ganges River. Many of Tagore's poems created a sense of nostalgia. In one of his poems, titled *Shah Jahan*, named after the Mughal emperor who built the Taj Mahal, Tagore lamented the end of the Mughal Empire, writing, "You are gone now emperor – Your empire has dissolved like a dream, Your throne is shattered, Your armies, whose marching shook the earth, Today have no more weight than the windblown dust on the Delhi road."[3] Tagore believed that the British Raj neglected the histories of the great Indian empires within their schools for Indian pupils. He wanted Indians to be proud of their ancestry, and sought to reassert their cultural brilliance both at home and abroad.

By the early 1900s, Tagore's writings had reached the international stage. He sought to inform the international community of the lives of India's poor and common people, and he had the ability to analyze their experiences with a penetrative depth of feeling that was singular in Indian literature. Tagore's literary output and later public speaking left a strong impression on American students and journalists. When he won the Nobel Prize for Literature in 1913 for a collection of poems titled *Gitanjali* (first published in English by the Indian Society of London in 1912), he was the first non-European to win the award. His accomplishment made him a revered literary figure on the international stage and created a demand for him to talk about poetry and literature. Fellow Indian independence activists such as Lala Lajpat Rai credited Tagore with drawing the interest of Americans and laying the groundwork for educating Americans about India from a non-British perspective.[4]

Tagore's Nobel Prize award in 1913 drew accolades from American newspapers such as the Philadelphia *Public Ledger*, which argued that Tagore's accomplishments displayed "how the races of the earth [were] ever drawing closer together, growing ever more ready to recognize and acclaim service, wherever the servitor and brother, far or near."[5] The *Outlook*, a weekly magazine in New York, similarly called Tagore's Nobel Prize award a turning point for the West's understanding of Eastern literature, as it placed Indian writers such as Tagore on the international stage and improved the "understanding of one hemisphere by the other."[6] Tagore also impressed American poets Ezra Pound and Harriet Monroe. In 1912, Pound, who was living in London at the time, lauded Tagore's poetry because his poems provided Western audiences with "the calm [they] need[ed] overmuch in an age of steel and mechanics."[7] Similarly, Monroe saw Tagore's poetry as a "tribute" to "all races and creeds" because it preached the universality of God.[8]

Tagore drew attention from American religious groups such as the Unitarians specifically in Urbana, Illinois, in part due to his connection to the Brahmo Samaj, an organization which his father Debendranath co-founded. Tagore was able to utilize his links with the Unitarians to secure guest-speaking opportunities at universities and Unitarian churches, especially in the American Midwest and the Northeast. In these, he attempted to persuade Americans that they could use India as a template to address race, caste, and class issues within the US, and argued against nationalism and ethnic nationalism, believing that nationalism was a root of racism and colonialism. Some of Tagore's trips to the US occurred during World War I, the global impact of which escalated his desire to encourage Americans to learn from the divisive nature of ethnic nationalism and avoid racial friction.

Tagore's Nobel Prize afforded him positive publicity from the American press in prominent newspapers such as the *New York Times* and *New York City Evening Post*. His 1916 and 1917 lecture tours were well attended, and Tagore briefly became an influential figure in the US despite the varying reactions to his critiques of nationalism in media outlets. Tagore's overall impact on American race relations was limited. In Tagore's case, the American public and the American government ignored his warnings against ethnic nationalism and ultimately the tail end of the 1910s saw the US Congress pass immigration restriction laws for Indians and other Asian groups, including the Immigration Act of 1917. The aftermath of World War I and the 1917 Russian Revolution further led to a heightened sense of xenophobia amongst the American public. By 1924, growing ethnic nationalism throughout the country had modified and changed Tagore's affinity for the US and reshaped his own aspirations for India. During Tagore's travels to the US prior to World War I, Tagore optimistically looked at the country as an example of a functional democracy which Indians could model their own nation upon. However, xenophobia and racial tribalism in the US eventually deterred Tagore from drawing upon the country as a source of inspiration for Indians.

Tagore's intellectual feats, including his Nobel Prize victory and lectures and writings on nationalism, showed Americans that Indians were not backward and subjugated. One of his aims was to change India's image as a nation of colonized, patronized, and downtrodden people. Americans such as J. T. Sunderland credited Tagore along with his contemporaries such as M. K. Gandhi and Lala Lajpat Rai for bringing India into public attention in America. He praised Tagore for rehabilitating negative stereotypes about Indians that may have existed in earlier years, such as Indians needing British colonialism to civilize them.[9] Journalists were at times impressed with Tagore's writings and public speaking ability; however, in some instances, American journalists saw him as an outlier amongst the greater Indian population and credited British colonizers for providing him a Western education.

Unlike his messages on colonialism, Tagore's attitude toward caste is less straightforward. Historian Nico Slate portrays Tagore as an Indian thinker who defended the "necessity" of the Indian caste system and portrayed it as a system which "harmonized different 'races.'"[10] However, sources exist in which

Tagore criticized the Indian caste system to his fellow Indian countrymen and referred to Hindus as hypocrites for decrying colonial rule in India while still following the caste system. Tagore at times attenuated the issues of caste to his American audiences. However, contrastingly, he urged Americans to learn from the racial divisions created by the Indian caste system within India and warned Americans that racial divisions from caste systems destroy the harmony of a nation.

When analyzing cosmopolitan thought zones, Kris Manjapra argues that we need to study nationalism and cosmopolitanism as dual, overlapping processes. Manjapra states, "If nationalism was the main political project of resistance in the anti-colonial era, cosmopolitanism was the main ethical project."[11] By this he means cosmopolitanism will also have to consider histories of anti-colonial nationalism to understand the circulation of ideas transnationally. Tagore's cosmopolitanism to some extent represents this anti-colonial nationalism based on his desire to unite Indians and his pride in his Indian heritage. However, Tagore in many cases during his trips to America argued for the abolition of all forms of nationalism, including the nationalist movement of colonized peoples such as Indians. Tagore's cosmopolitanism instead called for the ending of all nations based on ethnic and racial divisions both in India and throughout the world. As Tagore noted, "There is only one history – the history of man" and "I am not against one nation in particular, but against the general idea of all nations."[12] Therefore, Tagore's cosmopolitanism called for the absence of nationalist ideologies and instead saw the abolition of all forms of nationalism as a necessity to peace and racial harmony.

Tagore's Ideas on the Intersection of Caste and Race

As a strong advocate of Indian home rule, Tagore attempted to correspond with international figures and build relationships with Americans to enlist their support. A notable American with whom Tagore built a friendship with was Irish American New York lawyer Myron N. Phelps. Phelps had met with Indian mystic Swami Vivekananda in New York in 1895, but the details of this meeting are unknown to historians.[13] Phelps admired Vivekananda and the Vedanta Society.[14] Inspired by his love for and interest in India and Indians such as Vivekananda, Phelps founded the Indo-American National Association (IANA) in September 1907. The IANA aimed to assist Indian students in America, including providing them with facilities such as housing.

The organization promoted Indian independence in the American press and conveyed the sympathies of Americans toward Indian self-rule through the Indian media.

Tagore and Phelps occasionally corresponded with one another, and Phelps visited Tagore in Calcutta in 1912. In a series of letters to Phelps in 1909 and 1910, Tagore expressed his thoughts regarding caste in India and racism in America. In a 1910 letter, he drew parallels between caste in India and racial conflict in the US, and compared the "assimilation" of Indigenous Indians into a caste system to the genocide of Indigenous Americans. Tagore noted that both the conflict between European colonists and Indigenous Americans (1492 onwards) and that between the Aryan invaders of India and Indigenous Indians (circa 1500 BCE) were fueled by intolerance and inequality. Tagore believed that India, like America, was a geographical entity that many different ethnic groups called home, as opposed to the natural homeland of a singular ethnic or linguistic group. Both India and America were multicultural societies. However, the way in which these two societies dealt with Indigenous ethnic groups was very different from one another. Tagore argued that the Aryan invaders of India were far more merciful because their caste system "enabled races with widely different cultures and even antagonistic social and religious usages and ideals to settle down peacefully side by side."[15] In the Aryan invasion of India, the Indigenous people were assimilated into Aryan society, even if it was as servants and laborers, whereas in the European invasion of America, the bulk of American Indian people were killed through warfare and systematic genocide. Tagore stated,

> When, however, the white-skinned Aryans on encountering the dark aboriginal races of India found themselves face to face with the same problem [two races fighting over a shared homeland], the solution of which was either extermination, as has happened in America and Australia, or a modification in the social system of the superior race calculated to accommodate the inferior race without the possibility of either friction or fusion, they chose the latter.[16]

Nico Slate asserts that Tagore believed that "caste harmonized different 'races' and allowed India to avoid the divisiveness of Western racism."[17] Slate is correct in stating that Tagore saw the Indian caste system as a mixture of different races within a singular society and a more humane alternative to genocide. However, Tagore believed that Indian society was still very divided by "physical differences." He indicated that "it [had] never been India's lot to accept alien races as factors in her civilization."[18] Even though Tagore presented India's caste system as a more humane alternative to the systematic killings of Native Americans, he was aware that India had an internal "race problem" and that caste in India was a discriminatory system influenced by endogamy. While Tagore believed that White colonizers in the US chose to exterminate the Indigenous population rather than place them in a caste system, he noted that they had their own caste system as well. This caste system was the disenfranchisement of Black Americans and other racial minorities.[19]

Tagore did not necessarily view caste as distinct from racial discrimination in the US, since caste was ultimately a system in which a person had privileges based on hereditary traits. In the American system, especially in the US South, if an individual had non-White parents, they were denied the same privileges as White children such as attending a prestigious university like Emory or having access to the same public facilities as White people (although in some cases light-skinned Black Americans could pass as White). Even though in the Indian context Tagore saw caste as a system that brought multiple races together into a singular society, he used a two-tier racial system to define caste in India, in which the "superior race" (the white-skinned Aryans) asserted dominance over "the inferior race" (the aborigines). Tagore was aware of racial divisions in the Indian caste system as well as "color caste" in the US. Therefore, he inevitably viewed American racism and the Indian caste system as having many similarities, although the American system had far more "friction" and was "less peaceful" than the Indian version. The Aryan and non-Aryan distinctions were a major part of Tagore's argument and showed that Tagore believed that caste in India encouraged racial segregation.[20]

Tagore believed that caste in India had a positive impact of ensuring that trades were passed down through heredity but also understood that it restricted personal freedom. Tagore's analysis of the Indian caste system was primarily of its ancient origins, not of the usage of the caste system during British colonial rule. He accepted theories of the origins of caste in India by writers such as Arthur de Gobineau, Herbert Hope Risley, and William Wilson Hunter, and like other Indian Brahmins believed that high-caste Indians differed in race from low-caste Indians. Tagore had read Hunter's book *Indian Empire* and suggested that educated Bengalis read and translate it.[21] He leaned on Hunter's work as most Bengali intellectuals did because they had not yet created an alternative way of interpreting their own land and people.[22] Educated Indians throughout the late nineteenth and early twentieth centuries utilized British sources to understand India's history, and Hunter's books were widely translated and utilized in Indian schools. Tagore, however, was disappointed about this reliance on British literature amongst Bengali intellectuals, noting that "Englishmen write our histories, we translate them; Englishmen salvage our linguistics and grammar, we merely memorize them; even our knowledge of things that are near to our homes is heavily dependent upon Hunter."[23] Although Tagore used the term "Englishmen," he was likely referring to the British, since other British groups such as the Scottish and Welsh were also a part of the British Raj. Tagore wanted to challenge the British narrative of India's history and sought to create a positive impression of Indian culture transnationally.

Tagore's Impact as a Public Speaker in the United States

Tagore made a total of five trips to the US, first between 1912 and 1913, then between 1916 and 1917, between 1920 and 1921, 1929, and 1930. His first visit was in 1912 to see his son Rathindranath who was studying at the University of Illinois in Urbana-Champaign. He made subsequent visitations to the US to raise money for his university at Shantiniketan (near Calcutta).[24] Tagore's literary feats provided him with a celebrity status amongst White Britons and Americans. Therefore, during his first visit, where he spent his time primarily in Urbana, Illinois, Tagore sought to maintain a low profile because he was there to visit his son. Yet he was immediately recognized by the American press to the point where Tagore believed that he was being "stalked" by the media. While he insisted that he did not come to America to be "discovered by Americans," his son told the American press that his father was interested in spreading "a message to the western world." Rathindranath proved to be correct as Tagore accepted public-speaking opportunities at the University of Chicago, Harvard University, and Rochester, New York.[25]

While Tagore was in Urbana, he was invited by local Unitarian minister Reverend Mr Vail to speak on comparative religions at a local Sunday gathering in 1912. Tagore quickly formed an amicable relationship with the members of the group and was invited to speak subsequently. Tagore's relationship with the Unitarians he spoke to in Urbana ignited his career as a public speaker in the US. The shared affinity between Tagore and followers of Unitarianism was not a coincidence. Tagore's father Debendranath Tagore (1817–1905) was a social and religious reformer who was active in the Brahmo Samaj. Additionally, Unitarians had helped organize the 1893 World Parliament of Religions (WPR), which gave Indians such as Swami Vivekananda a platform to share their ideas. Vivekananda's primary motivation for traveling to the US was to raise money for his fellow Indians living in poverty but his success at the parliament also set a precedent for thinkers like Tagore to draw interest amongst White liberals and Unitarians. At the WPR, Vivekananda painted a tolerant and cosmopolitan version of India and claimed that India was accepting of people of all creeds. He emphasized that Hindus believed "not only in universal toleration," but also "accepted all religions as true." He gave several examples of India accepting refugees of "all religions and all nations of the earth," such as Jewish refugees escaping Roman, Muslim, and Christian persecution. Vivekananda condemned religious fanaticism and blamed religious fanatics for spreading violence and degrading human civilization. He noted how positive dialogue between different religions was necessary to create harmonious relations between people of different creeds and ethnic backgrounds.[26] Vivekananda's portrayal of Hinduism as a tolerant religion helped liberal-minded Indians such as Tagore construct connections with Unitarians who practiced a more cosmopolitan version of Christianity that valued equality for women and the abolition of slavery, which were reforms of great importance to Tagore.

In January 1913, Tagore was invited to speak at the University of Chicago by English professor and author Dr Edwin Herbert Lewis.[27] In December 1912, Lewis wrote to the president of the university, Harry Pratt Judson, requesting that he invite Tagore to deliver a series of lectures there. Judson had not heard of Tagore at the time, but he knew of Swami Vivekananda's talk at the WPR. Vivekananda's legacy in Chicago was somewhat mixed by 1912 amongst the academic community. Since Vivekananda's frequent criticisms of British rule in India, some American institutions were hesitant to invite Indian speakers who were unsupportive of British colonialism as the US was a strong ally of Britain.[28] Thus, Lewis specified in his request to Judson that unlike Vivekananda, Tagore was supportive of British rule in India.[29] Judson agreed to invite Tagore as a guest speaker, but he insisted that Tagore present a lecture on his own poetry, rather than on the religions of India, which was the topic Lewis requested. Judson was concerned about Tagore using the platform given to him by the university to build anti-British sentiment.

Tagore's early lectures in the US focused on Indian philosophy and literature. American audiences at the time were not exposed to his political ideologies or any potential anti-colonial sentiments. Therefore, his political and social impact was limited during his first visit to the US. He lectured again at the University of Chicago in January 1913, reading an essay titled the "Ideals of the Ancient Civilization of India," and in February 1913, he presented a philosophical paper at Emerson Hall at Harvard University to an enthusiastic audience, entitled "The Problem of Evil." Both readings were published by Macmillan later in the year as chapters in Tagore's philosophical book *Sadhana: The Realization of Life*.[30] Tagore gave a total of three lectures at Harvard during February. A notable attendee at his lectures was American poet T. S. Eliot, who was a student of Indian Philosophy and Sanskrit at the university.[31] Like Vivekananda, Tagore tried to present an idealistic view of ancient India to illustrate a positive impression of Indian culture.

Some Americans believed that Tagore was an exception amongst Indians rather than the rule. A columnist in the *New York Times* claimed that Tagore had only earned the Nobel Prize due to his "western education" and "Aryan extraction."[32] Instead of applauding Tagore for his accomplishments as an Indian, the columnist chose to credit Tagore's "white education" and racial categorization as an "Aryan." This response is comparable to the patronizing comments Vivekananda received from American journalists remarking on his "mastery of English," only "faintest indications of a foreign accent," and English education.[33] A reporter in Lawrence, Massachusetts, from the *Evening Tribune* highlighted his "swarthy complexion" but lauded Vivekananda as "a finely educated person" due to "his wonderful command of English and his power of argument," and specifically noted Vivekananda's "occasional quotation from Milton and Dickens," which the writer argued "showed that he was appreciative of the great English classics."[34] The reactions of these journalists to Vivekananda and Tagore tally with the attitudes espoused in Rudyard Kipling's "White Man's Burden," written in 1899 to support the American colonization of the Philippines. In the poem, Kipling asserted that White people were morally obliged to civilize non-White peoples, and to encourage their economic, social, and cultural progress through settler colonialism.[35] Furthermore, the journalists' reactions indicated that they believed that Western education could raise non-White people to a similar level of civilization as White people. Their arguments fit within the "White Man's Burden" narrative, which suggested that colonization and education could bring the "lower races" or castes to the same level as "Aryans." They believed that the British were responsible for educating and civilizing Indians, rather than acknowledging that Tagore and Vivekananda had attained their literary and intellectual feats through their own talents.

Tagore did not believe in the "White Man's burden," nor did he give credence to any civilizing mission of White European colonizers in India.[36] He loathed formal British education; he had only spent a day at the Presidency College in Calcutta, and his least favorite subject was English. Tagore did not believe, he claimed, that formal education could impact an individual. School teaching only stoked curiosity, but individuals had to follow and develop their intellectual pursuits outside of that system.[37] Hence, Tagore saw education as an individualistic endeavor that should be pursued through one's own interests, rather than qualifying it as an entity that was provided by society. However, Tagore did value formal education to some extent since he sent his son Rathindranath to study agricultural science in Illinois. It is, therefore, plausible that Tagore supported formal technical education, but he believed the arts and literature to be more personal and that they should be pursued by Indians from a non-British perspective.

After a short stay in Europe, Tagore traveled back to India in September 1913. Although he was a popular figure in both the US and western Europe, he preferred the quiet solitude of his home in Shantiniketan and wanted to escape the international celebrity status afforded to him by his Nobel Prize award.[38] While in Calcutta, Tagore became disturbed that the Indian youth was being educated by British colonizers. Likewise, he condemned the "Aryan supremacy" theorics of Indian Brahmins. In an essay titled "Chhatrasasantra," which was translated into English by the *Modern Review* in April 1916, he argued that Indian students were not learning their true history and condemned the biased "Aryan" supremacy version of India's history. Tagore noted that India belonged not just to "Aryans" but also to the "Dravidian civilizations" of India and Indian Muslims. Tagore called for an "undivided" version of Indian history, which incorporated and synchronized the histories of all groups in India to create unity.[39] Tagore pursued this goal by trying to create his own university in Shantiniketan called Visva-Bharati (eventually established in 1921). However, he needed funding for this, so he set out on another trip abroad. Europe was in the middle of a bloody war by then, so he isolated Japan and the US as the two primary locations in which he could raise money for his university.

Tagore first traveled to Japan in May 1916. However, he could not draw enough interest in his lectures and struggled to raise the money he needed for his university. Hence, he sailed for the US. In the following months, he conducted a coast-to-coast speaking tour in San Francisco, southern California, Salt Lake City, Des Moines, Chicago, Indianapolis, Detroit, Cleveland, and Boston.[40] Unlike his first visit to the US during which he primarily recited poetry and lectured on philosophy, his 1916 lecture tour was political. He explored topics such as nationalism, caste, and racial friction, hoping to inform Americans that xenophobia and division based on race would lead America into a war similar to that being experience by European nations.

Tagore framed his lectures around a speech titled "The Cult of Nationalism." In late 1916, he gave the speech in several cities and venues, including Portland, Louisville, San Francisco, Santa Barbara, Los Angeles, Pasadena, San Diego, Salt Lake City, Denver, Detroit, Milwaukee, Iowa State University, and Carnegie Hall in New York (organized by the Society of Ethical Culture), amongst others. While speaking in Portland, Oregon, at the Drama League of America at Lincoln High School, he admitted that India had "made grave errors in setting up the boundary walls between races," which implied that some races or ethnic groups were seen as superior to others. Tagore did not name which specific races were superior in India, but he was likely referring to lighter-skinned ethnic groups who were descended from the "Aryan" invaders of India and ethnic groups descended from the Scythians, which were a group of nomads who migrated from the Eurasian plains to India between the second century BCE and the fourth century CE. He criticized White Americans for using White supremacy and creating similar "boundaries" between races and excluding Black people and "Asiatics" as inferior groups.[41]

Tagore read the same speech at the Drama League of America in Cincinnati, Ohio, on November 9, and at the Board of Commerce Auditorium to a full audience in Detroit, Michigan, the following day. Tagore's speech was met with mixed reactions. A journalist from the Detroit *Free Press* called Tagore's speech "the most profound analysis of life and of the mechanism of commerce, of organized society and of Government that any modern ears have heard. The Rousseaus, the Jefferson, the Karl Marxes, the Bryees and the Wilsons seem superficial in the presence of this swarthy analyst." However, L. P. Moyle, a resident of Detroit, wrote a letter to the *Free Press*, arguing that the ideas in Tagore's speech represented a "sickly saccharine mental poison" and that Tagore "would corrupt the minds of the youth of our great United States" with his anti-nationalist sentiments.[42]

While some Americans disliked Tagore's anti-nationalist message, the reactions to his speeches were overwhelmingly positive and he attracted large crowds of over two thousand people. In November 1916, the Ohio *Dispatch* suggested that Tagore was an important and influential person but that he was losing some of his popularity because his anti-nationalist arguments alienated many of his followers, especially in the eastern part of the US since support for American involvement in World War I was high in that region of the country. However, the *Dispatch* was incorrect about Tagore's declining popularity. Weeks after the *Dispatch* article was published, he drew large and enthusiastic audiences in New Haven and New York. Despite the attempts of newspapers such as the *Dispatch* to discredit Tagore's ideas as being unpopular, American audiences remained receptive to his anti-nationalist message.[43] Tagore's Carnegie Hall lecture on November 21 was attended by over three thousand audience members, the largest crowd Tagore drew to any of his speeches.

The *San Francisco Examiner* noted that Tagore's speeches on nationalism had "stirred the intellectual world as the thoughts of no other contemporaneous writer ha[d] done" and that he had "taken San Francisco by storm."[44] In December 1916, the president of Yale University, Arthur Twining Hadley, presented Tagore with the Yale Bicentennial medal. Audiences filled to overflowing the halls and theaters where he spoke against the evils of nationalism, "at about seven hundred dollars per scold," which was the lecture fee Tagore charged per event.[45] A White undergraduate student at the State University of Iowa lauded Tagore's intelligence stating, "I thought that the Hindus were a bunch of people who needed to be taught; but now comes a Hindu who can really teach us Americans. For the love of Mike! Doesn't that beat all!"[46] Edwin Lewis similarly denied that Tagore's influence had declined. In January 1917, Lewis presented a paper at the Chicago Literary Club arguing that Tagore's anti-nationalist message was well-received by American soldiers who were fighting in the "Great War" and that Tagore had played a strong role toward uniting the East and the West through his poetry. In his 1917 essay "The Work of Tagore," Lewis suggested that soldiers were not singing "McAndrew's Hymn," a poem by British imperialist Rudyard Kipling, but were reading the poems of Rabindranath Tagore in their hospital beds. Lewis did not present evidence that he had seen soldiers reading Tagore's work, but he nevertheless believed that Tagore's role in spreading Indian literature to Western audiences was profound, and that he was an influential and important figure in modifying American opinion toward war and nationalism.[47]

While Tagore drew enthusiastic crowds throughout his lecture tours, some Indian revolutionaries in the US who were associated with the Ghadar Party criticized Tagore for not aggressively denouncing British rule in India during his tour of the US.[48] In October 1916, Ram Chandra, the president of the Ghadar Party, wrote a scathing letter in the *San Francisco Examiner* criticizing Tagore for accepting a knighthood from the British and for arguing that the British Raj was better for Indians than former rulers such as the Mughals. Chandra pointed out that British rule was far worse for Indians because under Mughal rule Hindus had been appointed to high positions, whereas the proportion of Indian to British officials in the government (local and central) was abysmal, and the drain of wealth to Britain remained in the realm of millions of dollars.[49] In response to Tagore's comments, Chandra and the Ghadar Party attempted to protest against Tagore's California lectures and block him from speaking. An incident on October 5, 1916, became violent when Professor Bishen Sing Mattu of Khalsa Diwan Society, a Sikh gurdwara (place of worship) in Vancouver, Canada, and two of his associates went to the Palace Hotel in San Francisco to meet with Tagore. They were attacked by Ghadar Party members Hateshi Singh and Jiwan Singh. Police arrested the attackers and Tagore immediately left for Santa Barbara. While Tagore downplayed the incident and denied knowledge of the attack, some newspapers such as the *San Francisco Examiner* deemed the attack to be an assassination attempt on him.[50] Throughout his lectures in the US, Tagore refrained from attempting to sway American opinion toward supporting Indian independence. He understood that the British Raj could limit his opportunities to travel abroad if he spoke out against it. Tagore had come to the US with the purpose of raising money for his university in Shantiniketan. He did not want to jeopardize losing his paid speaking opportunities in the US.[51]

Although reactions to Tagore's lectures were both positive and negative, they drew the attention of Macmillan Publishers and G. P. Brett visited Tagore in New York.[52] Macmillan published Tagore's key speeches on nationalism in an anthology of essays titled *Nationalism* the following year. Tagore wished to dedicate *Nationalism* to Woodrow Wilson because he believed that Wilson was an anti-colonialist who supported self-determination for nations such as the Philippines through gradual autonomy toward independence.[53] Wilson's plan for self-determination was somewhat vague and it was not clear if he supported self-determination for only European nations or also non-European nations. Historian Erez Manela argues that he did "not exclude non-European peoples" from his self-determination ideology as "matter of principle."[54] Nevertheless, Wilson believed that self-determination for colonial subjects should be granted by European nations in a guided, orderly manner.[55] Hence, the British Raj exploited Wilson's ideology and utilized the "White man's burden" to its advantage and argued that Indians were not ready or developed enough for immediate self-government. While Wilson supported self-determination for the Philippines, he did not support it for other colonial subjects in Porto Rico (Puerto Rico) and the Hawaiian Islands.[56]

Misguided regarding Wilson's self-determination policy, Tagore also failed to critique Wilson's lack of action toward ending discrimination for Indigenous and Black Americans in the US. While in principle, Wilson supported self-determination for some colonial subjects abroad, he did not support self-determination for Indigenous (Native) Americans. Denied citizenship, Indigenous Americans were essentially treated as colonial subjects with no rights under the US constitution even though they lived in the US. Wilson also did little to advance Black civil rights, he supported Jim Crow segregation, and his administration escalated discriminatory hiring policies against Black Americans for federal jobs. Wilson's administration continued the segregation of government offices that had begun under President Theodore Roosevelt and had continued under President William Taft.[57] Although Wilson did not directly segregate federal departments himself, he allowed his cabinet secretaries to enforce the divisions in federal departments. By the end of 1913, many departments, including the Navy, Treasury, and Postal Service, had segregated workspaces, restrooms, and cafeterias. Many agencies used segregation as a pretext to adopt Whites-only employment policies. Black employees were either fired or transferred to lesser facilities.[58]

Tagore's lack of awareness of the Wilson administration's racial discrimination against Black Americans showed that he was not particularly interested in the domestic politics of the US or its imperialist colonization of Puerto Rico, Hawai'i, and Guam, amongst others. Nevertheless, Tagore admired Wilson because he publicly preached an anti-war and anti-nationalist message and tried to negotiate a peace deal between the Allied and Central powers during World War I. Macmillan Publishers wrote to the president requesting his permission for the dedication. Wilson's adviser, Colonel Edward M. House, counseled against it because his British contact, Sir William Wiseman, Britain's special liaison agent in the US, warned him that Tagore was involved with Indian revolutionaries living in the US. Although Wiseman did not have any evidence that Tagore was involved with the Ghadar Party, Wiseman argued that Tagore had gotten "tangled up in some way" with the party because of the incident in San Francisco. In fact, Tagore was not involved with the Ghadar Party or any revolutionary activity whatsoever. Tagore wrote to President Wilson himself to clarify that the accusations against him were false and that he "despised" violent revolutionary methods. He never received a response from Wilson, and it was likely that the president never saw the letter because the Wilson administration prioritized concerns related to the war.[59]

Tagore intended to use his publication *Nationalism* to encourage American readers to avoid ethnic nationalism, a form of nationalism that highlighted racial differences and excluded ethnic groups outside of a nation's dominant culture. Perhaps Tagore's most significant essays in his Macmillan publication were "Nationalism in India" and "Nationalism in the West" which were based on his "Cult of Nationalism" lecture. Tagore criticized White Americans for failing to achieve racial unity. He argued against ethnic nationalism by illustrating racial problems in his own country. Tagore wrote and lectured amid World War I, during which various "nation-states" fought for greater control of Europe and colonial possessions in Africa and Asia. He was concerned that Europeans were making fatal mistakes by fighting each other instead of coexisting in a multicultural society. He believed that he needed to spread a strong anti-nationalist message to prevent Americans from supporting the same racialized ethnic nationalism that plagued the bulk of Europe during the war.[60]

Tagore traveled to the US during a contentious period for Asian immigrants. Due to ethnic nationalism, Asians were unwanted in the country by xenophobic White Americans. During the late nineteenth century, the US had experienced large-scale immigration by Chinese and Japanese immigrants on the West Coast. In response to Asian immigrants, some White Americans formed organizations to either limit Asian immigration to the US or prohibit new immigrants from attending schools for White Americans. Organizations such as the Asiatic Exclusion League (AEL) pressured the San Francisco school board to force all Japanese and Korean students to join their Chinese counterparts at the segregated Oriental School in 1906.[61] Additionally, in 1907 the AEL applied pressure on Congress to tighten existing immigration legislation, which led President Theodore Roosevelt to utilize an executive order to end migration by Japanese laborers from both Hawai'i and Mexico.[62] Similarly the AEL violently targeted Indian immigrants on the West Coast. The most notable incident was the Bellingham riots, which occurred on September 4, 1907, in Bellingham, Washington. The riots involved a mob of four hundred to five hundred White men, primarily members of the AEL, who intended to prevent East Indian immigrants from joining the workforce of the local lumber mills. The mob attacked the homes of South Asian immigrants, pushed them into the streets, beat them, and pocketed their valuables. Many Indian immigrants, fearing for their lives, left Washington, and fled to British Columbia to escape racial tensions.[63] None of the participants in the mob violence were prosecuted.[64] Tagore placed a strong emphasis on trying to change the xenophobic attitudes of White Americans by using racism and caste apartheid in India as a learning template to address racial division and ethnic nationalism in the US.

To encourage Americans to abandon growing nationalism within their society, Tagore used the Indian example of race and caste discrimination to show that if ethnic groups were divided, society could not prosper. He argued that India's racial problem – their lack of unity between various ethnic groups, whom Tagore referred to as races – was far more ancient than American racism. "From the earliest beginnings of history," he wrote, "India has had her own problem constantly before her – it is the race problem." It was a "social" problem rather than a "political" one and had yet to be solved by the Indian people.[65] Tagore criticized privileged White Americans for critiquing India's caste problem while creating caste systems within their own country. While he argued that India's race issue was comparable to American racism, he noted that India, unlike America, had at least attempted to solve the problems of race and caste without the use of violence and genocide as the Americans had done with the "Red Indian" (Native Americans) and the "Negro."[66] Tagore did not identify why he thought race was a "problem" in India. However, his usage of the term signified his view that human beings naturally divided themselves by physical differences and that race was the strongest indication of "physical difference."[67] He asserted that once India had solved its race and caste problem, it would help the rest of the world solve these issues as well.

Tagore believed that India had to assimilate its races and ethnicities, terms which he used interchangeably, into one singular society.[68] Tagore's comments in his "Nationalism in India" essay illustrated a more explicit condemnation of xenophobia and racialism amongst the Indian people in comparison to his comments in his 1909 conversation with Myron N. Phelps. In his letter to Phelps, Tagore suggested that even though caste created a society of segregation, it had successfully assimilated multiple races together without violence. He did not criticize endogamy as a hinderance to a unified Indian culture or India's functionality as a civilization. However, by 1917, Tagore unabatedly considered endogamous caste to be an ineffective method of assimilation. Tagore altered his views on caste for three reasons. First, Tagore became increasingly more aware about the oppression of lower-caste peasants by upper-caste Hindu leaders. Second, Tagore saw caste discrimination as practiced by Indian Brahmins to be an impediment to India's progress. Third, he theorized that a caste-influenced culture of endogamy and apartheid between various castes and between Hindus and Muslims prevented unity among Indians.[69]

Additionally, Tagore may have chosen to condemn ethnic and religious segregation in India more explicitly in his essays in *Nationalism* because of the growing ethnic nationalism in Europe and the US and the culmination of World War I. Tagore attributed the causes of World War I to ethnic nationalism. Various ethnic groups divided themselves up into nation states based on ethnicity and fought groups they deemed ethnically different. Ethnic nationalism was a common theme of the late nineteenth and early twentieth centuries across the world. The situation in India between various ethnic groups and races was not any different. Furthermore, Indians who lived apart in different villages were brought in greater contact with one another as a consequence of modernization and economic change. Migrations to urban areas through railroads and industrialization placed Indians of different ethnicities, religions, and castes into the same community. Tagore did not want Indian communities to become divided. He wanted harmony and unity between ethnic groups in India and he re-evaluated the effectiveness of caste as a viable assimilation technique.[70]

Deeming endogamous caste to be a failed method of assimilation, Tagore suggested that integration be facilitated by racial or ethnic intermarriage. He believed racial mixing was a global solution to racial discrimination and could solve both India and America's race problems. Tagore argued that "through scientific facility" or racial mixing the world would become "one country." Thus, Tagore saw "nationalism" as being a hindrance to solving racial inequality as it sought to establish different "nation states" divided by race, culture, and language. In "Nationalism in India," Tagore challenged ideas that divided "nation states" based on ethnic groups noting, "There is only one history – the history of man. All national histories are merely chapters in the larger one. And we are content in India to suffer for such a great cause." Tagore reasserted his dismay of nation states, stating, "I am not against one nation in particular, but against the general idea of all nations."[71]

Tagore's endorsement of racial mixing and the world becoming "one country" denote marked inconsistencies in his thinking. Only a year earlier in 1916, Tagore was quoted in the *Kewanee Ills Courier* as stating, "They [nations] must always exist as separate identities. The world would be unbeautiful and monotonous without variety. But no nation must predominate. Each one has a right to proper expression as part of a great unit. Any system which does not take this into consideration must produce evil." This shift in thinking caused papers such as the *Portland M.L. Press* to brand Tagore as a hypocrite, who did not believe in the "colorless cosmopolitan" world society that he preached in his essays and lectures. The paper also noted that during the Bengal Swadeshi movement (1905–1911), which involved the economic boycott of British goods and the revival of domestic products and production, Tagore was indeed a "nationalist" in the "Western" sense, meaning that he promoted Indian exceptionalism over working with Britain.[72] However, the *Minneapolis*

Tribune argued that during the Swadeshi movement, Tagore was "more concerned with the problems of his own country than with the problems of humanity." Therefore, Tagore was both a "nationalist" and an "internationalist" arguing for both the nation's autonomy for "self-rule" and awareness of its role in the global community. This evaluation by *The Minneapolis Tribune* was an accurate one, as Tagore believed in "self-rule" and the preservation of individual culture while still advocating the ideas of globalism and the intermingling of races. The *Milwaukee Wisconsin* also hinted that Tagore perhaps interpreted "nationalism" as having two separate meanings, one in regards to a nation's unified desire to free itself from foreign oppression, "Indian nationalism," and another in which a nation exploits another society for profit and gain and uses divide and conquer strategies to keep races divided, such as "Western nationalism."[73] Because some members of the American press perceived Tagore as having a double standard regarding "nationalism" in India and "nationalism" in the West, selected audiences deemed Tagore's ideas to not be genuine and his impact on Americans was partially blunted.

Akin to Swami Vivekananda, Tagore sought to place India on an international stage and make it an exemplar of inclusion for the rest of the world. Tagore believed that if the people of India, a very diverse society with many ethnic and linguistic groups, could live in harmony, then the US, a country with far fewer ethnic groups, could do the same. Similarly, Vivekananda painted a glorified picture of India as the epitome of spirituality and peace. Tagore, on the other hand, was more honest about race and caste friction in India to American audiences, but he maintained an outlook that India's caste system tried to harmonize different races into a singular society while caste in America sought to keep races apart. He did not defend India's caste system, but he noted that India had at least attempted to form some unity between different races by accepting various religions into its society. Tagore implored White American readers, "What have you done with the Red Indian and the Negro? For you have not got over your attitude of caste toward them. You have used violent methods to keep aloof from other races, but until you have solved the question here in America, [White Americans] have no right to question India."[74] Hence, Tagore used American racism as a shield against foreign criticism of the Indian caste system. He did not acknowledge that India's caste system was ingrained within its religious institutions and was an integral part of Hinduism.

Tagore presented caste in India to American audiences in a similar manner as Vivekananda, suggesting that India's caste system was not as violent and pervasive as American racism. However, while Vivekananda praised Hindus for their tolerance of other religions, he criticized them for caste prejudice and the extreme social inequality within the caste system. Like Vivekananda, Tagore was more critical of caste in India when writing to Indian audiences. In a 1908 essay in the Bengali journal *Prabasi*, Tagore told his Bengali countrymen that they were hypocrites for decrying colonial rule in India while still following the caste system. He similarly acknowledged to his Indian audience that "samaj" (religious society) was to blame for caste discrimination and claimed that because of caste discrimination, India "fail[ed] to do justice to herself."[75] Similarly, Vivekananda tried to enable caste reform by exploiting Hindu fears that their religion could become a minority religion if they did not end exclusionary caste policies such as caste segregation. Vivekananda warned his audience that British colonialism could influence low-caste Indians to become Christians or Muslims if Hindus did not reform their caste system and allow this group an avenue out of extreme poverty. He cautioned that discrimination against low-caste Indians and disparities in living standards was why "one-fifth of our people [former low-caste Indian Hindus] have become Mohammedans [Muslims]."[76] To maintain unity and harmony amongst Hindus and to avoid the conversion of low-caste Hindus to Christianity or Islam, Vivekananda endorsed caste reform more aggressively while speaking to Indian audiences.

Hence, both Vivekananda and Tagore believed that caste hierarchies and caste discrimination in India needed to end to unite the country and to give Indians a moral claim to denounce British colonial rule. However, to American audiences, Vivekananda and Tagore wanted to show that Indians were already as capable, if not more capable than Americans, to cope with self-rule and self-determination. They therefore, at times, downplayed the pervasiveness of caste discrimination in India.

While Tagore saw similarities between caste in Indian society and racial discrimination in American society, he believed that the motives behind the implementation of these systems were different. He was critical of the Indian caste system, but he believed that its motivation stemmed from the "production of commodities" and that its chief objective was the perfect satisfaction of social needs. Conversely, in American society, racial conflict was "guided by the impulse of competition whose end is the gain of wealth for individuals."[77] Therefore, Tagore argued that American racism was propagated by capitalism, whereas the Indian caste system was a more "rational" system that had merely failed by creating finite social divisions and hierarchies.

Tagore presented nationalism, race, and caste as overlapping concepts. He argued that in small nations such as Switzerland, nationalism was not quite as divisive as it was in larger nations such as India and the US. He asserted that Swiss nationalism was less problematic because the "races" of Switzerland were all of "the same blood," therefore they could intermarry and had common birth privileges. By maintaining that the "races" were of "the same blood," Tagore once again used the terms "race" and "ethnicity" interchangeably. He noted that in a larger nation such as India, the greater differences in races had created "physical repulsion," which had led to caste differences. He believed that the "physical repulsion" the various races in India had for one another presented many difficulties in forming unity within Indian society. He thought that unless this "physical repulsion" was lessened and Indians intermarried with different races and religious groups, Indians would never "shed blood for one another except by coercion or for mercenary purpose[s]." Therefore, in Tagore's view, racism and "caste differences" within Indian society prevented Indians from uniting and successfully defeating British imperialism.[78] Tagore never specified what "physical differences" prevented Indians from intermarrying. However, he equated "physical differences" to "different castes." Thus, he encouraged a comparable caste narrative to scientific racists such as Herbert Hope Risley, who claimed that Indians practiced endogamy based on physical features, such as small differences in skin color and bone structure, particularly the ratio of nose width to height. Risley argued that castes with the "finest nose" were at the top of the social ladder, and Indians with "the coarsest" noses belonged to lower castes.[79]

In addition to interrogating America's "attitude of caste" toward Black and Indigenous Americans, Tagore criticized American attitudes toward Asian immigrants. In an interview with the New York City *Evening Post* on November 20, 1916, he considered the anti-Asian Immigration Bill that was being discussed by Congress. The bill would later be passed as the Immigration Act of 1917 (Asiatic Barred Zone Act) on February 5, 1917. Building on the Chinese Exclusion Act of 1882, the Immigration Act of 1917 further broadened immigration restrictions and excluded Indians, Afghans, and Arabs, amongst other non-White groups from Asia, but made an exception for Russians from areas west of the Ural Mountains because they were fair-skinned and phenotypically akin to White Europeans.[80] Tagore contended that this legislation was politically and economically motivated. He believed that the US government might have received pressure from the British to deny entry to Indian immigrants out of fears that other Indians abroad were engaging in anti-colonial activism. Furthermore, he noted correctly that the US government feared that Indian students in the US were a threat to US citizens who were looking for work as qualified Indian graduates added increased competition to the job market.[81]

Tagore's strong awareness of American racism, as exemplified by his writings in *Nationalism*, makes it curious that he downplayed the racial motivations behind the Immigration Act of 1917 in an interview with the *Evening Post*. In earlier correspondence, Tagore had mentioned that racial animosity and "color caste" in Western societies led to the exclusion of "Asiatics from European colonies."[82] Therefore, Tagore was cognizant of anti-Asian racism in Western society, and had been very critical of it in his private letters. What was even more curious was that just a month earlier, on October 4, 1916, during an interview with the *Bridgeport Standard* in Connecticut, Tagore had noted that America was the "only nation engaged in solving the problems of race intimacy."[83] He praised the US for "permitting all races entry and widening the ideal of humanity." Tagore's inconsistent portrayal of American racism in his public interviews and private letters proved that he was more willing to criticize American racism privately than publicly.[84] This may have been because Britain had a strong alliance with the US and the British government could revoke Tagore's travel privileges if he was too aggressive in his disparaging of Britain and the US. The British government in India was monitoring the activities of Indians abroad and was concerned about Indians in the US using the country as a base to convey anti-British propaganda and build alliances with Americans to overthrow them. British agents such as Sir William Wiseman falsely believed that Tagore was involved in conspiring against the British government in India.[85]

After the passage of the Immigration Act of 1917, Tagore's view of America and American culture became more negative. Although he visited the US on three more occasions – first between 1920 and 1921, then again in 1929 and 1930 – he did not receive the same reception as previously. While Tagore's 1916 trip to America helped him raise enough money to open his university, Visva-Bharati, he had planned to raise an additional five million dollars for the institution during his 1920 trip to America; however, his fundraising effort failed.[86] America's changing political climate contributed to Tagore's declining popularity as the US government and public opinion became less welcoming to immigrants. The US judiciary further racialized immigration restrictions in 1923 after the *United States v. Bhagat Singh Thind* Supreme Court case deemed that only members of the "white" or "Caucasian" race were eligible for American citizenship and stripped many non-Europeans of their citizenship. Thus, the US government endorsed racial and ethnic nationalism and solidified the definition of the "white race" as Americans and immigrants with White European ancestry only. Hence, Tagore's anti-nationalist message was not as sought after by American audiences as it was during

Wilson's presidency. During his 1920–1921 trip, Tagore mostly recited poetry and literature at women's clubs, and he had a brief profitable lecture tour in Texas after failing to draw enough interest in New York to raise additional funds for his university.[87]

Unable to fulfil his requirements in the US, Tagore traveled to Germany where he was a far more popular figure. By 1921, Tagore's plays were in high demand on the major stages of Germany in Berlin, Munich, and Frankfurt. Rabindranath Tagore's books sold more copies in Germany between 1917 and 1924 than in any other country.[88] His response from the German public was so strong that he wrote to his friend, Anglican priest and Christian missionary Charles Freer (C. F.) Andrews stating, "It has been a wonderful experience in this country for me! Such fame as I have got, I cannot take at all seriously. It is too readily given, and too immediate."[89] Because of the interest he drew there, Tagore saw Germany as a desirable alternative to the US for raising funds for his university.

In his 1924 travelogue recounting his trips to America, Tagore admitted that he was disillusioned with the idea that Americans believed in equality and cooperation between different ethnic groups. He criticized Americans for following purely individualistic goals such as gaining materialistic wealth and possessions. He similarly asserted that some Americans had an "antipathic" and xenophobic attitude toward Asians, Germans, Russians, and their own Black citizens. Tagore did not specify which Americans were xenophobic toward these groups but since he referred to anti-German xenophobia, he was likely referring to White Anglo-Saxon Americans. The xenophobic attitudes toward Germans likely stemmed from the culmination of World War I, with the German state and German people representing a threat to the Anglo hegemony of Great Britain, America's ally, during World War I. The Russian Empire had been an ally of Britain and the US during World War I, but the Russian Revolution of 1917 and the newly formed Bolshevik government was perceived by Britain and the US as a threat to capitalism. Thus, Tagore, an ardent anti-nationalist, believed nationalism in the US had become worse after the war, based on the negative attitude amongst Americans toward Germans and Russians. His pleas to Americans to avoid ethnic nationalism throughout his 1916 and 1917 lecture tour and in his 1917 book *Nationalism* had been ignored by much of the American public. He asserted that xenophobic nationalist attitudes toward immigrants from foreign nations represented the "mob psychology" of the American people and this xenophobic mob psychology was the very backbone of American "political civilization."[90] He related the "mob psychology" of White Americans to the lynchings of Black Americans, noting that "[in America] Negroes are burnt alive, sometimes merely because they tried to exercise their right to vote, [which is] given to them by law."[91] Tagore's negative illustration of American culture marked a shift from his earlier representations of American culture when he believed that Americans were working to create "race intimacy." While Tagore left America disappointed and discouraged by the nation's failed potential to become a positive representation of race harmony on a global level, it was not a total loss for him. There were those among his White American audience that had had their xenophobic attitudes toward India altered by Tagore.

Akin to Vivekananda, Tagore did not immerse himself in the Black American experience. He came to America to raise money for his university and, like Vivekananda, he primarily lectured to wealthier White audiences. He also did not prioritize the Black American struggle in his lectures because he believed that it was more urgent for him to inform Americans about the flaws of ethnic nationalism, primarily because he understood that to be the cause of World War I. Hence, he interrogated race in the context of nationalism, and he used the example of friction between races and ethnic groups in India to encourage Americans to create racial unity within their own country to avoid the same division that existed between races and religious groups in India. Tagore asserted that America could learn from the failures of the Indian caste system, which divided racial, ethnic, and religious groups. He urged his American readers to eliminate their own system of caste toward Black Americans and Native Americans.[92] After the war, Tagore was disappointed that he was unable to impact and change the xenophobic attitudes of Americans toward the people of Asia and the Soviet Union. He looked at American animosity toward Asians and Soviets as an example that he did not want India to follow.

Tagore's experiences in America modified his vision and aspirations for India. Although the US was a wealthy nation and Tagore claimed that "Western people have made their money," their pursuit of money represented "utter vanity." He argued that the pursuit of money was a form of "imaginary freedom" because Americans were too attached to material possessions. Additionally, he believed that the chase for financial acquisitions motivated European nations as well as the US to pursue expansionist or colonial policies. In some ways, Tagore pitied the American upper-class's attachment to wealth and material possessions. He did not want Indians to emulate upper-class Americans, noting that "[w]e, in India have to show what is the truth." "The truth," according to Tagore, was "moral force" (peace, non-confrontation, and harmony) rather than "brute force" (warfare, colonization, and using natural resources for material gain). By the early 1920s, Mahatma Gandhi was rising to prominence in India and his promotion of non-violence to challenge colonialism was keenly felt by Tagore. He thought that Gandhi could show Americans this "moral force" since he was "devoid of all material resources." India under Gandhi's leadership could "raise the history of man from the muddy level of physical conflict" and allow India to serve as an example of peace and tolerance. His goal during his trips to America was not to just raise money for his university but also to spread an anti-nationalist message that could end warfare and colonization. However, he fell short in his mission. Tagore came to hope that perhaps Gandhi's example of asceticism could accomplish what he could not. He asserted that creating international peace through "moral force" was more important than Indian "Swaraj" (self-rule) as the idea of treating India as a "Nation" was borrowed from the West.[93] Just as Tagore envisaged Indian independence as having a global impact, Indians from the Ghadar Party had similar ambitions of ensuring that an independent India could benefit the rest of the world.

Notes

1. Rabindranath Tagore, *Selected Poems of Rabindranath Tagore*, ed. William Radice (London: Penguin Classics, 2005), 24.
2. Ibid.
3. Ibid., 79.
4. Dipesh Chakrabarty, "Friendships in the Shadow of Empire: Tagore's Reception in Chicago, circa 1913–1932," *Modern Asian Studies* 48, no. 5 (2014): 1161–1187, 1162; Lala Lajpat Rai, *Young India*, January 1918.
5. Stephen N. Hay, "Rabindranath Tagore in America," *American Quarterly* 14, no. 3 (1962): 439–463, 445.
6. Ibid.
7. Chakrabarty, "Friendships in the Shadow of Empire," 170.
8. Ibid., 169.
9. J. T. Sunderland, "Communications: India's Need of Foreign Propaganda," *The People*, May 16, 1926.
10. Nico Slate, *Colored Cosmopolitanism: The Shared Struggle for Freedom in the United States and India* (Cambridge: Harvard University Press, 2012), 58.
11. Vinayak Chaturvedi, "Cosmopolitan Thought Zones: South Asia and the Global Circulation of Ideas," *Journal of Global History* 6, no. 3 (November 2011): 538–539.
12. Ibid., 28–29.
13. Arvind Gururao Ganachari, "Myron H. Phelps (1856–1916): An Early American Advocate of India's Freedom," *Proceedings of the Indian History*

Congress 52 (1991): 650–651; Alan Raucher, "American Anti-Imperialists and the Pro-India Movement, 1900–1932," *Pacific Historical Review* 43, no. 1 (1974): 83–110, 86.

14. Harald Fischer-Tiné, "Indian Nationalism and the 'World Forces': Transnational and Diasporic Dimensions of the Indian Freedom Movement on the Eve of the First World War," *Journal of Global History* 2, no. 3 (2007): 325–344, 333; Raucher, "American Anti-Imperialists and the Pro-India Movement, 1900–1932," 83.

15. Rabindranath Tagore to Myron N. Phelps, August 1910, in *Selected Letters of Rabindranath Tagore*, ed. Krishna Dutta and Andrew Robinson (Cambridge: Cambridge University Press, 1997), 74–77.

16. Ibid., 74–77; While Tagore was correct that European colonizers of America used violence, displacement, and warfare against Indigenous Americans, more than half of the Indigenous population died from the effects of diseases such as measles, smallpox, and cholera. Arthur C. Aufderheide, Conrado Rodríguez-Martín, and Odin Langsjoen, *The Cambridge Encyclopedia of Human Paleopathology* (Cambridge: Cambridge University Press, 1998), 205.

17. Slate, *Colored Cosmopolitanism*, 58.

18. Tagore to Phelps, *Selected Letters of Rabindranath Tagore*, 74–77.

19. Ibid.

20. Ibid.

21. Rabindranath Tagore, "Bharatbarser Itihas: Hemlata Devi" (1903), British Library, London.

22. Pritam Mukherjee, "William Wilson Hunter and Colonial Bengal Historiography Literature Modernity," PhD diss. (Jadavpur University, 2015), 300.

23. Rabindranath Tagore, "Safalatar Sadupay," in *Rabindra Rachanabali* Vol. 13 (Kolkata: West Bengal Government, 1990), 70.

24. According to Stephen N. Hay, Tagore spent a total of seventeen months in the US during these years and it was the longest amount of time he spent in any country outside of India and the United Kingdom; Hay, "Rabindranath Tagore in America," 439.

25. Hay, "Rabindranath Tagore in America," 442.

26. Swami Vivekananda, "Response to Welcome" (speech, Chicago, September 11, 1893), Belur Math, https://belurmath.org/swami-vivekananda-speeches-at-the-parliament-of-religions-chicago-1893/, accessed August 2021.

27. Chakrabarty, "Friendships in the Shadow of Empire," 1165.

28. William C. Reuter, "The Anatomy of Political Anglophobia in the United States, 1865–1900," *Mid America* 61, no. 2 (1979): 117–132.

29. Chakrabarty, "Friendships in the Shadow of Empire," 1168.

30. Ibid., 1162.

31. Jeffry M. Perl and Andrew P. Tuck, "The Hidden Advantage of Tradition: On the Significance of T.S. Eliot's Indic Studies," *Philosophy East and*

West 35, no. 2 (1985): 116–131; "A Timeline of Tagore's Life and Work," http://www.rabindratirtha-wbhidcoltd.co.in/Rabisarani/event/VZlSX RFWwJlUsRmdT1WNXJ1aKVVVB1TP, accessed January 30, 2021.

32. *New York Times*, November 15, 1913, 10; *New York Tribune*, November 14, 1913.

33. "Swami Vivekananda Tells of Ancient Faith Speaks Again Tonight," *Daily Iowa Capitol*, November 28, 1893.

34. "Swami Vivekananda Tells about the Religion of High Caste Indians," *Evening Tribune*, Lawrence, Massachusetts, May 16, 1894. Note: There are several other accounts in the American Newspaper Reports section in Vol. 9 of *The Complete Works of Swami Vivekananda* where American reporters frequently compliment Vivekananda's mastery of the English language while praising his Western education.

35. Christopher Hitchens, *Blood, Class, and Empire: The Enduring Anglo–American Relationship* (New York: Nation Books, 2004), 63–64; *The Oxford Companion to English Literature*, 6th edition (New York: Oxford University Press, 2006), 88.

36. K. Dutta and A. Robinson, *Rabindranath Tagore: An Anthology* (Saint Martin: Saint Martin's Press, 1997), 127, 210, 324.

37. K. Dutta and A. Robinson, *Rabindranath Tagore: The Myriad-Minded Man* (Saint Martin: Saint Martin's Press, 1995), 50.

38. Rabindranath Tagore to Somendrachandra Devbarma, October 12, 1913.

39. Mohit Chakrabarti, *Rabindranath Tagore: Diverse Dimensions* (New Delhi: Atlantic Publishers and Distributers, 1990), 134–135.

40. Hay, "Rabindranath Tagore in America," 445–447.

41. Rabindranath Tagore, "Nationalism in the West," in *Nationalism*, 11–61 (New York: Macmillan, 1917), 15.

42. Rabindra Smaraka Grantha, "Rabindranath in America – Cincinnati, Ohio & Detroit, Michigan," Rabindranath Tagore – A Search for Creativity of Rabindranath (Blog), March 3, 2012, http://sesquicentinnial.blogspot.com/2012/03/rabindranath-in-america-cincinnati-ohio.html, accessed February 2021.

43. Hay, "Rabindranath Tagore in America," 448–449.

44. Ibid., 446.

45. Ibid., 445.

46. Sudhindra Bose, "Sir Rabindranath Tagore at the State University of Iowa," *Modern Review* 21, no. 2 (February 1917): 216–220, 220.

47. E. H. Lewis, *The Work of Tagore* (Chicago: Chicago Literary Club, 1917), 16; Chakrabarty, "Friendships in the Shadow of Empire," 1177.

48. The Ghadar Party was a revolutionary group of Indians located in the US who sought to overthrow the British empire through armed revolution.

49. *San Francisco Examiner*, October 5, 1916, 22.

50. Hay, "Rabindranath Tagore in America," 450; Subrata Kumar Das, "Tagore's Crisis in America: An Overview," https://www.academia.edu/9554036/Tagore_s_Crisis_in_America_An_Overview, accessed November 15, 2020.

51. Sunderland, "Communications." Sunderland noted that Tagore's hesitancy towards openly criticizing British Rule in India to American audiences might have been influenced by the fact that Britain could deny Tagore opportunities to visit America if he were to make statements in favor of Indian independence.

52. "A Timeline of Tagore's Life and Work."

53. John Milton Cooper Jr., *Woodrow Wilson* (New York: Knopf Doubleday Publishing Group, 2009), 249.

54. Erez Manela, *The Wilsonian Moment: Self-Determination and the International Origins of Anticolonial Nationalism* (New York: Oxford University Press, 2007), 25.

55. Arnulf Becker Lorca, *Mestizo International Law: A Global Intellectual History 1842–1933*, Cambridge Studies in International and Comparative Law (Cambridge: Cambridge University Press, 2015) 259.

56. Woodrow Wilson, "State of the Union 1913," December 2, 1913; Daniel Immerwahr, *How to Hide an Empire: A History of the Greater United States* (New York: Picador, Farrar, Straus, and Giroux, 2019), 4. Immerwahr notes that Wilson referred to Puerto Rico and Hawai'i as colonies. However, to portray the US as a non-colonial nation, American officials referred to their colonial possessions as "territories."

57. Manu Karuka, "Black and Native Visions of Self-Determination," *Critical Ethnic Studies* 3, no. 2 (2017): 77–98, 81–82; August Meier and Elliott Rudwick, "The Rise of Segregation in the Federal Bureaucracy, 1900–1930," *Phylon (1960–)* 28, no. 2 (1967): 178–184.

58. Kathleen L. Wolgemuth, "Woodrow Wilson and Federal Segregation," *The Journal of Negro History* 44, no. 2 (1959): 158–173; David Levering Lewis, *W.E.B. Du Bois: Biography of a Race 1868–1919* (New York: Henry Holt and Company, 1993), 332.

59. Erez Manela, "Imagining Woodrow Wilson in Asia: Dreams of East–West Harmony and the Revolt against Empire in 1919," *The American Historical Review* 111, no. 5 (2006): 1327–1351, 1342; Rabindranath Tagore, *The English Writings of Rabindranath Tagore*, ed. Sisir Kumar Das, 3 vols. (New Delhi: Sahitya Akademi, 1994–1996), 2; Hay, "Rabindranath Tagore in America," 451–452.

60. Hay, "Rabindranath Tagore in America," 445.

61. K. R. Arnold, *Anti-Immigration in the United States: A Historical Encyclopedia* (Westport, CT: Greenwood Press, 2011), 48–52.

62. Ibid.

63. Erika Lee, "The 'Yellow Peril' and Asian Exclusion in the Americas," *Pacific Historical Review* 76, no. 4 (November 2007): 537–562, 551;

Gerald N. Hallberg, "Bellingham, Washington's Anti-Hindu Riot," *Journal of the West* 12 (January 1973): 163–175; Erika Lee, "Hemispheric Orientalism and the 1907 Pacific Coast Race Riots," *Amerasia Journal* 33, no. 2 (2007): 19–48.

64. Robert E. Wynne, "American Labor Leaders and the Vancouver Anti-Oriental Riot," *Pacific Northwest Quarterly* 57, no. 4 (1966): 172–179, 174.

65. Rabindranath Tagore, "Nationalism in India" (1917), in *Indian Philosophy in English: From Renaissance to Independence*, ed. Nalini Bhushan and Jay L. Garfield, 22–36 (New York: Oxford University Press, 2011), 23.

66. Ibid., 23–24

67. Ibid., 34.

68. Ibid.

69. Rajarshi Chunder, "Tagore and Caste: From Brahmacharyasram to Swadeshi Movement (1901–07)," *Sahapedia* (September 19, 2018).

70. Tagore, "Nationalism in India," 24–34.

71. Ibid., 28–29.

72. L. M. Bhole, *Essays on Gandhian Socio-Economics* (Delhi: Shipra Publications, 2000), ch. 14: "Swadeshi: Meaning and Contemporary Relevance."

73. Ramananda Chatterjee, "Rabindranath Tagore in America," *Modern Review* 21 (June 1917): 660–661.

74. Tagore, "Nationalism in India," 23–24.

75. Ramachandra Guha, "Traveling with Tagore," in Rabindranath Tagore, *Nationalism* (London: Penguin Classics, 2010), 7–8, https://www.i-house. or.jp/programs/wp-content/uploads/2015/06/Tagore-essay_R.Guha_.pdf, accessed August 24, 2020.

76. Ibid.

77. Tagore, "Nationalism in India," 31–32.

78. Ibid.

79. Crispin Bates, "Race, Caste and Tribe in Central India: The Early Origins of Indian Anthropometry," *Edinburgh Papers in South Asian Studies* no. 3 (1995): 1–35, 22; Thomas R. Trautmann, *Aryans and British India* (New Delhi: Vistaar Publications, 1997), 203.

80. Christopher A. Airriess, *Contemporary Ethnic Geographies in America* (Lanham, MD: Rowman and Littlefield, 2006), 39; Seema Sohi, "Immigration Act of 1917 and the 'Barred Zone,'" in *Asian Americans: An Encyclopedia of Social, Cultural, Economic, and Political History [3 volumes]: An Encyclopedia of Social, Cultural, Economic, and Political History*, ed. Xiaojian Zhao and Edward J.W. Park, 534–535 (Santa Barbara, CA: ABC-CLIO, 2013).

81. Chatterjee, "Rabindranath Tagore in America," 663.

82. Tagore to Phelps, *Selected letters of Rabindranath Tagore*, 74.

83. Hay, "Rabindranath Tagore in America," 458; Manela, *The Wilsonian Moment*, 92.

84. Ibid.

85. Hay, "Rabindranath Tagore in America," 450.
86. Ibid., 452.
87. Ibid., 453.
88. Kris Manjapra, *Age of Entanglement* (Cambridge: Harvard University Press, 2014), 72, 99.
89. Martin Kämpchen, "Rabindranath Tagore and Germany," *Indian Literature* 33, no. 3 (May–June 1990): 109–140, 109–112.
90. Rabindranath Tagore, "A Monotony of Multitudes" (1924), in *From the Outer World* , ed. Oscar Handlin and Lilian Handlin, 57–64 (Cambridge: Harvard University Press, 1997), 60–61.
91. Ibid., 60.
92. Tagore, "Nationalism in India," 23.
93. Tagore, "A Monotony of Multitudes," 60–64.

2
Lala Har Dayal, Taraknath Das, and the Ghadar Party

By the 1910s, the Indian independence movement was well under way. Intellectuals such as Rabindranath Tagore, apprehensive about drawing scrutiny from the British government, hesitated to use the US as a base for actively spreading Indian independence propaganda. However, Indians such as Lala Har Dayal and Taraknath Das rejected such qualms as they sought to build an internationalist coalition to fight against White supremacy and colonialism. The center of this coalition was the Ghadar Party, a political organization created by Har Dayal and other Indian revolutionaries such as Sant Baba Wasakha Singh Dadehar, Baba Jawala Singh, Santokh Singh, and Sohan Singh Bhakna in 1913 in Astoria, Oregon. Mark Naidis argues that the Ghadar Party built alliances with the Irish independence movement and was primarily a promoter of Indian nationalism, seeking only to liberate India from the British. However, the party also had a platform of global decolonization and establishing democracy for all colonized peoples was one of their goals.[1]

The Ghadar Party operated primarily along the West Coast, in states such as California and Washington due to the larger Indian population in the region, and as a result it did not reach many Black or Indigenous Americans, who lived in other areas of the US.[2] Similarly, Ghadar Party members did not actively try to enlist Black Americans, focusing instead on the anti-colonial and self-determination struggles of subjects of European colonization. Lala Har Dayal, however, did compare the Black American experience to the situation of Indians under British colonialism, and theorized that American racism mirrored caste discrimination in India. Other Ghadar Party members such as Das and Ram Chandra believed that the condition of Indians under British rule was akin to the experience of Black slaves in the US prior to the Civil War. However, the party as a whole did not see the plight of Black Americans in the early twentieth century as a direct parallel to their own struggle in India, and they did not believe that the Black American struggle was one of self-determination. That outlook, and the fact that Har Dayal only led the Ghadar Party until 1914, may offer an additional explanation as to why the organization did not foster solidarity with African Americans.

Overall, the Ghadar Party prioritized anti-colonial alliances with groups such as the Irish republicans rather than African Americans. The Ghadar Party did not see African Americans as being engaged in an anti-colonial struggle against White Americans; therefore, relationships between Black Americans and the Ghadar Party were not frequent. However, W. E. B. Du Bois and Taraknath Das looked at the Irish anti-colonial movement in similar ways. They believed that Irish independence could be a springboard for other anti-colonial movements and could help stagnate global White supremacy. Hence, both Indians and African Americans could benefit from Irish independence and utilize it to advance their own causes.

While communication between Ghadar Party members and Black Americans was sparse, the National Association for the Advancement of Colored People and W. E. B. Du Bois offered support to Taraknath Das and his organization, the Friends of Freedom for India (FFI). Through the FFI, Das was able to have some localized impact in the US. He managed to tie the Indian independence movement to other anti-colonial struggles such as the Irish independence movement and urged sympathetic Americans to stand against the British Raj. The FFI gained some local American followers and supporters for Indian independence in cities like Philadelphia. However, ultimately the organization failed to gain widespread Indian independence support and its impact was short-lived. In 1923, after the US Supreme Court ruled naturalized citizens from India were not "white," Das lost his citizenship. However, he remained in the US, obtained a Ph.D. from the School of Foreign Service at Georgetown University, and became a Professor of Political Science at Columbia University in 1925.

The Ideas and Impact of the Ghadar Party

During the early 1900s, Indians began to settle in North America, most notably on the West Coast of America and in Vancouver, Canada. Canadian steamship companies, acting on behalf of Pacific coast employers, recruited Sikh farmers with promises of economic opportunities in British Columbia.[3] Indians faced a great deal of hostility from members of the Asiatic Exclusion League, an organization formed in 1905 amongst White Americans and

Canadians to prevent the immigration of people of Asian origin.[4] Due to the cold welcome that they experienced in the Pacific Northwest and following the 1907 Bellingham Riots, during which White mobs attacked Indian residents, many Indians eventually resettled in San Francisco. There, Indian intellectuals formed the Ghadar Party in 1913: a multi-ethnic, multi-religious organization aimed at ending British rule in India. The Ghadar Party was led by the Indian intellectual and anarchist Lala Har Dayal.

Har Dayal was born in 1884 to a high-caste Kayastha family in Delhi. He studied at the Cambridge Mission school, a Christian missionary initiative led by graduates of the University of Cambridge. He received his bachelor's degree in Sanskrit from St. Stephen's College, Delhi, and his master's degree in the same subject from Punjab University. In 1905, he received two scholarships from Oxford University for his higher studies in Sanskrit. While at Oxford he quickly became a staunch believer in anti-colonialism and began exploring anarchist ideas. As a result, he resigned his scholarship and returned to India in 1908 to further Indian political institutions and to rouse his countrymen against British rule, but the government thwarted his work. Advised by his friend and fellow Indian revolutionary Lala Lajpat Rai, Har Dayal returned to Europe. He traveled through France and Germany, disseminating anti-British propaganda, hoping to lead an anti-colonial struggle against the British. However, Har Dayal felt lonely and isolated in Europe and moved to Algeria. There too he was unhappy and pondered going to either Cuba or Japan but instead traveled to the island of Martinique. From there he journeyed to the US, hoping to further propagate his anti-colonial ideology.[5]

Har Dayal arrived in the US in 1911, where he served as secretary of the San Francisco branch of the Industrial Workers of the World. He briefly studied Buddhism at Harvard University but left for San Francisco in April to recruit Indian workers in California for the cause of Indian independence, and developed contacts with Punjabi farmers in Stockton, California. Punjabis, a great majority of whom were Sikhs, had started emigrating to the West Coast around the turn of the century. Having experienced hostility from the Canadians in Vancouver, they ended up disaffected with both British rule in India and White supremacy in Canada. Har Dayal tapped into this sentiment and recruited them to the Ghadar movement.[6]

Although Har Dayal primarily dealt with the struggles of his fellow Indians, both at home and abroad, he drew strong parallels between American racism and the Indian caste system. Har Dayal noted, "Race introduced the first inequalities in Hindu society. The distinction between the Aryans and the aborigines was the thin end of the wedge that finally destroyed the unity of Indian society itself." These "racial distinctions," according to Har Dayal, were the root of the Indian caste system. He argued that the "white" and "Black" racial distinctions in the US mirrored the "Aryan" and "non-Aryan" divisions that represented the Indian caste system; thus similar racial hierarchies were formed in both Indian and American societies.[7] Following Har Dayal's theory, in both Indian and American societies caste was created by the "dominant race," hence perpetuating a racial hierarchy. Har Dayal claimed that the political subjugation of one race by another was inevitable in colonial conquest, which he referred to as "social conquest." Racism was an inherent outcome of social conquest. Political power could be wielded through military force, but "social conquest" required more than just military force because the colonized peoples had to be conditioned to believe that they were members of an inferior race.[8] Har Dayal spent three years in the US. In April 1914, he was arrested by the US government for spreading anarchist literature. However, he skipped bail and fled to Switzerland, eventually making his way to Berlin, leaving Ram Chandra as the president of the Ghadar Party.[9]

Like Rabindranath Tagore, Har Dayal believed that ethnic nationalism was a growing global problem. While in Berlin, he posited that there were many similarities between American ethnic nationalism and European imperialism. He argued that Germans believed that other races, both inside and outside Europe, were inferior to the German people. He noted that German attitudes toward Asians mirrored American attitudes toward Blacks: "Some Americans defended slavery on the grounds that negroes really belonged to a different species. The Germans look upon all nations European and Oriental the same way."[10] By making these observations in Germany, Har Dayal concluded that nationalism, imperialism, and racism were intertwined. Thus, although the marginalization of Black Americans was not a form of imperialism, the Black American experience mirrored the exploitation of colonial subjects in Africa and Asia.

Due to similarities between the marginalization of Indians under British rule in India and Asians and Blacks in the US, the Ghadar Party engaged in activism geared not only to improve the lives of Indians in India but to end non-democratic rule in other colonial nations. In an "Open Letter to the People at Large," the Ghadar Party argued that "in a country either everyone has democracy or no one. The world is like one country today, so either everyone in the world has democracy, or no one has it long." By analyzing oppression as a global problem, the Ghadar Party did not limit itself solely to India, but also sought to promote activism through a global lens. The party claimed that it sought to "educate and organize the masses of the world to fight injustice."[11] According to historian Seema Sohi, the Ghadar Party and Lala Lajpat Rai both aimed to turn the Indian independence movement into one of the "great emancipation movements in history" which could serve as a "model and inspiration for the rest of the colonized world."[12]

Although the Ghadar Party wished to unite the masses of various disenfranchised groups, the party did not draw much support from Black Americans or other racial minorities. It did not energetically seek out Black American support and searched primarily for other Indians and White Americans in the US who were sympathetic toward Indian independence. The party did receive some support from White Americans such as feminist writer Agnes Smedley, who joined the Ghadar Party because it was anti-capitalist and condoned women's education. Smedley had grown up in poverty and by the age of nine understood class inequality in the US, having been inspired by class struggles such as coal miner strikes. She aided the party by publishing anti-Allied propaganda during the war using German funding.[13] Smedley was a supporter of other anti-colonial efforts, including those of Lala Lajpat Rai's India Home Rule League of America, exemplifying her unconditional backing in the fight against British colonialism.[14]

Because of its anti-colonial sentiments, Ghadar Party affiliates, including Smedley, were exposed to scrutiny from the British and American governments. The military intelligence of both countries feared that the Ghader Party was conspiring to overthrow British rule in India. The organization particularly had a loyal following in the Indian province of Punjab. When the British learned of the party's anti-imperialist activities, it exiled many of its leaders to Canada and the US.[15] Despite these roadblocks, Chandra continued to try and garner American support for the Ghadar Party. He envisaged the US as an ideal nation for enlisting support for Indian independence because it was the "land of the free." He believed that Americans such as Abraham Lincoln had broken the "shackles of the downtrodden race and set the Negro free."[16] Since Chandra believed that the US had reversed its racial wrongs by abolishing slavery, he thought Americans, including the US government, would be sympathetic to Indians trying to achieve freedom from the British Raj.[17] However, Chandra had an idealistic image of the US and neglected the fact that the country did not practice racial equality. Immigration law excluded Chinese immigrants, and Jim Crow laws in the US South treated Black Americans as second-class citizens.

In July 1916, Chandra wrote a set of articles in the *New York Times*, arguing that the only difference between an educated Indian and an educated American was their skin color. To gain American support, Chandra suggested that he wanted India to become a democratic republic like the US. In a following article, Chandra directly addressed President Woodrow Wilson, comparing the goals of the Ghadar Party to those of American revolutionaries during the Revolutionary War. However, while Chandra condemned British colonialism in India, he curiously praised the US's involvement in the Philippines as being a more benevolent form of colonialism. Chandra claimed to support colonialism in the Philippines because he believed that, unlike British rule in India, the US was not using Filipino labor and sacrificing the welfare of Filipinos to enrich the US.

It was interesting that Chandra used the term "benevolent colonialism." When the US declared rule over the Philippines in 1898, President William McKinley used the term "benevolent assimilation" to describe American rule in the Philippines.[18] Hence, it was likely that Chandra analyzed the colonization of the Philippines from a pro-American perspective. Nevertheless, he contradicted the earlier aims of the Ghadar Party which followed the motto" "Either everyone in the world has democracy, or no one has it long." Har Dayal similarly noted that American rule in the Philippines was less exploitive than British rule in India and called it "benevolent assimilation." Chandra and Har Dayal's comments suggested that Ghadar Party leaders were willing to be flexible and forgo their aims for global decolonization to gain American support for decolonization in India.[19] Both Har Dayal and Chandra consistently criticized British colonial rule but ignored American colonial rule in Puerto Rico, Hawai'i, Guam, the American Samoa, and Wake Island, and defended US colonialism in the Philippines.[20] It is possible that Har Dayal and Chandra did not see American colonies such as Guam and Puerto Rico as colonial possessions. Historian Daniel Immerwahr notes that much of the American public "in their heads did not include places like the Philippines" as part of an American colonial empire and largely only considered the US as a "union of states bounded by the Atlantic, the Pacific, Mexico and Canada."[21] Hence, it was likely that Ghadar Party leaders, like much of the American public, did not see American "territories" as part of a colonial empire. Hence, the organization did not incorporate America's overseas "territories" into their decolonization platform.

Chandra did not receive a reply from President Wilson. Additionally, Chandra's articles and open letter to President Wilson did not get him the American support he desired. In March 1917, he was arrested by US federal agents in New York for violating the neutrality laws of the US by trying to instigate a rebellion against a World War I ally of the US, the UK. A year later, during his trial, Chandra was assassinated by Ram Singh, a fellow defendant who believed that he was diverting funds (mostly from Germany) for the Ghadar Party for his own personal use. Singh was immediately shot dead by a court marshall.[22]

Although the Ghadar Party did not receive much backing from prominent Americans after the American government cracked down on Indian revolutionaries, one member of the party, Taraknath Das, managed to gain some American and Irish support through other organizations. Disappointed with the Ghadar Party's lack of impact, Das decided to align himself with Lala Lajpat Rai and his India Home Rule League of America. In March 1918, Das founded the FFI, along with Rai, American feminist Agnes Smedley, and Salindranath Ghose. The organization drew inspiration and support from the similarly named Friends of Irish Freedom, an Irish republican group formed in New York in 1916.[23] Additionally, they were championed by the Industrial Workers of the World and the Socialist Party to advocate for the rights of immigrants to engage in political activity. Even the historically anti-immigrant American Federation of Labor (AFL) endorsed the FFI's mission. In 1920, the California branch of the AFL explained that they supported the FFI because the "interests of the proletariat are identical everywhere in the world." The California branch of the AFL encouraged international solidarity amongst the working class because they believed that their alliances would "shatter" the "shackles of slavery and bondage [low-wage labor]" due to the "latent power of the people."[24]

However, shortly after the founding of the FFI, Das, Ghose, and Smedley were arrested by the American government for violating the US neutrality laws and were tried as part of the Hindu–German Conspiracy in San Francisco. Their prosecution was due to their supposed involvement with the Japanese and German governments toward forming an alliance with these nations to free India from the British. Smedley had received financial support from Germany to support revolutionary activities against the British government in India,[25] and Das did go to Germany on the eve of World War I to secure funds for an armed insurrection in India. He even took part in an unsuccessful German–Indian endeavor to destroy a British-controlled railway along the Suez Canal and then traveled to China and Japan to organize the Pan-Asiatic League and promote India's independence.[26] Smedley had her bail paid off by John Haynes Holmes and her charges were eventually dropped. Upon her release, she became the executive secretary of the FFI. Das was sentenced to twenty-two months in Leavenworth prison by an all-White jury.[27]

Aside from being imprisoned, Das risked losing the naturalized American citizenship granted to him in 1914, and faced being surrendered to British authorities for conspiring against an American ally. Multiple allies attempted to help Das retain his citizenship. Socialists Rose Strunsky and Robert Morss Lovett, who became the temporary president of the FFI, publicized the cases in *Dial* magazine, which was the chief publication of Transcendentalists.[28] The NAACP similarly displayed its solidarity with Das after he was imprisoned by writing a plea in *The Crisis* on his behalf to not have him deported back to India. In a 1919 edition of *The Crisis*, the NAACP advocated for Das to remain a US citizen. They argued that if he was forced to surrender his citizenship and be deported to India, the British government would execute him. This plea by the NAACP displayed their sympathy for Indians such as Das, arguing that he was simply trying to "free [his] country from the rule of [the British]."[29] Similarly, New York Senator Joseph I. France of Maryland, a supporter of Indian Home Rule, argued against legislation to deport Indian activists not only because he believed that they would be executed upon their arrival in India but also because such an action was "inconsistent ... with the long and honorable tradition of this country as a land of refuge for the oppressed."[30] The US Congress did not pass laws that allowed the deportation of naturalized citizens. Hence, Das was able to remain in the US. The NAACP's plea on Das's behalf was not influential in preventing Das's deportation, but it marked an example of alliance between Indian independence advocates and American civil rights activists. Das was able to retain his citizenship until 1923 when the Supreme Court ruled that Indians were not "white" in the *Thind* verdict, thereby voiding all previously granted citizenship.[31] He was able to remain in the US as a teacher, however, and in 1924, he married Mary Keatinge Morse (Mary Das), a White founding member of the NAACP, strengthening his ties to the association and the Black American struggle.[32]

Das understood that American society was fractured and divided by race. He, therefore, deemed it important for Indians to stand at the forefront of racial equality, otherwise independent India would be a fragmented society with racial divisions like the US. Das continued his activism for Indian independence after he had served his twenty-two-month prison sentence. During a December 1920 speech at a national conference held in New York for the FFI, Das warned his audience that Indians must not only seek independence from the British but also prevent a potential independent

India from becoming "a tool" for "those capitalistic, imperialistic nations whose business it is to subject men of another color and creed." While Das did not specifically mention the US by name, it was apparent that his stern warning was for Indians not to align themselves with nations who exploited their racial minorities. Das suggested that forming an alliance with capitalist and imperialist nations was detrimental to the morality of Indian nationalism, declaring that the Indian nationalist movement was "fighting for an ideal, a world ideal, where human life will be the supreme value rather than property being the standard of value. We are fighting against racial and class injustice."[33]

In his statements, Das tied capitalism to both race and class injustice. He argued that aligning India with capitalist nations would cause further racial and class division since capitalism increased income and wealth inequality and the protection of private property. This perspective echoed the anti-capitalist viewpoints of his fellow Indian countrymen, Lala Lajpat Rai and Rabindranath Tagore. Instead of seeking the aid of American capitalists, Das argued that Indian nationalists should continue to draw inspiration and alliances from the Irish republicans. Unlike the US, which had an alliance with the British, and was a colonial nation due to its activities in the Philippines, Das believed that Irish republicans were the antithesis of British imperialism.[34] The Irish republicans, Sinn Fein, maintained an anti-capitalist platform and were fighting against the British for Irish independence.[35] Sinn Fein's anti-capitalist platform and its involvement in an independence struggle which mirrored that of India's made the Irish republicans a far more valuable ally than the US. In the aftermath of the Irish revolution which cemented the Republic of Ireland as an independent nation in 1920, Eamon de Valera, the president of the Sinn Fein party of Ireland, published a pamphlet through the FFI titled *India & Ireland*. In this pamphlet, which was also read as a speech in New York City hosted by the FFI, de Valera shared a message which compared the common anguish experienced by subjects under British rule in India and Ireland. De Valera displayed solidarity with Indians by criticizing the Amritsar massacre of 1919 in Punjab ordered by General Reginald Dyer. British authorities had responded to the gathering of a few hundred peaceful protestors with gunfire which led to the loss of at least 379 Indian lives.[36] According to British civil servant Sir James Houssemayne Du Boulay (1868–1943), the British opened fire on Indian protesters because they believed a Ghadar inspired uprising was imminent.[37] De Valera also had ties to the Ghadar Party and was presented with an engraved sword by party members on July 21, 1919.[38]

In the aftermath of the Amritsar massacre, more Americans became sympathetic to the Indian independence struggle. In 1920, ten thousand American citizens along with Indian revolutionaries mobilized in Philadelphia to protest against the slaughter of innocent civilians in the incident. In an article in the *Independent Hindustan,* its official newspaper, the Ghadar Party acknowledged the American protests in Philadelphia as a small victory for the Indian independence movement and claimed that American support exemplified Philadelphia's recognition of the "sister Republics of Ireland and India." The Indian revolutionaries in the protest were part of the FFI and thus an example of solidarity between the FFI and some members of the American public. After the protest concluded, five thousand Americans remained for a mass meeting at the Knickerbocker Theater. At the meeting, S. N. Ghose, who was the national organizer of the FFI, made a case to the American public alongside Das for Indian independence. The audience's overwhelming support for Indian independence epitomized growing American sympathy for the cause. The Ghadar Party responded with glee that "full-blooded Americans [could] not but feel happy at India's Revolutionary movement."[39]

Because the FFI for India had a desire to fight racial and class injustice alongside the Indian independence movement, Black Americans such as W. E. B. Du Bois aligned themselves with the organization and pledged their support. Du Bois recounted the aims of the FFI in a 1921 article in *The Crisis,* asserting that British rule was "opposed to the welfare of all Indian people."[40] Just as Black Americans such as Du Bois expressed solidarity with Indians, Das understood the Black American struggle through his wife Mary Das's work with the NAACP. He hoped to use his insights to inform his American and Indians friends on the similarities between caste discrimination and American racism. In a June 1925 letter to J. T. Sunderland, Das theorized that the US had its own "caste system" by "outlaw[ing] the Chinese, Japanese, and Hindus, as outcastes" through the Immigration Act of 1924, which in the aftermath of the *Thind* decision effectively banned all new immigration from Asia and placed quotas on immigration from eastern European nations as well. Das referred to America's exclusion of Asians and denying them naturalized citizenship as a "a new caste-system based upon race-hatred and color prejudice [that] has arisen which is going to poison human relations between the people of Asia – particularly the people of India, China and Japan on the one hand and the world of Whitemanism on the other!!!"[41]

Like Tagore, Das used caste as an analogy for race relations in America and believed that caste was a transnational system because it had parallels in many countries. Because of the repressive "caste system" based on "color prejudice" in the US, Das shifted to a Pan-Asiatic outlook for Indian independence. He was inspired by Polish writer and anti-communist activist Ferdynand Antoni Ossendowski's 1922 book *Beasts, Men, and Gods* which argued that Asian nations under the leadership of Japan could unite to fight against the "supremacy of white races." Das had spent some time in Japan in 1905, briefly studying at the University of Tokyo before he was forced to escape to the US after the British renegotiated a 1902 Anglo-Japanese alliance which provided Japanese support of British interests in India in return for British support for Japanese progress into Korea.[42] Das left Japan in 1905 as he was pressured by Japanese authorities to leave the nation because the British demanded that the Japanese curtail seditionist activity in their country against the British Raj.[43] Hence, he believed that Japan had formed an alliance with the British. However, in 1923, any Anglo-Japanese alliance was terminated by the British as tensions between America and Japan had increased during the early 1920s and the British did not want to be bound to Japan if they went to war with the US.[44] After the Anglo-Japanese alliance ended, Das believed that his vision for Pan-Asian unity between Japan, India, and China was possible, and he favored an alliance with Asian nations over the US.

Writing in Lala Lajpat Rai's newspaper *The People*, which was primarily read by the Indian youth in Punjab, Das reiterated the Ghadar Party ideology of universal decolonization. Advocating for full "Asian Independence" from any foreign colonization, he argued that all the Asian nations should work together in liberating themselves from foreign rule. He believed that "India with her 320,000,000 people" was a "great factor" in "The Awakening of Asia" and the "progress of humanity."[45] Furthermore, Das called upon India's youth to "vigorously oppose all forms of intolerance and barriers of creed, colour, race, and class antagonisms." Das believed that Rabindranath Tagore was the greatest living teacher of the values of equality, and he praised the efforts of Tagore's university in Shantiniketan in providing an education for the Indian youth which was not taught by the British Raj.[46] Das tried to enlist J. T. Sunderland to join Tagore's work at his university. While Sunderland did not teach at Tagore's university, he helped promote Indian independence in the US, countering American conservatives who justified British colonialism, such as Katherine Mayo. Sunderland sought to build on Tagore's work in America and promote Indian culture and portray the Indian people as being fit for self-rule through his book *India in Bondage: Her Right to Freedom* published by Prabasi Press of Calcutta in 1928.[47]

Just as Das believed that racism in America was a form of caste, both Taraknath and Mary Das theorized that caste discrimination in India mirrored the Black American experience. In October 1925, Das wrote to J. T. Sunderland that Mary Das had written an article in a Madras journal comparing the lived experiences of Indian untouchables to Black Americans, hoping that more Americans would become aware of Indian caste discrimination.[48] Unlike Swami Vivekananda who tried to hide the evils of caste in India from White liberals to paint an idyllic view of India, Das believed that it was necessary to give the international community, including both Americans and Indians, an honest view. Das believed that "no good" could "be accomplished by covering up the sore-sports [caste discrimination] of the Indian [primarily Hindu] body-politics." In a 1927 letter reprinted in Lala Lajpat Rai's newspaper *The People*, Das condemned untouchability as "an awful and abominable condition of social and economic slavery" which mirrored the social condition of "Negro slaves of North America."[49]

Like Tagore, Das saw caste in India as being a divisive system that prevented unity between the Indian people. Additionally, like Tagore, he theorized that caste was not a unique Hindu system. Das saw caste as being a universal system that could be applied to any context where an ethnic, religious, or racial group faced exclusion by a dominant mainstream group. Das came to understand this through his own experiences with racism in the US based on his non-European heritage. Historian Gerald Horne notes that Das's experiences, including being denied opportunities to rent apartments and lodge at upscale hotels due to his "Hindu" background while in Manhattan, may have pushed him to take a more aggressive stance against untouchability.[50] However, Das did not explicitly specify that he believed that racial segregation in America was as pervasive as Indian untouchability and he posited that the social conditions of untouchables was more like chattel slavery than contemporary racial segregation. He emphasized his analogy between Indian untouchability and American slavery by paraphrasing Lincoln's 1858 "House Divided Speech," stating that "a nation cannot and should not remain half-slave and half-free."[51]

Just as Das made several analogies between race in American and caste in India, he similarly conjectured that caste in India mirrored Russia's class system before 1917, namely its historic serfdom. Das warned upper-caste Indians that unless the social and economic slavery of India's "untouchables" was remedied quickly, low-caste Indians would likely launch a violent revolution like the Russian Revolution of 1917, culminating with the destruction of the Indian upper class and the formation of a Marxist society. Das referred to the

Russian Revolution as a form of retribution against the Russian aristocracy and Russian upper class for the "oppression suffered by the majority of the Russian people." He believed that the only reason a similar Marxist revolution in India had not yet occurred was due to the "submissiveness and docility among the so-called 'untouchables' whose souls seem to have been crushed by the centuries of oppression."[52] However, Das ignored that the Marxist revolution in Russia was instigated by the intellectual class and not launched by the masses. Hence, the Russian Revolution was a Marxist struggle that was waged through the cooperation of multiple social classes, and it was not a clear template for "untouchables" to follow.

Perhaps the most notable claim by Das was that if the social and economic slavery of Indian "untouchables" continued to exist, and if the Indian aristocracy and intellectuals of India were not "rigorously fighting" against "untouchability," then the people of India did not "deserve any better lot nationally and internationally than what they are receiving at the hands of their alien rulers and those who proclaim and uphold the false doctrine of 'White Supremacy!'"[53] Das's statement showed how his wife had modified his beliefs regarding unconditional Indian independence. While Das was in America, he worked toward liberating India from British colonialism, even risking his own freedom and US citizenship to achieve that goal. Although trying to utilize the US as a base for promoting Indian independence propaganda did not prove effective, his understanding of American slavery and racial discrimination transformed his outlook on the validity of Indian independence's moral claims unless untouchability was annihilated. Das proclaimed that the removal of untouchability and "Racial Equality" should be at the forefront of "Indian nationalism." In making this assessment, Das tied Indian nationalism and anti-untouchability into one unified movement. He suggested, "Nationalist India should oppose all forms of direct, indirect or veiled communalism in its political program." Das used Abraham Lincoln's quotation that "a nation cannot and should not remain half-slave and half-free" as an example as to why immediate caste reform was necessary.[54]

Like Tagore, when Das first arrived in the US in 1906, he saw potential for the nation to serve as an example for race assimilation and liberty for peoples and creeds. Aside from seeking asylum from British persecution, Das remarked that he was originally inspired by Swami Vivekananda's disciple Sister Nivedita to come to America and study political science at the University of California, Berkeley, and build alliances for Indian independence.[55] However, over time, especially as the US passed laws excluding Asians, he gradually lost faith in the country as a viable ally for Indian independence. Like Tagore, Das believed that Western nationalism was a form of imperialism and "national expansion at the costs of others." Das contrasted Western nationalism with Indian nationalism, commenting that Indian nationalism was "actuated by the idea of the recovery of [India's] national integrity and sovereignty."[56] Nevertheless, Das believed that Indian nationalism had to incorporate caste reform into its program to achieve unity and give Indian independence activists a moral edge over the racialized "caste system" of nations such as the US and the British Raj. Although Das shifted his anti-colonialism activism to a Pan-Asiatic outlook, he did not completely abandon the US as a potential ally for Indian independence despite its position as a White supremacist society. Das believed that "American public opinion" was instrumental to "the British Empire's security." He understood that America was a powerful force in world politics and its public opinion helped secure "Ireland's freedom."[57] Hence, although Das saw the US as a racist society, he still believed that Indians had to win over American public opinion in order to pressure the British to give them their freedom.

While Das saw some parallels between American slavery and the Indian caste system, he did not go back to India to become an anti-caste advocate. Instead, he stayed in the US as a professor of political science at Columbia University and became a Fellow at Georgetown University. He was not the only Indian independence advocate who used American racism to understand caste in India and push for its reform; his friend and fellow Indian independence activist Lala Lajpat Rai also considered the parallels between the two.

Notes

1. Mark Naidis, "Propaganda of the Gadar Party," *Pacific Historical Review* 20, no. 3 (1951): 251–260.
2. Nishant Upadhyay, "Ghadar Movement: A Living Legacy," *Sikh Formations* 10, no. 1 (2014): 1–3.
3. Padma Rangaswamy, *Namasté America: Indian Immigrants in an American Metropolis* (University Park: Pennsylvania State University Press, 2000), 42.
4. Gerald N. Hallberg, "Bellingham, Washington's Anti-Hindu Riot," *Journal of the West* 12 (January 1973): 163–175; Erika Lee, "Hemispheric Orientalism and the 1907 Pacific Coast Race Riots," *Amerasia Journal* 33, no. 2 (2007): 19–48.
5. Emily C. Brown, *Har Dayal: Hindu Revolutionary and Rationalist* (Tucson: University of Arizona Press, 1975).

6. E. C. Brown, *Har Dayal*; Seema Sohi, "Repressing the 'Hindu Menace': Race, Anarchy, and Indian Anticolonialism," in *The Sun Never Sets: South Asian Migrants in an Age of U.S. Power*, ed. Vivek Bald, Miabi Chatterji, Sujani Reddy, and Manu Vimalassery, 50–74 (New York: New York University Press, 2013), 58.

7. Lala Hardayal, "The Social Conquest of the Hindu Race and the Meaning of Equality" (San Francisco: Hindustan Ghadar Party, December 1913), p. 5, folder 3, box 2, South Asians in North America Collection.

8. Lala Hardayal, "The Social Conquest of the Hindu Race," reprinted from December 1909 article in *The Modern Review Calcutta*.

9. Naidis, "Propaganda of the Gadar Party," 252.

10. Lala Hardayal, *Forty-four Months in Germany and Turkey* (Westminster: P.S. King & Son, Ltd., 1920), 15.

11. Hindustan Ghadar Party, "An Open Letter to the People at Large," San Francisco, California, USA.

12. Seema Sohi, *Echoes of Mutiny: Race, Surveillance, and Indian Anticolonialism in North America* (New York: Oxford University Press, 2014), 67.

13. Ruth Price, *The Lives of Agnes Smedley* (Oxford: Oxford University Press, 2005), 63–66.

14. Alan Raucher, "American Anti-Imperialists and the Pro-India Movement, 1900–1932," *Pacific Historical Review* 43, no. 1 (1974): 83–110, 96.

15. Om Gupta, *Encyclopedia of India, Pakistan and Bangladesh* (Delhi: Gyan Books, 2006), 780.

16. Gerald Horne, *End of Empires: African Americans and India* (Philadelphia: Temple University Press, 2008), 48.

17. Ibid., 49.

18. President William McKinley, "Benevolent Assimilation Proclamation," December 21, 1898.

19. Naidis, "Propaganda of the Gadar Party," 255; Sohi, *Echoes of Mutiny*, 70.

20. Daniel Immerwahr, *How to Hide an Empire: A History of the Greater United States* (New York: Picador, Farrar, Straus, and Giroux, 2019), 4.

21. Ibid.

22. Naidis, "Propaganda of the Gadar Party," 253.

23. Robert A. Hill, *Marcus Garvey and UNIA Papers*, vol. 1: 1826–August 1919 (Los Angeles: University of California Press, 1983), lxxiii.

24. "California Labor Stands for Freedom of India," *Independent Hindustan* (September 1920): 72.

25. Price, *The Lives of Agnes Smedley*, 63–66.

26. "Taraknath Das," The Library at University of Washington, Special Collections, https://www.lib.washington.edu/specialcollections/collections/exhibits/southasianstudents/das, accessed May 1, 2021.

27. Raucher, "American Anti-Imperialists," 96.

28. Ian Frederick Finseth, "The Emergence of Transcendentalism," *American Studies and The University of Virginia* (The University of Virginia),

http://xroads.virginia.edu/~MA95/finseth/trans.html, accessed August 6, 2020; Arthur Versluis, *The Esoteric Origins of the American Renaissance* (Oxford: Oxford University Press, 2001), 3.

29. *The Crisis* 19, no. 2 (November 1919): 78.
30. Paul Teed, "Race Against Memory: Katherine Mayo, Jabez Sunderland, and Indian Independence," *American Studies* 44, no. 1/2 (2003): 35–57, 40.
31. "Taraknath Das," The Library at University of Washington, Special Collections.
32. Ibid.
33. Taraknath Das, "International Aspects of the Indian Question," *Independent Hindustan* 1, no. 6 (February 1921): 130–131.
34. Ibid., 130.
35. Kevin Rafter, *Sinn Féin, 1905–2005: In the Shadow of Gunmen* (Dublin: Gill & Macmillan, 2005), 219.
36. Eamonn de Valera, "Address Delivered at the India Freedom Dinner of the Friends of Freedom for India, on February 28, 1920, at the Central Opera House, New York City," *India & Ireland*, Friends of Freedom for India, New York, 1920.
37. Emily Brown, "Book Reviews; South Asia," *Journal of Asian Studies* 32, no. 3 (May 1973): 522–523.
38. Naidis, "Propaganda of the Gadar Party," 254.
39. George Franklin, "Philadelphia Rings the Liberty Bell of India," *Independent Hindustan* (October 1920): 44.
40. Friends of Freedom for India Pamphlet (1916), Slide 403, Reel 5, W. E. B. Du Bois Papers; W. E. B. Du Bois, "The Woes of India," *The Crisis* 22 (May 1921): 27.
41. Taraknath Das to J. T. Sunderland, June 17, 1925, in Tapan K. Mukherjee, *Taraknath Das: Life and Letters of a Revolutionary in Exile* (Jadavpur: National Council of Education, 1998), 266–267; Nico Slate, *Colored Cosmopolitanism: The Shared Struggle for Freedom in the United States and India* (Cambridge: Harvard University Press, 2012), 57.
42. Robert Joseph Gowen, "British Legerdemain at the 1911 Imperial Conference: The Dominions, Defense Planning, and the Renewal of the Anglo-Japanese Alliance," *Journal of Modern History* 52, no. 3 (1980): 385–413.
43. Neilesh Bose, "Taraknath Das (1884–1958), British Columbia, and the Anti-Colonial Borderlands," *BC Studies* 204 (2020): 67–88, 71.
44. Malcolm D. Kennedy, *The Estrangement of Great Britain and Japan* (Los Angeles: University of California Press, 1969), 54.
45. Taraknath Das, "Review of Beasts, Men and Gods," *The People*, March 7, 1926.
46. Taraknath Das, "Young Asia and World Peace," *The People*, August 8, 1926.
47. Teed, "Race Against Memory," 35.
48. Horne, *End of Empires*, 135.

49. Taraknath Das to Lala Lajpat Rai, *The People*, August 2, 1927 (featured in the October 6, 1927, edition of *The People*).
50. Horne, *End of Empires*, 135–136.
51. Taraknath Das to Lala Lajpat Rai, August 2, 1927.
52. Ibid.; Abraham Lincoln, "House Divided," Illinois Republican State Convention, Springfield, Illinois, June 16, 1858.
53. Taraknath Das to Lala Lajpat Rai, August 2, 1927.
54. Ibid.; Horne, *End of Empires*, 136.
55. T. Das, "Young Asia and World Peace."
56. Ibid.
57. Taraknath Das, "American Policies Today," *The People*, January 16, 1927.

3

Lala Lajpat Rai and W. E. B. Du Bois

While Rabindranath Tagore and Taraknath Das did not travel to the US to learn about American racism, Lala Lajpat Rai specifically journeyed there to understand the Black experience. Rai was born in 1865 to a Jain family in the Punjab Province. His father was a teacher of the Urdu language at the Government Higher Secondary School where Rai also studied as a child. In 1880, Rai attended the Government College at Lahore to study law, graduating four years later. During his time at there, Rai began to grow disillusioned with British rule. In 1886, he moved to the village of Hisar in Haryana to practice law and founded the Hisar district branch of the Indian National Congress and the Arya Samaj, a Hindu reform movement.[1] Like the Brahmo Samaj, the Arya Samaj campaigned against caste discrimination, and they supported widow remarriage and women's education.[2] The organization also had an internationalist outlook and established chapters in British colonies with Indian populations, such as South Africa, Fiji, Mauritius, Suriname, Guyana, and Trinidad and Tobago.[3] Rai was an active participant and campaigner during the early years of the organization's existence.[4] Like the Arya Samaj, Rai had an internationalist philosophy toward advocating for Indian independence as well as social reform. In 1914, he quit practicing law to dedicate himself to the Indian independence movement fully. That same year, Rai planned a six-month trip to the US to collect material for a book on the plight of Black Americans. However, while he was in the US, the British categorized him as a political exile for criticizing British rule and he was not allowed to return to India until the end of 1919.

During his five-year stay in the US, Rai had a considerable impact on Americans. He formed alliances and garnered support for Indian self-rule from Irish nationalists, American civil rights activists, and other American anti-colonialists. In addition to seeking out support for Indian self-determination, the strife of Black Americans was a central part of Rai's advocacy. Rai wanted to understand how the Black American struggle related to the plight of Indians under the British Raj, and he also sought to compare American racism to the Indian caste system. Additionally, he wanted to assess what elements of American society could provide a useful model for the development of India. Rai was inspired by W. E. B. Du Bois to study race relations, along with caste and class systems, transnationally and formed an important friendship with Du Bois while in the US.

Like Rai, Du Bois had an internationalist outlook toward uplifting people of color and the two men bonded over their shared goal of fighting colonialism and White supremacy. At the Pan-African Conference held in London in July 1900, organized by the Trinidadian barrister Henry Sylvester Williams, W. E. B. Du Bois contended that the greatest problem of the twentieth century was "the problem of the color-line." He played a leading role in drafting a letter titled "To the Nations of the World" to European leaders, appealing to them to advocate against racism, to grant colonies in Africa and the West Indies the right to self-government, and demanding political and other rights for African Americans.[5] Du Bois was astute in his assessment that the "color-line" was the integral issue of the twentieth century. Imperialism and colonialism had rapidly increased amongst European powers throughout the nineteenth century and his home country, the US, was similarly trying to assert imperial dominance in the Philippines, Hawai'i, and Guam. Thus, Du Bois deemed that it was important to not only address racism at a local level but also transnationally. Du Bois believed that developing strong, strategic alliances with Indian figures was instrumental since British colonialism was a form of White supremacy.[6]

Du Bois's views on race were shaped from a variety of different international perspectives throughout the early part of the twentieth century. He lauded sociologist Jean Finot's 1906 work *Race Prejudice,* which argued against theories about the superiority of the Aryan race. Du Bois as well as Mohandas Gandhi were inspired by reading Finot's book, which became a key component of both Du Bois and Gandhi's understanding of racial science, and Gandhi recommended it to several of his associates.[7] Finot was also an organizer and attendee at the First Universal Races Congress in London in July 1911 which Du Bois had attended. In addition to Finot, the Congress was assembled by prominent humanists Felix Adler and Gustav Spiller, a leader in the British Ethical Union.[8] The meeting sought to increase cooperation between the "races of mankind" through a "Congress where the representatives of the different races might meet each other face to face" and "further the cause of mutual trust and respect between Occident and Orient."[9] Representatives from fifty countries attended the Congress and fifty-eight papers were presented by members of twenty countries.[10] Du Bois credited Finot for challenging the racial science pushed by racial anthropologists, stating, "[T]he conception of races as of so many watertight compartments into which human beings can be crammed as if they were so many breeds of horses or cattle, has had its day."[11]

Du Bois similarly learned about race from an Indian perspective from Bengali humanist writer Dr. Brajendra Nath Seal at the First Universal Races Congress. Seal in his speech argued that races were "growing developing entities and that one should not regard races as unchangeable accomplished facts." He asserted all races and ethnic groups had a common social history and humanity was universal. Each race had its share of the characteristics of inferiority; therefore, it was "impossible to arrange the main groups of men in an ascending scale of physical development."[12] Du Bois agreed with Seal as he believed that the social environment of White supremacy had led to the subjugation of both Black Americans and Indians in their respective countries. Like Seal, Du Bois believed that Black Americans and Indians could achieve the same intellectual capabilities and economic standards as White Americans and Europeans if they were not forced to live in an environment of White supremacy.[13] Because of the shared marginalization of Indians and Black Americans by White supremacy, Du Bois consistently sought out transnational alliances throughout the early twentieth century, particularly with Indians, and his most notable Indian ally and friend was Lala Lajpat Rai who often cited Du Bois in his writings, both during his time in the US and during the 1920s when he returned to India.

Rai's Understanding of "Caste" and the Plight of Black Americans

Rai noted that he was specifically inspired by Du Bois's work *The Souls of Black Folk* to seek parallels between caste in India and racial discrimination in the US.[14] Intrigued by the writings of Du Bois, Rai came to the US in 1914 to study the "Negro problem on the spot" and to write a book on the issue.[15] Rai only planned to spend six months in the US but he ended up staying until 1919 (except for a six-month journey to Japan) after being made a political exile by the British government.[16] Rai had briefly visited the US for three weeks in 1905. His tour covered New York, Buffalo, Chicago, Philadelphia, and Boston. Additionally, Rai visited Sikh communities along the West Coast and Booker T. Washington's Tuskegee Institute in Alabama, a school that provided trade school education to Black Americans. During his travels, he gained a strong awareness of the various racial issues that were plaguing American society, concluding that America was a society predicated on White supremacy. Yet he was impressed with its ethnic diversity, noting that "[t]here are Filipinos, Cubans, Indians (both Red and East), Arabs, Syrians, Chinese, Japanese," and "almost every nationality [was] in fairly good strength [and] publishes its own organs."[17] Like Tagore, Rai's first impressions of the US were mixed. He understood the prevalence of White supremacy but believed that the influx of new nationalities and the growing melting pot of various ethnic groups in the US could gradually create racial harmony.

After his travels throughout the American South and reading Du Bois's works, Rai saw Black Americans as the "pariah of America." Rai theorized that there was "some analogy between the Negro problem of the United States of America and the problem of depressed classes in India."[18] Rai noted that the main similarity between the two groups was their lowered social status within their respective societies. Because the Black American experience mirrored the Indian untouchable experience, Rai was eager to learn about the struggles of Black Americans and was accompanied by the Tuskegee Institute principal, Booker T. Washington, on a tour of Black communities in the US South. During his tour with Washington, Rai met numerous Black American leaders, including John Hope, the president of Morehouse College, and George Washington Carver, the renowned scientist.[19] After his tour was completed, in 1916, Rai published a book in New York titled *The United States of America: A Hindu's Impressions and a Study*. In the book, Rai dissected the issues faced by Black Americans as well as the similarities and differences between their struggle and the Indian caste system. Rai hoped that his book could provide his Black American friends, such as Du Bois, with his international perspective on the problems of the Black community as well as assess the "practical usefulness" of American ideas for the development of India.[20] While Rai conducted research for his book, Du Bois assisted Rai by providing him reference letters to gain access to libraries.[21] Additionally, both men conversed about race relations at Du Bois's office, home, and civic club.[22]

Through his research and interactions with Du Bois, Rai concluded that that there were cogent similarities between the way White Americans subjugated Black Americans to a lower social status during the Jim Crow and slavery eras, and the way the Aryan conquerors of India treated Indigenous Indians.[23] He argued that caste in India was a hierarchical system that treated the lowest members like slaves. Furthermore, Rai noted that the principles and reasons for caste in India, which were to preserve the privileges of the ruling class, were not unique to Hinduism or Indian society. He asserted that "the caste system in India owed its origin to probably the same considerations and causes as are to be found at the bottom of the caste feeling in America." Rai argued that all non-Europeans faced some form of "caste discrimination" in the US. He defended his reasoning with claims that Chinese and Japanese and mixed-race Blacks who had a similar skin color to some Whites were marginalized. The "bar of color" applied just as strongly to a light-skinned Black man as it did to a "dark-skinned" Black man.[24] Rai used W. E. B. Du Bois as an example of a mixed-race Black man who had not received a higher status even though he had White ancestry. However, Rai ignored that Du Bois had attended Harvard University and that a low-caste Indian would not have had the same opportunities in India.

Rai noticed that the second-class treatment of Black Americans with traceable White ancestry was different from caste in India. In India, social mobility for children could be achieved through inter-caste marriage. Conversely, interracial marriages in the US did not improve the offspring's social status unless the child could pass as White. Rai believed that the American caste system operated on the condition "Once a Negro, always a Negro." Rai claimed that even light-colored Black Americans such as Dr Hope, who was president of Morehouse College, whom Rai described as being "as fair-coloured as a white man or woman can be," still "had to give up his seat on the streetcar to the 'most ignorant, dark-coloured, white scoundrel.'"[25] Rai in his assessments did not understand that Southern states often enforced Jim Crow laws based on phenotypical appearances. Hence, a lighter-skinned Black American could often pass for White and could access White facilities.

While Rai believed that caste existed in Western society, he argued that the "color line" was not the only measure of caste line there. Rai asserted that "a century ago," there were also four castes in European society. The serf was the lowest of the four groups, alongside monarchs, lords, and knights. According to Rai, the serfs had no "freedom of action'" and were born into their social class with no prospect of reaching a higher social class. Since Rai believed that there was a lack of social mobility in the European classes, he viewed European feudalism as being a caste system as well.

Therefore, Rai did not necessarily believe that class and caste struggles were independent of one another and often caste and class were overlapping concepts. Rai ultimately believed that any system that suppressed social mobility was a caste system.[26] Additionally, Rai acknowledged the rigidity of American caste, noting that he had several encounters with White Americans who had very negative attitudes toward Black people. From these encounters, Rai concluded, "[T]he prospect of the disappearance of the caste feeling in America, in the near future at least, seems to be very meager."[27]

Rai's assessment of the US being a caste society was similar to Gunnar Myrdal's illustration of race relations in American society. Myrdal believed caste accurately described racism in the US because "group prejudices against particular persons or types of people [Black Americans, Asians, and Hispanics] dominate[d]" the outlook of the "average [White] American" more so than any Marxist-type class struggle.[28] However, Myrdal analyzed caste in terms of race only and theorized that if Americans stopped being racist, America's "caste system" would disappear. In his conceptualization of caste, Myrdal did not believe that capitalism and economic class had any relevance or role in perpetuating caste, contrary to Rai's characterization of the situation in the US. Like Rabindranath Tagore, Rai blamed American capitalism for the disenfranchisement and exclusion of "Asiatics" from the US. Rai attributed negative American attitudes toward Indian immigrants to fears over labor market competition. Rai also inculpated capitalism for the enslavement of Blacks in the US South, maintaining that the economy of the South relied on "Negro laborers" but both the North and the South did not want skilled "Asiatic" immigrants in the US because they would compete with White laborers for jobs.

While Rai saw the power dynamics between White and Black Americans as comparable to the Indian caste system, he chose to express the contemporary plight of Indians publicly as an issue of colonialism. He considered caste to be a secondary issue. In Rai's view, India first had to gain independence from the British before it could address its internal problems of caste and religious communalism. At an Intercollegiate Socialist Society meeting in New York in 1917, Rai attempted to link the Black American and Indian struggles as a common fight against White supremacy, stating, "The problem of the Hindu and of the negro and cognate problems are not local, but world problems."[29] He made this comment alongside Du Bois, displaying a sense of global solidarity with Du Bois and other Black Americans,[30] but also prompting the US War Department to write to Du Bois expressing concern over Rai's words. The War Department alleged that "Mr. Lajpat Rai seem[ed] anxious for trouble" and asked Du Bois whether or not Rai's speech addressed "the negro question in this country?" Du Bois ignored the War Department's concerns and enthusiastically continued his alliance with Rai.[31]

Both Rai and Du Bois continued to work together and built connections with Irish independence supporters as well, and both attended a meeting in Chicago of the People's Movement and Unity Club organized by Rev. Pat. H. O'Donnell, an Irish Sinn Feiner, in March 1919. Similarly, Du Bois and Rai were members of the League of Small and Subject Nationalities, which sought to achieve independence for oppressed nations such as Ireland and India, and supported the self-determination struggles of ethnic groups in eastern Europe.[32] According to Rodger Nash Baldwin, a founder of the American Civil Liberties Union, Rai was a passionate supporter of the Irish independence cause and he commonly attended "meetings of Friends of Irish freedom (FIF)," an Irish American republican organization. Baldwin noted the Rai's ability to speak and write "like a scholar" captivated many Irish Americans and made Indian independence a focal point alongside Irish independence at FIF meetings. Baldwin argued that Rai made "common cause with the Irish in the struggles against the British empire," thus linking the anti-colonial movements of Indians and the Irish. Baldwin, who joined Rai's Friends of Freedom for India organization, lauded Rai as India's most able spokesmen to "plead India's cause." Baldwin claimed that that he knew of no other Indian who had the "authority," "wealth of information," and the "grounded passion" that Rai displayed.[33]

Rai's Anti-colonial Activism in the United States

Aside from directly working with Du Bois to promote independence for the Irish, Rai formed his own organizations to help enlist support amongst Americans and Irish nationalists for Indian home rule. In November 1917, Rai founded the India Home Rule League of America (IHRLA) in New York City. The organization shared similar goals as the Ghadar movement on the West Coast but was a more moderate, less militant concern and publicly only advocated for "home rule" or dominion status rather than unconditional independence.[34] Rai was able to inspire Americans such as Agnes Smedley to join the IHRLA. Smedley first heard Rai lecture at Columbia University in March 1917. In her autobiography, Smedley noted that Rai introduced her to "the movement for the freedom of his people" and showed her "that it was not only an historic movement of itself, but it was part of an international struggle for emancipation.... It was not a distant movement."[35]

To circulate its views to the American public, the IHRLA published a monthly journal titled *Young India*. In the inaugural issue in January 1918, Rai complained that the American people did not understand "real India" as much of their knowledge was derived from British sources or Christian missionaries. In response, Rai declared that the mission of the IHRLA would be to educate the American public about Indian affairs and British colonialism.[36] Rai contended that many Westerners believed that Indians were heathens, who needed to be civilized through Western education and Christianity, asserting that various missionaries had advocated this idea and "Reverend fathers who in their benevolence have been sent to convert and comfort the [Indian] heathen" to Christianity.[37]

Like Tagore, Rai questioned American Christians for consistently criticizing India's caste system while not resolving the problem of caste within their own societies. He believed that Christianity was a central theme in creating racial caste hierarchies in the US and noted that the Hindu Aryans never applied the color bar as rigidly as Christian Whites in the US.[38] Rai's criticism of racism amongst White American Christians mirrored Swami Vivekananda's condemnation of apartheid within American churches.[39] Vivekananda, in particular, lauded the racially inclusive nature of Islam and encouraged White American Christians to adopt a similar policy, arguing that in a mosque people of all races prayed side by side but in America he had yet to see "a church where the white man and the negro can kneel side by side to pray."[40] However, Rai believed that some Christian sects had begun having a less condescending view of Eastern religions, which had the potential to lead to a more racially cosmopolitan form of Christianity. Rai credited Tagore for changing the attitudes of some Christian groups. Although Rai did not mention these groups by name, he was likely referring to the Unitarians. Rai had appointed J. T. Sunderland as vice president of the IHRLA and invited him to write the foreword to his 1916 book *Young India*. Thus, Rai, like Tagore, had a favorable view of American Unitarians and believed that the Unitarians could be American allies for achieving Indian independence.

At a November 1918 dinner at the Grand Hotel in New York City, organized to celebrate the one-year anniversary of the IHRLA, Sunderland compared the potential independence of India to the abolition of slavery in the US in the aftermath of the American Civil War. Sunderland suggested that Rai and other Indian figures should seek alliances with Americans like those "whose heart throbbed for the freedom of the slaves ... in the days of the Civil War." By making such a suggestion, Sunderland linked India's independence movement to America's fight against slavery. Oswald Garrison Villard, another guest at the dinner, seconded this notion and argued that India's independence movement shared many principles with anti-slavery activism during the American Civil War. Villard quoted an 1854 Abraham Lincoln speech in which Lincoln had stated, "No man is good enough to govern any other man, without that other man's consent."[41] Lincoln had delivered the speech to criticize the Kansas–Nebraska Act, which permitted the expansion of slavery into the Kansas and Nebraska territories if White settlers living in those territories supported it. Lincoln argued that slaves were people, not animals, and consequently White settlers needed their consent to utilize their labor. Villard used Lincoln's quote to suggest that British dominion over India lacked a similar form of consent from Indian natives as white Americans lacked from Black Africans whom they had enslaved.[42] Villard's grandfather was William Lloyd Garrison, a prominent abolitionist during the early 1800s. Thus, Villard followed in the footsteps of his grandfather, and used the example of American slavery to criticize other systems of oppression elsewhere in the world.

The IHRLA was able to foster some American interest for Indian independence. Within a year of its foundation, the organization had nine hundred American and Indian members in at least ten American cities. Villard, who was the owner of the *Nation*, assisted the IHRLA by bringing in his writers Henry R. Mussey and Freda Kirchwey to assist the *Young India* organ. John Haynes Holmes, who was a Unitarian minister in New York and a founding member of the National Association for the Advancement of Colored People (NAACP), was another active member in the IHRLA. Holmes, like Villard, was previously a member of Myron N. Phelps's Society for the Advancement of India in 1909, and Holmes became a fervent supporter of Indian independence after meeting Rai and reading his books. Additionally, wealthy German American banker Jacob Schiff made an undisclosed financial contribution to the organization, although he was not a member.[43]

Through the IHRLA, Rai was successful in his efforts to bring awareness to issues of British colonialism and gained greater support amongst Americans for Indian home rule. Furthermore, the IHRLA supported the British war effort during World War I and believed that Indian cooperation with Britain would convince the latter to grant India dominion status and eventually full independence. In December 1919, Lala Lajpat Rai returned to India after his exile had ended. In November 1919, the League of Oppressed Peoples (LOP), an organization led by American attorney Dudley Field

Malone, held a special farewell dinner for Rai. The executive committee consisted of Rai, Irish playwright Francis Hackett, Allan McCurdy, American archeologist Arthur Upham Pope, and psychoanalyst Dr Gregory Zilboorg. The farewell dinner was sponsored by W. E. B. Du Bois, J. T. Sunderland, and Oswald Garrison Villard, and supported the self-determination of nations such as India, China, Ireland, and Korea. At the dinner, Dudley compared Rai to "pioneers of liberty" such as Gilbert du Motier and Marquis de Lafayette, a French military officer who played a pivotal role in the American Revolutionary War. Villard followed Dudley's speech by offering Rai the "continued interest and help of America in India's struggle."[44] Villard did not offer specifics on how Americans would continue to assist Rai, but he pledged moral support from White American internationalists and anti-colonialists.

According to J. T. Sunderland, Rai's lectures and addresses, which he delivered in many parts of the country, were greatly influential toward helping sympathetic Americans understand the negative aspects of British colonialism in India. Rai promoted the cause of Indian self-rule, while speaking at many colleges, labor unions, and women's groups in Boston, Washington, DC, Atlanta, New Orleans, Chicago, Los Angeles, and San Francisco.[45] Sunderland stated, "[T]he influence of Rai in America in all these ways was very great. I doubt if any five years of his important work in India has accomplished as much in aiding the Indian people on their way toward their goal of freedom as these five years in this country."[46] Along with Rai, Sunderland credited Rabindranath Tagore for building a great reputation in the US. Sunderland believed Rai and Tagore's influence on American supporters of Indian independence could push America to help India achieve independence. According to Sunderland, it was a shame that Rai left America in 1919, believing that had he remained he would have added even more to his "influential and far-reaching work," and drawn even more American support for the Indian cause.[47] While Sunderland believed that Rai could have gained a larger and even broader following if he had remained in the US, it is possible that, like Tagore, his impact would have faded during the 1920s. The internationalist intellectual climate of the 1910s was followed by growing xenophobia and ethnic nationalism in the 1920s. Additionally, immigration laws denied Indian immigrants and residents the same opportunities they had in prior decades.

Aside from researching the plight of Black Americans, like Tagore, Rai became a respected figure amongst many influential Americans and his work in the US caused multiple senators to voice their support for Indian home rule, including Joseph France of Maryland, Asle Gronna of North Dakota,

George Norris of Nebraska, and Joseph McCormick of Illinois. Senator France publicly thanked him for "rendering a valuable service in acquainting the people of America with the grave problems which confronted the people of India."[48] Sunderland similarly noted that Rai opened American eyes to "the real character of British rule in India," and proved that Britain's "civilizing mission" in India was not beneficial for the Indian people.[49]

During his five-year stay in the US, Rai served as a nexus between some of the leading civil rights activists in America, like Du Bois and Villard, and Indians fighting for freedom and social justice. He played a pivotal role in the exchange of ideas and viewpoints between the two groups which were used advantageously by both sides. After returning to India, Rai applied what he learned in America to his activism in India and continued to advocate for Indian home role. Additionally, he sought to bring greater awareness of the plight of Black Americans to his Indian countrymen and regularly leaned on DuBois as a source of inspiration.

Notes

1. Jugal Kishore Gupta, *History of Sirsa Town* (New Delhi: Atlantic Publishers & Distributors, 1991), 182.
2. Madhu Kishwar, "Arya Samaj and Women's Education: Kanya Mahavidyalaya, Jalandhar," *Economic and Political Weekly* 21, no. 17 (1986): WS9–24.
3. S. Vertovec, *The Hindu Diaspora: Comparative Patterns* (London: Routledge, 2000), 29, 54, 69.
4. L. L. Rai, *The Arya Samaj: An Account of Its Aims, Doctrine and Activities, with a Biographical Sketch of the Founder* (London: Longman Publishing, 1915).
5. W. E. B. Du Bois, "To the Nations of the World" (speech, London, July 25, 1900), in *My Life and Work*, ed. Alexander Walters, 257–260 (NY: Fleming H. Revell Company, 1917).
6. W. E. B. Du Bois, *The Souls of Black Folk* (New York: New American Library, 1903), 19.
7. Anil Nauriya, *The African Element in Gandhi* (Delhi: Gyan Publishing House, 2006).
8. W. E. B. Du Bois and David L. Lewis, *W.E.B. Du Bois: A Reader* (New York: Macmillan, 1995), 44–47.
9. Ulysses G. Weatherly, "The First Universal Races Congress," *The American Journal of Sociology* 17, no. 3 (1911): 315–328, 316.
10. Ibid., 318.
11. W. E. B. Du Bois, "The First Universal Races Congress," in *The Oxford W.E.B. Du Bois Reader*, ed. Eric J. Sundquist (New York: Oxford University Press, 1996), 59.

12. "The First Universal Races Congress," *The Independent* 70, August 24, 1911, 401–403.
13. David Kopf, *The Brahmo Samaj and the Shaping of the Modern Indian Mind* (Princeton: Princeton University Press, 1979).
14. Lala Lajpat Rai, *The United States of America: A Hindu's Impressions and a Study* (Calcutta: Brahmo Mission Press, 1916), 389.
15. Ibid., 77.
16. Harish K. Puri, "Lajpat Rai in USA 1914–1919: Life and Work of a Political Exile," https://theprg.files.wordpress.com/2009/07/puri-lala-lajpat-rai.pdf, accessed May 1, 2021.
17. Manan Desai, "*Oh Niagara!* Lala Lajpat Rai at Niagara Falls in 1905," September 1, 2017, https://www.saada.org/tides/article/oh-niagara, accessed March 1, 2021.
18. L. L. Rai, *The United States of America*, 77.
19. Nico Slate, *Colored Cosmopolitanism: The Shared Struggle for Freedom in the United States and India* (Cambridge: Harvard University Press, 2012), 38.
20. L. L. Rai, *The United States of America*, iii.
21. Ibid., v; Slate, *Colored Cosmopolitanism*, 38.
22. Babli Sinha, "Dissensus, Education and Lala Lajpat Rai's Encounter with W.E.B. Du Bois," *South Asian History and Culture* 6, no. 4 (2015): 462.
23. L. L. Rai, *The United States of America*, 104.
24. Ibid., 389.
25. Ibid., 392.
26. Ibid., 396.
27. Ibid., 395.
28. Gunnar Myrdal, *An American Dilemma, Volume I: The Negro in a White Nation* (1944; reprint in New York: McGraw Hill, 1964), lxx–lxxi; Gyanendra Pandey, *Race, Caste, and Difference in India and the United States* (New Delhi: University of Cambridge Press, 2013), 22–23; Daniel Immerwahr, "Caste or Colony? Indianizing Race in the United States," *Modern Intellectual History* 4, no. 2 (2007): 275–301, 281.
29. Slate, *Colored Cosmopolitanism*, 38.
30. "Explosion of Asia as Menace to Peace," *New York Evening Post*, September 22, 1917, 14; Dohra Ahmad, "'More Than Romance': Genre and Geography in Dark Princess," *ELH* 69, no.3 (2002): 775–803.
31. Slate, *Colored* Cosmopolitanism, 38.
32. Robert A. Hill, *Marcus Garvey and UNIA Papers Volume I* (1826–August 1919) (Los Angeles: University of California Press, 1983), 434.
33. "Tribute from Roger Nash Baldwin," *The People*, April 13, 1929.
34. Paul Teed, "Race Against Memory: Katherine Mayo, Jabez Sunderland, and Indian Independence," *American Studies* 44, no. 1/2 (2003): 35–57, 40.
35. Puri, "Lajpat Rai in USA," III.
36. Lala Lajpat Rai, *Young India*, January 1918.

37. Ibid.

38. L. L. Rai, *The United States of America*, 293.

39. Swami Vivekananda, "The Future of India," *The Complete Works of Swami Vivekananda*, Vol. 3 (Mayavati: Advaita Ashrama, 1927), 293.

40. Swami Vivekananda, "The Great Teachers of the World" (delivered at the Shakespeare Club, Pasadena, California, February 3, 1900), in *Complete Works of Swami Vivekananda*, Vol. 4 (Mayavati: Advaita Ashrama, 1927); Swami Vivekananda, "The Way to the Realisation of a Universal Religion" (delivered in the Universalist Church, Pasadena, California, January 28, 1900), in *Complete Works of Swami Vivekananda*, Vol. 2 (Mayavati: Advaita Ashrama, 1927).

41. Abraham Lincoln, "Peoria Speech" (speech, Peoria, Illinois, October 16, 1894).

42. Dixie, "Our First Anniversary Dinner," *Young India* 1 (December 1918): 24–25.

43. Alan Raucher, "American Anti-Imperialists and the Pro-India Movement, 1900–1932," *Pacific Historical Review* 43, no. 1 (1974): 83–110, 94–95.

44. "Farewell Dinners," *Young India* 3, no.1 (January 1920): 11–14, 11.

45. Seema Sohi, *Echoes of Mutiny: Race, Surveillance, and Indian Anticolonialism in North America* (New York: Oxford University Press, 2014), 68.

46. J. T. Sunderland, "Communications: India's Need of Foreign Propaganda," *The People*, May 16, 1926.

47. Ibid.

48. Sohi, *Echoes of Mutiny*, 68.

49. Sunderland, "Communications: India's Need of Foreign Propaganda."

4

Lala Lajpat Rai in India

After Rai returned to India in December 1919, he sought to apply what he had learned in America to his own activism in India. Inspired by the Rand School of Social Science, Rai formed the Tilak School of Politics in 1921 to educate underprivileged Indians. He also started his own newspaper, *The People*, to circulate his ideas on caste and racial science, and his opinions on Gandhian non-violence tactics. Rai's views regarding the effectiveness of Gandhian techniques evolved throughout the 1920s. At the start of the decade, he supported Gandhi's non-violence strategy. However, Rai questioned passive resistance as a viable method for overthrowing White supremacy and the British Raj following the failure of the non-cooperation movement in 1922 and his exposure to Du Bois's articles in *The Crisis* describing the mass lynchings of Black Americans in the 1921 Tulsa race massacre. Rai came to see violent encounters as an inevitability during social clashes predicated upon race and class. Sadly, this violence came to claim Rai's life. On October 30, 1928, Rai himself led a protest against the British to challenge their lack of inclusion of Indians on the Indian Statutory Commission, which was a group of seven White British members of parliament chosen by the British government to study constitutional reform in India. During the protest, British police superintendent James A. Scott ordered the police to attack the protesters and Scott personally assaulted Rai. Rai died a month later, never recovering from the injuries inflicted upon him.

Up until his death, Rai's outlook continued to evolve. Alongside his thoughts on violent protest, his perception of caste changed throughout the 1920s. While Rai saw India's caste problem as a secondary issue early in the decade, by the tail end of his life, Rai had brought the matter to the forefront of the Indian independence movement. He actively sought the abolition of caste discrimination and sub-castes even to the point that he considered postponing

Swaraj to solve the issue of caste. This showed that Rai actively sought caste reform and advocated for the abolition of sub-castes. In the many articles that Rai wrote in *The People*, he condemned caste discrimination explicitly and stressed that India could never achieve unity and become a functional democracy so long as caste discrimination remained.

Rai's relationship with W. E. B. Du Bois has been assessed by some scholars to be a relatively insignificant aspect of Rai's life; Suraj Yengde suggests that Rai abandoned the solidarity that he created with Black Americans in the US and used racial-caste theories to defend the racial superiority of high-caste Indians over Indian untouchables and Black Americans.[1] Yengde argues that Rai had chosen to "side with the white castes of America," and that he had found a "natural home in the white caste values of America" such as endorsing racial hierarchies that disparaged Black Americans as an inferior group. Although Yengde acknowledges Rai's relationship with Du Bois, he considers it to be a relatively small part of Rai's activism and suggests that Du Bois had very little impact on Rai's thinking and values.[2] However, Rai's interactions with American civil rights activists, his portrayal of Du Bois as a valuable ally in his journalism and his writings, and his persistent loyalty to the National Association for the Advancement of Colored People (NAACP) prove that Rai displayed solidarity with Black Americans, and that he was committed to the Black civil rights cause even after leaving the US. In his final letter to Mary White Ovington in 1928, Rai reiterated that his "interest in the welfare of the coloured races of the coloured people of the United States has never slackened."[3]

Rai overtly denied that there was a racial difference between caste groups in India, and sought to unify all Indians. He consistently supported the advancement of both Black Americans and Indian untouchables until his death. Rai believed that caste was a hinderance to Indian unity and the creation of new sub-castes by the British further divided Indians based on caste, class, and racial lines. Like Rabindranath Tagore, Rai saw immutable caste divisions as creating false ethnic divisions between Indians. This manipulated the Indian populace into seeing themselves as distinct groups rather than building a unified movement that created a cosmopolitan Indian identity. To Rai, these caste and religious divisions hindered the creation of an Indian nationalist identity that was devoid of caste, creed, and race which could serve as a counter to the ethnic nationalism which Tagore aptly warned Americans was happening within Europe and the US during the 1910s. Although Rai blamed Hindus for implementing the caste system, he believed that the British had modified it and made it more rigid by adding sub-castes that categorized an increasing percentage of the Hindu population as low-caste. Hence, anti-colonial activism for Rai included caste reform and abolishing the sub-castes created by the British Raj. Rai, however, believed that religious divisions in India between Hindus and Muslims served as an even larger hindrance to Indian unity than caste and saw it more pertinent at times to highlight religious divisions in India over caste divisions.

Throughout the 1920s, Rai continued his alliances with multiple NAACP leaders, considering both Oswald Garrison Villard and W. E. B. Du Bois as viable allies for Indians in fighting against White supremacy. Maintaining an internationalist outlook in the fight against White supremacy, he utilized the NAACP newspaper, *The Crisis*, and Villard's newspaper, *The Nation*, to inform the Indian people about the Black American struggle. Rai believed that the NAACP was a valuable American ally for Indians and encouraged NAACP figures such as Mary White Ovington to transform the organization into a transnational movement assisting both Indians and Black Americans.

Rai was an important and revered transnational figure, and his death in 1928 had an impact on multiple NAACP figures. After Rai's passing, Du Bois, Villard, and Ovington praised his anti-colonial activism and appreciated his support for the Black American cause.[4] Du Bois, in particular, saw Rai as a martyr for Indian independence and used Rai's death to stress the urgent need for India's liberation. Additionally, Rai became a martyr amongst some Punjabi Indian revolutionaries. Bhagat Singh along with fellow revolutionaries Shivaram Rajguru, Sukhdev Thapar, and Chandrashekhar Azad sought revenge against Officer Scott. However, they accidently shot the wrong officer, John P. Saunders, on December 17, 1928. In response to their actions, British authorities executed Singh and his co-conspirators in March 1931. Jawaharlal Nehru praised Singh for attempting to defend the "honour of Lala Lajpat Rai," proving how Rai was an iconic, esteemed, and important figure who shaped the Indian youth and inspired them to advocate for Indian independence.

Lala Lajpat Rai's Activism in India

While in New York City, Rai found a kinship with various American left-wing figures. In 1914, he was introduced to Columbia University economist Edwin A. Seligman by Sidney Webb, an early member of the Fabian Society, a British democratic socialist organization. Through Seligman,

Rai was invited to meetings at the American Sociological, Economic, and Statistical Associations and he developed a keen interest in the social sciences. After attending various lectures, Rai sought to better understand socialist ideologies and purchased the works of Marx and other socialist classics.[5] This interest led him to visit the Rand School of Social Science in New York City, a school founded in 1906 by members of the Socialist Party of America. The Rand School aimed to provide education to groups regardless of social or economic class. In November 1918, Rai briefly lectured there as Indian educator and publicist, giving a total of six lectures on "Asia in World Politics."[6] Other notable lecturers included W. E. B. Du Bois and Oswald Garrison Villard.

Rai admired the fact that the Rand School was an institution "which imparted instruction to people whose circumstances did not permit of their using regular universities and colleges for improving and developing their knowledge of Politics, Economics, and Social Sciences." His appreciation for the school and its altruistic philosophy inspired Rai to create his own institution for the underprivileged in India called the Tilak School of Politics. Rai stated, "I owe a great deal of my education in Politics and Sociology to my stay in New York and the ideas I borrowed from there was the need of institution of that kind in my own country."[7] He noted that "[w]ithin a year of my landing [in Bombay in February 1920] I began to form my plans for establishing a School of Politics somewhat on the lines of the Rand School in New York."[8] Rai argued, "One of the essential features of the scheme of the Tilak School of Politics was the provision of the training to young men destined for the political and social service of the country." Alongside the Tilak school of Politics, Rai also created the Servants of the People Society, a non-profit social service organization to produce activists within India and to "enlist and train national missionaries for the service of the motherland."[9]

The impact of the Rand School on Lala Lajpat Rai was unavoidably significant. It symbolizes how American socialists influenced Rai's vision for India. Before encountering the Rand School, Rai noted that he believed that "some kind of education was better than no education" and that even an upper-class Indian with a British education could assist India's "progress towards freedom." However, after his experiences at the school and his interactions with the American left, Rai believed that it was urgent and necessary for Indians to learn about social sciences through a non-British lens, without which India could not "make satisfactory process."[10] It was essential, he felt, for Indians to receive an education that did not deter them from anti-colonial politics. Rai believed that the biased British education provided in India was the "most important of all of [India's] problems."[11] British education hindered Indian independence to Rai's mind, because it encouraged educated Indians to support British rule and discouraged critical thinking.[12] Rai noted that he himself was encouraged to support British rule by British educators at the Government College of Lahore where he studied law in the early 1880s. He credited his experiences in the US and his socialist education through the American left and the Rand School for helping him break free from his formative learning: "During this stay [in New York] I learnt and unlearnt much. Some of the American institutions attracted me and I used them both as a lecturer and a student on and off."[13] Because Rai understood that upper-class Indians may have been socially conditioned to support British colonial rule, he sought to instead recruit lower-class uneducated Indians to study at the Tilak School of Politics since their minds could be molded to become more active proponents of Indian independence.

The Tilak School of Politics played an integral part in developing and building the future of Indian politics, as well as in supporting the Indian independence movement. The school educated prominent Indians such as Indian independence activist Purushottam Das Tandon; politician and second chief minister of Gujarat, Balwantrai Gopalji Mehta; and the second prime minister of India, Lal Bahadur Shastri. Indian revolutionary Bhagat Singh was also a student at the school from 1921 until at least 1924.[14] Rai named the school after his mentor, Indian independence leader Bal Gangadhar Tilak who was notoriously referred to by the British as "the father of Indian unrest."[15] Tilak was one of the first and strongest advocates of Indian self-rule. Tilak and Rai had formed a friendship during the first decade of the twentieth century when they were both part of the Indian National Congress, a political party which represented Indian interests. However, both men decided to leave the party in 1907 because it was dominated by a moderate faction. Led by Gopal Krishna Gokhale, the moderates sought Indian independence through constitutional means and cooperation with the British government. Conversely, Tilak advocated radical methods such as protest, boycott, and agitation which Rai supported.[16] While Tilak and Rai had a strong relationship, Tilak clashed with Gandhi. Tilak did not believe in "total non-violence" and advocated achieving Swaraj by any means necessary. He expressed these views to Gandhi, but Gandhi did not take Tilak's advice and instead decided to continue his strict adherence to non-violent tactics.[17] While Rai was aligned with Tilak, he was also a supporter of Gandhi's approach and asked him to host the opening ceremony for the Tilak School of Politics in November 1921.

The naming of the school after Tilak was somewhat ironic. The school was founded by Rai to raise the social status of low-caste and underprivileged Indians, but Tilak himself was opposed to social reforms regarding untouchability and had refused to sign a petition for the abolition of untouchability.[18] Tilak's anti-caste views intertwined with his misogyny. He opposed inter-caste marriage, particularly a match where an upper-caste woman married a lower-caste man, which signified that he believed that a Brahmin woman's social status depended more on whom she married than a Brahmin man's. Additionally, Tilak was against providing education to women, unlike Rai.[19] Rai's desire to honor prominent Indian nationalists caused him to ignore the discriminatory caste and gender ideologies of some of its leaders. He himself was vehemently against untouchability, but he overlooked the fact that some of his allies endorsed caste ideologies. Rai was willing to work with Indian nationalists who were caste sympathizers because he believed that the remedying of caste and gender discrimination would follow if Indians were given independence.

Rai communicated the ideas of the Servants of the People Society through a weekly newspaper called *The People*. He was the main author of this organ but allowed other intellectual thinkers such as Taraknath Das, C. F. Andrews, and J. T. Sunderland to contribute. The paper explored mostly Marxist viewpoints toward revolution, politics, and economics. Rai himself was very critical of capitalism, which he believed was intertwined with the marginalization of non-Europeans across the globe, a view shared by his friend W. E. B. Du Bois. Rai was not present and did not have an active role in the early years of the Tilak School of Politics because he was imprisoned by the British government in December 1921 for participating in the non-cooperation movement in 1920.[20]

After his release from jail in 1923, Rai became a frequent contributor to *The People*. The non-cooperation movement was, however, short-lived and ended in February 1922. In his autobiography, Jawaharlal Nehru blamed the collapse of the movement on the Chauri Chaura incident, which was a violent clash between policemen and non-cooperation protesters.[21] Gandhi was a strict believer in the practice of *ahimsa* (non-violence) and, therefore, decided to halt the non-cooperation movement because of the violent event. Nehru criticized Gandhi for calling off the movement, noting that the Indian people were finally uniting against the oppressive British government in India.[22] Like Nehru, Rai expressed skepticism over Gandhi's political leadership at this point, deeming "non-violence as an impossibility from the practical point of view." He thought that the "occurrence of violence at some place or other could not have been averted by the best efforts of leaders and the masses."[23]

Rai's Views on the Effectiveness of "Non-violence"

Individuals such as Rai and Nehru likely showed a lack of confidence in the methods of "non-cooperation" because they were radical or unconventional for the time. The recent successful revolutions such as the Irish War for Independence from 1919 to 1921 and Russian Revolution of 1917 had been implemented through militant tactics; therefore, Indians did not have any tangible evidence that Gandhi's tactics would gain them independence. The economic boycott of British goods and withdrawing of participation from the labor force was not a proven method that Indians could rely upon to secure independence from the British.[24]

Rai's skepticism about non-violence increased after reading Du Bois's writings in *The Crisis*. Intrigued by Du Bois's activism and his fight against White supremacy, Rai urged Indians to read the NAACP newspaper. He claimed that he had learned a great deal about the spirit of Black Americans from it. While Rai had supported non-violence during the non-cooperation movement, he mentioned that Du Bois did not shy away from supporting militant self-defense by Black Americans in response to the violent actions of White Americans against them. Rai referred to Du Bois's endorsement in *The Crisis* of "Black Tulsa" fighting against White lynchers by forming a squadron of Black riflemen. "Black Tulsa" was a reference to the Tulsa race massacre in May 1921, the "single worst incident of racial violence in American history."[25] The violence involved thousands of White people rampaging and destroying Black neighborhoods in retaliation for an alleged assault on a seventeen-year-old White woman by a nineteen-year-old Black man in an elevator. In response, the Black residents of Tulsa took up arms to defend themselves against the White mobs. Du Bois praised these fighters because "they killed the [white] beasts rather than lie down and fawn ... to save a worthless pride."[26]

Rather than criticize Du Bois for endorsing physical self-defense, Rai praised him and Black Americans for "fighting the battles of all coloured peoples on earth."[27] Crucially, Rai explicitly used this tragedy in the American context to question the effectiveness of passive resistance in India. Studying the Tulsa race massacre, Rai pondered that perhaps some degree of militant resistance might be needed to fight against oppression. Rai, like Nehru, was frustrated by the failure of the Indian non-cooperation movement, leaving him eager to learn about how Black Americans were fighting their own struggles.[28]

Even though Rai supported the inherent right of all oppressed people to engage in an armed revolt against a violent regime, he could not definitively endorse it as the most effective method specifically for the Indian independence movement. Rai believed that Indians were not mentally equipped to ignite an armed revolt because they were too docile, gentle, and spiritual to start a military campaign against the British Raj.[29] Additionally, Rai considered the situation in India to be different from that of Black Americans; the latter were severely outnumbered by their oppressors whereas Indians were still the majority group in their country. Therefore, perhaps different methods of protest and retaliation were necessary for both groups and a large-scale economic boycott could be effective for Indians. The British Indian economy, after all, depended more on the Indian worker than the American economy depended upon Black labor.

Aside from Du Bois's influence, there were other factors that made Rai question the effectiveness of total non-violence. Rai noted that recent successful socialist revolutions such as the Russian Revolution of 1917 were successfully implemented through violent methods. He theorized that socialist and communist revolutionaries endorsed violent methods because "socialists and communists believe that capitalism can only be destroyed by the same methods which helped create it, which is war." Rai himself was anti-capitalism and supported socialism. He was of the opinion that most Hindus were naturally anti-war through conviction of faith. However, he asserted that the "pacifism of the 'no war under any circumstances' kind has not yet been found anywhere in the civilised world." Therefore, Rai thought, perhaps Hindus had to modify their "anti-war" beliefs in order to successfully achieve independence.[30] In some ways Rai saw the Russian Revolution as a practical parallel to the Indian independence because it involved the masses overthrowing a small number of elites.

Rai's Continued Appreciation for Du Bois

Rai's consistent praise for Du Bois in his articles proved that the American was a role model for Rai's own activism. In a 1926 article in *The People*, titled "The Clash of Colour," Rai referred to Du Bois as a "personal friend" and mentioned that he had had several meetings with Du Bois, including the "privilege of enjoying his hospitality in his own home." Rai noted that as a colored man himself, and as a member of a "disinherited and dispossessed race," he and Du Bois "had something in common" with one another that led them to establish a friendship. Rai made a comparison of Du Bois's racial status in America and what it would be if he lived in India, remarking that if a "mixed-race Eurasian" such as Du Bois lived in India, he would be given the same privileges as a White man. However, in the US, a "Euro-African" remains a "coloured man for all generations and times." Through this racial classification of Du Bois, Rai suggested that racial classifications in British India were not as rigid as those in the US. Rai, as in his previous considerations of race in the US, did not understand its fluid nature; he ignored the phenomenon of racial passing and did not realize that some Americans that were legally Black could construct their own racial identities.

Although Rai had also formed a friendship with Booker T. Washington while in the US, he evaluated Du Bois's methods of activism to be more effective and beneficial for disenfranchised groups in the long term than Washington's willingness to accept money from White capitalists to educate Black Americans.[31] While Rai praised Washington as an educator and credited him for providing Black Americans a vocational education through the Tuskegee Institute, he criticized him for receiving aid from "white capitalists" to build the institution. Rai argued that because of Washington's willingness to accept capitalism as a system that could uplift Blacks, White Americans were more agreeable to his form of activism. In Rai's view, constructive work with White capitalists to dismantle racial conflict was an impossibility because capitalism naturally dehumanized Black Americans and Indian laborers, treating them as a commodity that could be exploited.

Rai supported Du Bois's vision to fight against White supremacy through an anti-capitalist lens. In addition to a racial struggle, Du Bois conveyed the plight of Black people as an issue of economic marginality. In his 1903 publication *The Souls of Black Folk*, Du Bois argued that White capitalists excluded Black Americans from an economic mainstream that prided itself specifically on its virtues as an "inclusive capitalist system" which created opportunities for White Americans with limited financial means.[32] Rai regarded *The Souls of Black Folk* as a key source for his understanding of the Black struggle. He agreed with Du Bois that racial equality could not be achieved so long as capitalism reigned in America. Rai argued that conflicts of "race and colour" originated from economic causes, "the desire of profit and gain and power," and thus any cooperation with capitalists was antithetical toward achieving racial equality. Because of Du Bois's anti-capitalist views,

Rai believed that Du Bois "stood for a dignified, clean, honorable but a manly fight with the oppressors and exploiters of his race."[33] Additionally, it is likely that Rai saw the Tuskegee Institute as an American parallel to his own education at the Government College of Lahore. Since the Tuskegee Institute was funded by White Americans and the Government College of Lahore was funded by the British, Rai believed that this form of education deprived its students of the critical thinking skills that allowed them to question White supremacy and British colonialism.

Du Bois's influence also pushed Rai to question the religious institutions of American society. Rai criticized the hypocrisy of White Christianity in the US and stated, "[H]ow far it is from Christ may be imagined from the awe-inspiring, blood-curdling details of Negro lynchings which take place in that land of liberty and freedom every year." However, Rai noted that this hypocrisy regarding White Christianity did not just exist in America but "all the world over," stating that it was the "same in India, and in the U.S.A, and Great Britain."[34] Rai's criticisms of Christianity mirrored those of Swami Vivekananda, who had argued to American audiences that Christians were hypocritical in asserting the inclusivity and tolerance of their religion when in reality White Christians supported British imperialism in India and did not address the violent marginalization of Black Americans in the US. Also, Rai was critical of White Christian missionaries in India because they sought to push "anti-Indian" propaganda to maintain the rule of the British Raj.[35]

Both Du Bois's writings on lynchings and Rai's own experiences in America modified the latter's outlook on religion. During his stay in the US, Rai witnessed that religious differences between South Asians living in America did not cause the same friction between them as they did in India. Rai noticed that in the US, White Americans discriminated against all South Asians regardless of their caste or religion. Rai believed that the social status of South Asians in the US was comparable to how Black Americans were regarded by White Christians. Even if Black Americans were Christians, their skin color took precedence, and White Christians considered them to be an inferior sect of society. The treatment of all non-White individuals in the US led Rai to discuss the potential of abolishing all religious institutions in India on several occasions with fellow Punjabi exile, S. Nihal Singh.[36] In some ways Rai saw racial friction between Whites and non-Whites in America as a parallel to that between Hindus and Muslims in India. For Rai, Jim Crow segregation was akin to communal segregation in India.

Rai's Internationalism and Ideas about Race in a Global Context

Inspired by Du Bois's global outlook, Rai aggressively tried to link the Indian independence movement and the plight of Black and Asian Americans to a larger global struggle against White supremacy. Both Rai and Du Bois theorized that immigration restrictions against Asians and Africans preserved the racialized economy of imperialism which prioritized White workers in upper-middle-class professions. That was why Rai believed that the British Raj attempted to prevent permanent Indian emigration to the British Isles and only allowed Indians temporary work. Similarly, the US did not let their "Asiatic" citizens such as native Hawaiians into the mainland and restricted immigration from Asia after the Immigration Act of 1924.[37] Rai concluded that both the British Raj and the US government tried to limit non-White migration because they wanted to keep White citizens separate from "colored subjects" and they did not want the children of "colored subjects" to compete with White children and have access to social mobility. In Rai's view, British and American authorities feared that the intermingling of races could lead to racial conflict and, therefore, they encouraged the idea that the White race is the only race fit to govern and others "must occupy a subordinate position for all time to come."[38]

Because Rai believed that the American government and the British Raj marginalized its subjects in the same way and limited their opportunities to migrate to White-majority countries, he strategized his activism transnationally and lobbied for human rights for all marginalized people of color. In 1926, Rai traveled to London to speak at the World Migration Congress in June. At the Congress, Rai criticized the discriminatory immigration laws levied toward people of color by the British and US governments. The Congress was organized by the International Federation of Trade Unions and the Labour and Socialist International and attended by delegates from twenty-three countries, seventeen of which were in Europe.[39] The Labour and Socialist International was an international organization of socialist and labour parties, active between 1923 and 1940.[40]

Rai understood that Western nations relied upon "coloured workers" for profit. In his speech, he argued that Indians were taken forcefully from their homeland to work in different parts of the British Empire as indentured servants, including in "Natal, Fiji, Guiana, West Indies, and later to other places," yet both Europe and America did not allow voluntary Indian immigration into their countries. Rai blamed capitalism and imperialism for making the poorer classes of the world "ignorant, dirty and uncivilized" and for the exclusion and segregation of different races. He warned that through capitalism and racial discrimination, Western nations were "throwing the whole weight of the coloured workers of the world in the scale against [Western capitalism]."[41] Rai argued that whether racism or economic concerns motivated exclusionary migration policies was irrelevant as they both led to subordination, exploitation, exclusion, and segregation.

By using the term "coloured world," Rai linked people of color from different areas of the world together, unifying them into one shared struggle against racism and capitalism. This terminology further suggested that the experiences of people of color were completely different and independent from those of White Americans. Rai's speech at the World Migration Conference signified a growing solidarity between the colonies of the colored world. He mentioned that if Western nations were willing to form a migration policy that was "considerate and humane, we of Asia will help and cooperate with the greatest possible goodwill," suggesting that he was willing to make mutual compromises.[42]

Socialist politician and anti-war activist A. Fenner Brockway noted that the original sub-committee for the conference were exclusively White Europeans. To give Rai an opportunity to speak at the event, Brockway gave up his spot on the sub-committee to him, also making sure that the entire sub-committee was not made up of White Europeans. Brockway noted that Rai made an "effective speech in favour of racial equality" and his efforts lead to the sub-committee extending consideration of the issue. Furthermore, Rai had "moved an amendment to the original resolution urging that race and colour should not be made a barrier to migration."[43] However, Rai's statements at the Congress were refuted by other speakers such as William Kitson from Australia who only supported European migrants to his country as long as "they could be absorbed without detriment" to Australian workers. Delegates from New Zealand similarly advocated for a migration policy based on "social and racial grounds."[44] After a vote, Rai's amendment was not passed by the sub-committee.

Rai's reasons for advocating international migration in many ways mirrored Rabindranath Tagore's. Both Rai and Tagore believed that international travel and migration would lead to the assimilation of various races and ethnic groups through interracial marriage, which would in turn defeat White supremacy. Rai argued that much of the world was already racially mixed. He stated, "Countless centuries of migrations, of war, of conquest, of changes of ideas and ideals [had] introduced heterogeneity in every country." Rai did not believe in the need for racial segregation since different races had mixed into a homogenous society. He used the example of "experiments in racial blends" in Central and South America as evidence that people from different races and cultures could exist in a singular society.[45]

However, in a separate London meeting with Oswald Garrison Villard, Rai contradicted his argument that some societies had mixed different races into a homogenous society. He told Villard that the Indian struggle against the British was not unique and that "in every country, in every state" there were wars "between race and race, colour and colour, and class and class." Rai conveyed to Villard that he believed that both the US and India shared common dynamics between race, color, and class, noting that just as the British Raj marginalized Indians, Europe and America relegated "Jews and Asiatics" to second-class citizens. Villard responded that he understood that there would "be a reaction in the favour of human ideals in the next 20 years" and argued that Gandhi's "remedy for [India's] political troubles was the most effective that human genius could invent." Villard mentioned that if only Indians could "act up to" Gandhi's plans, they would "achieve their desire in no time."[46] Rai, however, told Villard that Indian independence through Gandhian techniques was "unattainable" as "one hundred and fifty years of foreign rule, with its foreign system of education and administration has taken away the soul out of our intellectuals." Rai asserted that Indians could not "afford to boycott Government service or the professions allied to it" and thus educated Indians were an asset to the British Raj in suppressing any large-scale Gandhian movement.

Rai wrote about his conversation with Villard in *The People*, telling his readers that Villard was a friend of "all subject peoples, oppressed nations, and suppressed classes." Attempting to contextualize the Indian struggle as part of a global movement against White supremacy, Rai was adamant in portraying Villard as an individual whom his Indian readers should see as an unwavering ally of the struggles of all colored peoples, including those in India. He urged Indians to read Villard's newspapers for more insight. Villard owned *The Nation*, a progressive liberal-leaning paper founded in 1865 as a successor to Villard's grandfather William Lloyd Garrison's antislavery paper, *The Liberator*.[47] *The Nation* did not circulate outside the US; however, Villard consistently used it to argue against imperialism and expansionism and support the Indian independence struggle, as well as civil rights for Black Americans. Rai's depiction of Villard showed that he viewed him as a figure for moral support in whom both Indians and Black Americans could have faith in.[48]

In addition to recognizing upper-class Indian support for British rule as an obstacle for Indian independence, Rai blamed American eugenicists Lothrop Stoddard and Madison Grant for bolstering both British rule in India and the marginalization of Black Americans in the US.[49] Both authors argued that the Nordic race (Anglo-Saxons, Germans, Scandinavians) were the superior one and synonymous with the Aryan race. Hence, according to Stoddard and Grant, Nordics had an inherent right to rule the world. Furthermore, Rai blamed Stoddard and Grant for influencing laws confining the "coloured man" to Asia and Africa and preventing his migration to Europe and America because they did not want non-White laborers competing with their White counterparts. Stoddard's racist beliefs were especially hostile to Black people. He claimed that they were fundamentally different from other groups, had no civilizations of their own, and had contributed nothing to the world. Stoddard opposed interracial mixing between White and Black Americans on the grounds that it would degrade White American civilization.[50]

Stoddard's 1920 book *The Rising Tide of Color Against White World-Supremacy*, with an introduction written by Madison Grant, was praised by President Warren G. Harding, and it helped bolster segregation and anti-immigration policies. At a 1921 speech in Birmingham, Alabama, Harding cited Stoddard's work as evidence that Jim Crow was necessary to prevent "racial amalgamation." He claimed that social equality between Black and White Americans was not a possibility. Harding also signed the Per Centum Act of 1921, which restricted immigration from southern and eastern Europe, limiting both Italian and eastern European Jews from emigrating to the US. Stoddard categorized eastern European Jews as being "Asiatics" and argued for restricting "Mediterranean" groups such as the Italians from emigrating to the US, contending that if they reproduced with "Nordic" Americans, it would threaten "Nordic" racial purity in the country.

While Harding used Stoddard's work to bolster arguments favoring social inequality between White and Black people, his writings conversely inspired some Black Americans to begin to look at their own struggle as part of a larger global struggle against White supremacy. Although Stoddard believed that the White "race" was the dominant race, he ultimately believed that White supremacy and White colonialism would eventually end. According to Stoddard, nations such as Japan were going to expand their influence in the Pacific, the people of India would throw the British out, and the Islamic world would grow militant and begin hostilities against the West. Black columnists in newspapers such as Baltimore's *Afro-American*, the third most read Black newspaper with a circulation of around twenty thousand in the early 1920s, welcomed Stoddard's book as positive news. Columnists noted that since the "colored races" vastly outnumbered Whites globally, marginalized groups of color could defeat White supremacy. Additionally, some Black journalists believed if anti-colonial struggles such as the Indian independence movement succeeded, it could also provide a route and source of inspiration to pursue Black equality in the US.[51]

Like Black journalists writing for the Baltimore *Afro-American*, Rai understood that Stoddard and Grant's work intended to warn White Americans and White Europeans that the "colored" races were growing in population and that they could eventually overthrow the "white man's world dominion." Rai, however, noted that he did not think that most British colonial officials believed that colonized subjects in Asia and Africa would ignite a united movement against White supremacy and British colonialism. Rai noted that "the logical consequence" or response by the British to a growing "revolt" against their colonial rule would be for White colonial settlers to return to their own lands (Europe) and leave the "coloured people" to their fate and abandon the cry of the "white man's burden."[52] Rai did not anticipate Indians instigating a large-scale revolt against the British because powerful upper-class Indians supported British rule. The British could rely on upper-class Indian support to maintain their rule primarily because they were willing to enforce and support caste privileges.

Rai also criticized Stoddard and Grant for misrepresenting the Hindu usage of caste by arguing that the Hindu caste system was intended for racial segregation and to prevent interracial marriage. In his 1916 book *The Passing of the Great Race*, Grant referred to the Hindu caste system as "a record of the desperate efforts of the conqueror classes in India to preserve the purity of their blood" and he argued that just like Jim Crow laws, the Hindu caste system separated the "dominant" races from the "lesser" races.[53] Although, Rai admitted that Hindus practiced caste segregation, he referred to Grant and Stoddard's arguments regarding the racialization of the Indian caste system as "the result of confused thinking and utter nonsense." Rai denied that there were racial difference between Indians. He argued that all civilizations originated in Asia and "the non-white element in European blood is almost as common as the so-called Nordic element." He concluded his critique of Stoddard and Grant by proclaiming that "the whites have all kinds of blood in their veins – Black, brown, yellow, and red." Rai also maintained that "a new race is being born in the two Americas [North and South], which is a mixture of all these racial values." Therefore, Rai asserted that White American eugenicists had misinterpreted the Indian caste system and both American and Indian societies already had a large population of "mixed race" individuals. He believed that Indians should not "feel very much concerned over the prognostications of Stoddard's and Grant's." The problem in India was primarily a problem of "creeds," Rai affirmed, rather than race, and religious unity was the ultimate priority for Indians. He believed the fate of the "whole coloured world" lay in the hands of Hindus and Muslims.[54]

Rai's Developing Views on Caste

Rai's views on the problems of caste quickly evolved from seeing them as secondary issues to understanding the need for urgent reform. Perhaps the greatest motivator that forced Rai to bring caste to the forefront of Indian independence movement was the anti-Indian propaganda advanced by American historian and White nationalist Katherine Mayo in her 1927 book *Mother India*. Mayo had been a research assistant for Oswald Garrison Villard for his 1910 biography of abolitionist John Brown, but her own views endorsed White Anglo-Saxon Protestant Nativism.[55] She wrote extensively in opposition to non-White and Catholic immigration to the US and propagated false stereotypes of Black Americans as sexually aggressive toward White Anglo-Saxon women.[56] Based around her travels and experiences in India, *Mother India* critiqued India's treatment of its female population as well as the treatment of untouchables. The British government funded her trip to India and she received both hospitality and research assistance from British officials.[57] The book, intended for British and American audiences, was an indictment of Indian culture and Indian desire for self-rule. Her work was a bestseller in the US and Great Britain, selling over 140,000 copies in less than a year. It had a powerful influence on the American people's view of India, thus weakening India's moral claim to self-determination.[58] In response to the success of her work, the finance minister of the Government of India personally expressed gratitude to Mayo for countering nationalist propaganda and showing her fellow Americans "the difficulties of the English in their task in India."[59]

Rai believed that international opinion needed to be favorable toward Indian self-determination to pressure the British to grant India freedom.[60] Rai was threatened by *Mother India*'s popularity. His writings in *The People* signified that that he believed that Mayo's negative representation of India as a caste-ridden society could alienate international allies from the Indian independence movement. In response, Rai dismissed Mayo's arguments and suggested that she only visited India with a mission to vilify the Indian people, not to promote caste equality. He accused her of exaggerating the number of untouchables in India (she had reported that there were as many as "60 million"). According to Rai, the true number was far lower as "a caste reckoned as untouchable or depressed in one locality [was] not necessarily so in another." Rai also pointed to an extreme spike in untouchability in recent years, citing British census records stating that in 1917, there were 31 million, but in 1921, 53 million untouchables were reported. Rai believed that Mayo and the British government deliberately "raised the figure to 60 million" to fuel anti-Indian propaganda.[61]

Rai was correct that British colonial officials used census-determined sub-groups to decide which group of people were qualified for which jobs in the colonial government, and which groups could be excluded as unreliable.[62] During the early twentieth century, the British consistently modified caste groupings in every census classification. Rai criticized the British government for complaining about Hindu caste but then creating greater sub-castes and making caste a larger issue than it was in the past. Rai called this "a deliberate policy of distinguishing between castes and castes in many matters within their jurisdiction." He also accused the government of sanctioning special grants for the education of Europeans and Anglo-Indians but not doing this for untouchables. Thus, Rai concluded that "the Government of India, as at present constituted is not vitally concerned in the uplift of these classes," and "[i]t maybe they want to keep them in their present state of backwardness as a trump card against our claim for full responsible government."[63] Since the British government refused to help educate untouchables, Rai constructed his own plan for their education, which mandated that "all local governments provide facilities for the education of untouchables and other depressed classes particularly by reserving seats in teachers training classes for them and also opening all public services to them." Additionally, Rai suggested that "one crore [ten million] rupees" be designated by the government toward the education of "untouchables."[64]

Although Rai believed Mayo's claims about Indian untouchability were exaggerated, he admitted that caste was a pervasive issue in much of the Hindu community. Rai understood that the upper castes had a significant input into British census classifications. He correctly saw that the expansion of caste was a collaborative effort by British rulers and Indian elites to exercise their privilege over the masses.[65] To lessen the rigidity of these caste ideas, Rai argued, Indians first had to abolish the existence of sub-castes and even suggested that "Swaraj be postponed until this reform has been effected." Rai, however, proposed the postponement as a temporary measure. He was a firm unconditional believer in India's right to self-rule. It was an ideology he never wavered from.[66] Rai argued that despite the flaws of the Indian caste system, "[n]o kind of national rule will be worse than foreign rule, even if it is accompanied by a certain amount of disorder, anarchy, and class dominance. Foreign rule breeds all kinds of social, economic, and moral evils." Rai noted that the worst of these include "the slave mentality" and "the habit of dependence" upon British goods and their capitalist system which destroyed the self-sufficiency of Indians.[67]

Rai deduced that Mayo's criticism of India's caste system was hypocritical because caste ideologies in the US were just as strong as those in India. He noted that White Americans had developed a caste system of their own which ran "almost parallel to the distinction between caste-Hindus and the untouchable Hindus in India." He asserted that the American caste system was designed to differentiate White from Black people and to also separate other examples of caste, such as the religious communalism that segregated Jews from non-Jews. Additionally, Rai theorized that there was a "3rd line of caste, between Europeans and Asiatics, the Chinese, and Japanese, and the Hindus on the Pacific Coast are almost as much discriminated against as the Negroes."[68]

While Rai saw many similarities between the Indian caste system and the racialized caste system in America, he noted that one major difference was that the US was "a democracy and a Republic with universal adult suffrage." Rai's claim was not accurate. In reality, many Black Americans could not vote. Even though federal law permitted Black Americans to vote, in many Southern states, African Americans faced extreme intimidation at the polls, coupled with literacy tests and poll taxes. Hence, although Black Americans were given the right to vote, voting itself was still difficult for them. While Rai incorrectly described America as a functional democracy, he argued that unless caste was annihilated in India, it would not be a functional democracy and would lead to tremendous instability. According to him, "as long as caste exist[ed] in its present form in India, the foundations of any democracy would not be stable." Consequently, Rai argued that "the time has come for some vigorous and concentrated action being taken for the abolition of caste distinctions by and among those who do not believe in them and who are anxious that these distinctions and restrictions should go."[69] Rai believed in the urgency of caste reform not only to salvage the Indian independence movement and counter criticism from colonial sympathizers such as Mayo, but he also understood that caste divided Indians. Rai stated, "Caste must go if Hindus have to be consolidated into one living, powerful, social organism" and he implored that "caste must also be done away with if India is to ever be a real democracy."[70]

In response to encountering Katherine Mayo's critiques of Indian society, Rai sought to write a book titled *Unhappy India* (1928) that illustrated America's treatment of its racial minorities. Rai sought to prove that the US was a "caste society," showing that Americans who criticized caste in India were hypocrites. Rai wrote to W. E. B. Du Bois to ask him for "recent literature" regarding the "treatment of Negroes in the United States and also about the activities of the Ku Klux Klan." Rai additionally asked for "telling pictures" of the "cruelties inflicted on [Black Americans] by the whites of America."[71] While Rai was still a fervent supporter of the advancement of Black Americans, his main reason for this request was to produce a similar book about American life as the one Mayo produced regarding Indian life. In response to Rai's message, Du Bois sent him the last six editions of *The Crisis* along with a photo of a Black man being lynched. Du Bois also sent a manuscript of a book he was working on titled *Dark Princess* (1927), which was a novel about a Black man's romance with an Indian princess for which he asked Rai to provide feedback.[72] The exchange of these letters provides an example of how both Rai and Du Bois depended on each other for first-hand knowledge when writing about the issues of their respective societies. Both men understood that they needed one another to understand the plight of the other context accurately. However, Rai and Du Bois did not discuss India's "caste problem" in this exchange. The foundation of solidarity between these two men was based primarily around a shared "racial struggle" rather than one that sought to interrogate the specific internal problems of Indians and Black Americans. Du Bois's knowledge of India's problems dealt primarily with India's struggle with the British. He did not yet have a strong grasp of India's internal caste problems.

Rai used the evidence gained from his interactions with Du Bois to counteract Mayo's points that Indians were unfit to rule. Rai pointed out that even though White Americans had a "class of untouchables amongst themselves" (Black Americans), they "never abdicated their right to self-government or allowed other people to question it." Furthermore, Rai used Du Bois's examples of lynchings to display the extreme cruelties that White supremacists directed toward Black Americans and he argued that the Ku Klux Klan was not merely a fringe society but "the embodiment of the exclusive spirit in America." Rai was correct in assessing that the Ku Klux Klan was the "the exclusive spirit" in America. The Klan had experienced rapid growth throughout the 1920s and had expanded membership dramatically to a 1924 peak of 1.5 million to 4 million, which was between 4 and 15 percent of the eligible population, and nearly one in five of the eligible Indiana population were members.[73] Because of the growth of racist organizations such as the Ku Klux Klan, Rai claimed that the US had no right to use the Indian caste system as a reason to hold Indians unfit for self-determination.[74]

When comparing Indian untouchability and racial discrimination in the US, Rai at times suggested that racial discrimination in the US was a more violent system because of the lynchings African Americans were commonly subjected to by White racists. However, Rai did not consider caste to be a lesser moral issue than American racism. Rai himself had stated that India could not have a functional democracy unless caste were abolished. Rai sought to rectify the issues of caste within Indian society, as exemplified by his willingness to postpone the Indian independence movement until sub-castes were removed, his desire to boost education funding for low-caste Indians, and his calling for "caste distinctions" to be annihilated. Even though Rai believed that the treatment of Black Americans was more severe than Indian untouchability, his "ranking" of these social aspects did not display any lack of commitment to eradicating them from Indian society. Rai did not use the example of American racism to absolve Indians of their role in enabling caste discrimination. He used it as an example to show that "caste ideologies" existed in America as well, and to prove that "foreign rule" was not better equipped to dismantle the problems of caste than Indians themselves.[75]

While Rai shielded India's caste system from the international community, he actively tried to encourage urgent caste reform within India. Although he believed caste existed "in some shape or form all over the world," he admitted that in other countries caste was not as "rigid and exclusive as it is in Hinduism," which he referred to as the religion's "greatest curse." Hence, Rai did not minimize the problem of caste. He believed that Hindus would never unite, unless they broke "the centrifugal influences" of caste.[76] Rai argued that caste in Hinduism was so rigid and resilient that it manifested itself in the Indian diaspora, noting that "[w]hen Indians travel abroad, they intermingle and have friendly relations with people of other castes and religions however when the time comes for someone in their family to marry, they will revert back to caste rigidity."[77]

Rai admitted that encouraging Indian nationalists to modify their rigid caste ideologies was a daunting task because nationalists presided over and took part in "establishing caste institutions." Hence, nationalism and caste discrimination in India was intertwined and "caste loyalty was openly and persistently exploited by the so-called nationalists." While Rai did not specifically address these nationalists by name, he proved that even though he was willing to work with caste sympathizers such as Tilak and Gandhi, he had the courage to criticize them. He considered caste to be an integral problem for India that the Indian nationalist movement had to address. Gandhi himself had pursued a strategy of Indian nationalism that kept the Indian caste system in place because he believed that separate representation in the Indian parliament for "depressed classes" would divide the Hindu community into two groups.[78] Hence, Gandhi and Rai had opposing views on how caste reform impacted the Indian independence movement. Gandhi thought that allowing social and economic mobility for lower castes would divide the Indian population and cause "class struggle and class war."[79] Rai believed that rectifying the issues of caste would unite the Indian people and he supported class mobility for all Indians.[80] Although Rai never criticized Gandhi explicitly for his lack of caste activism, he did not censor viewpoints in his newspaper which lambasted Gandhi for not bringing caste to the forefront of the Indian independence movement. In February 1927, *The People* printed an article in its letter page which condemned Gandhi's lack of caste activism. The article questioned the morality Gandhi's program of "Swaraj," especially the fact that it did not place emphasis on reforming the "attitudes towards [caste amongst] the educated classes and masses."[81]

Although Rai took an active approach in trying to reform caste through his journalism, advocating for the abolition of sub-castes, and condemning Indian nationalists who supported caste, his efforts never produced any real results. Rai's life ended abruptly on November 17, 1928. While the British parliament denied that Rai was murdered, W. E. B. Du Bois as well as doctors who attempted to treat Rai believed his death was caused by being personally assaulted by British police superintendent James A. Scott.

Shortly before his passing, Rai sent correspondence to Mary White Ovington, an American suffragist, journalist, and co-founder of NAACP. Ovington revealed the context of Rai's letter in a tribute after he died. In his letter, Rai stressed the importance of the work of the NAACP as its activism was not only beneficial to colored individuals in the US, but to "all the coloured people of the world." Rai believed that the efforts of White-led organizations toward the advancement of "colored races" showed individuals that they had White allies and gave them some reassurance that there were "some white people who can be fair and just to them and who are making earnest efforts to establish a really good international tone." Rai also mentioned that he was anticipating a "colour clash in the near or remote future" and that "the policy of the imperialist dominance by white races" was creating a strong bitterness amongst colored individuals in the world "against the insolence and defiance of the white races."[82]

Rai perceived the activism of Ovington to be "the only silver lining" to growing friction between White and non-White races. He understood that the only peaceful solution to racial friction was for "white allies" to take charge as mediators to resolve the problems of racial discrimination.[83] His conversation with Ovington suggested that just as Rai believed that advantaged Indians had to try and convince other higher-caste Indians to modify caste prejudices, privileged Whites similarly had to persuade the White masses to challenge America's racial hierarchy and British colonialism. As he had written about Oswald Garrison Villard being a viable partner for Indians and Black Americans in their struggles for racial equality, Rai believed that Ovington could also serve as a "white ally" who could provide moral support for both groups. Additionally, Rai saw both Villard and Ovington as people who could help create further transnational dialogue between people of color to address the global problems of "imperialist domination" through White supremacy. Rai's comments largely followed a trend of his increasing lack of faith in the effectiveness of the Gandhian movement, and his comments and letter to Ovington suggest that before his death he was actively searching for allies in the US to assist Indian independence.

In addition to Ovington, many other prominent American activists paid tribute to Rai's memory, including W. E. B. Du Bois. Du Bois recounted his interactions with Rai both in his home and his office. Although he saw Indian independence as a necessity even before Rai's passing, the need for Indian self-rule became much more urgent following his murder because it proved that British authorities were willing to use violence to suppress the Indian people. According to Du Bois, when a man of Rai's stature is "beaten to death by a great civilized government then indeed revolution becomes a duty of all right-thinking men." He stressed the urgent need for revolution following the proof that Indians were denied human rights during a peaceful protest. In his tribute, Du Bois stated, "[O]ut of the blood of [Rai's] martyrdom very soon a free coloured nation will arise." Du Bois made a further analogy between the struggles of Indians and Black Americans stating, "[T]he people of India, like the American Negroes, are demanding day to day things not in the least bit revolutionary, but things which every civilized white man has long taken for granted."[84]

Villard, editor and owner of *The Nation* magazine, also paid tribute to Rai, noting how he was "profoundly impressed by [Rai's] ability, his philosophy, and his calm and understanding appreciation of the realities of the Indian situation." Furthermore, he commemorated Rai's bravery and his "readiness to suffer imprisonment or anything else on behalf of the cause which he valued more dearly than life itself."[85] J. T. Sunderland also praised Rai for his efforts to combat imperialism, comparing Rai's activism against the British government to the efforts of slavery abolitionists in the US. Sunderland argued that even though these abolitionists were portrayed as enemies of America by pro-slavery Americans, in truth, they were America's "best friends" because the "American nation was incomparably better off when it became all free, than she was when part free and part slave." Sunderland also believed that through his activism, Rai was trying to make Britain better by urging it to respect the Indian people's right to self-determination, writing that Rai was "so true a friend [to Britain] that he wanted to save her from committing what he believed to be a great wrong, a great crime against 320 millions of human beings, who have as much right to freedom and self-government as have the people of Great Britain and North America." Tying India's freedom struggle against the British to the American Revolutionary war, Sunderland drew a parallel between Rai and the American founding fathers such as Samuel Adams, Benjamin Franklin, and Thomas Jefferson, noting that if India failed to get independence through peaceful means such as those advocated by Gandhi and Lajpat Rai, India would be "driven to seek it by arms" as the American revolutionaries did.[86]

The reactions described here prove how Rai was revered as a transnational symbol for the advancement of colored individuals by American activists. Rai's consistent interactions with Ovington and Villard also showed that he too viewed activism through a global lens, believing that Indian activists needed to look at the problems of their nation through a transnational scope rather than confining themselves to local issues. Rai's final letter to Ovington was an example of how Rai viewed international White allies as a necessity in the fight against White supremacy, while his exchanges with Du Bois displayed his consistent kinship and solidarity with Black Americans.

Rai understood the importance of focusing on issues outside his nation and dismantling White supremacy globally.[87] Throughout the 1920s, he applied what he had learned from his experiences in America to his Indian activism. While Rai was primarily concerned with the issues in his own country, he never lost sight of race, class, and caste issues globally, with his primary focus being the US. It was the global and transnational issues of colored people that became the nexus of his ideas for activism in India. Rai's efforts at the World Migration Conference demonstrate how he used his position to improve the status of individuals outside his home country. Through his writings and interactions, Rai established Black Americans as a strong ally in fighting against colonialism and White supremacy. Rai, along with Du Bois, aggressively meshed the struggles of Black Americans and Indians together into a common strife for advancement. Additionally, Rai along with American counterparts such as Du Bois created a joint struggle against racial discrimination demonstrated by their internationalist writings and speeches against White supremacy.

In the Indian context, Rai primarily tried to enable caste reform but did not manage to produce any impact before his death. Although he blamed the British for manipulating caste to divide Indians by increasing sub-castes, Rai acknowledged that Indians were at fault for condoning caste ideologies and continuing its practice and he believed Indians had to transform caste radically to be a more egalitarian society. Mohan Lal, the secretary of the Achhut Uddhar, a peasant organization in Punjab, noted that before Rai died, he "moved a resolution in the [General] Assembly for a grant of one crore rupees to spread free education among [the depressed classes]."[88] The resolution was defeated by a narrow margin due to government opposition. Due to his efforts, Lal labelled Rai "the father of mass movement among depressed classes and greatest champion of their rights and liberties." Lal had also noted that in 1924, Rai had told him to "remove untouchability, for all practical purposes, within the next twelve months," but Lal concluded that Rai's goals were "too optimistic" for India which he called a "tradition-ridden country." Hence, Rai made clear efforts to challenge caste discrimination in India, but ultimately he was only one man who could not change the culture of an entire religion.[89]

Aside from rigorously challenging caste in India, Rai ultimately gained first-hand knowledge of the Black American struggle from his stay in the US from 1914 to 1919. He continued to learn about the struggles of Black Americans throughout the 1920s from Du Bois. Likewise, Du Bois gained knowledge of the Indian anti-colonial struggle. After Rai's death, Du Bois saw the Indian independence movement as an urgent priority and the interactions between him and Rai encouraged Du Bois to seek out dialogue with other figures from India such as Rabindranath Tagore and M. K. Gandhi in the years following Rai's death.

Notes

1. Suraj Yengde, "Castes of Mind: On the Intersection of Race and Caste," review of *Caste: The Origins of our Discontents*, by Isabel Wilkerson, *The Baffler* no. 56, March 24, 2021.
2. Ibid.
3. Mary White Ovington, *The People*, January 3 and 10, 1929.
4. Nico Slate, *Colored Cosmopolitanism: The Shared Struggle for Freedom in the United States and India* (Cambridge: Harvard University Press, 2012), 127–128.
5. Chris Moffat, *India's Revolutionary Inheritance Politics and the Promise of Bhagat Singh* (Cambridge: Cambridge University Press, 2019), 39.
6. Ibid., 41.
7. Lala Lajpat Rai, "Servants of the People Society and Tilak School of Politics," *The People*, March 7, 1926. Note: All the articles from *The People* were accessed through the Nehru Memorial Museum & Library in New Delhi through microfilm.
8. Moffat, *India's Revolutionary Inheritance Politics*, 41.
9. L. L. Rai, "Servants of the People Society and Tilak School of Politics."
10. Moffat, *India's Revolutionary Inheritance Politics*, 31.
11. Ibid., 36; Lala Lajpat Rai, *The Problem of National Education in India* (London: George Allen & Unwin Ltd, 1920), 31.
12. Lala Lajpat Rai, "Introduction," in Lala Har Dayal, *Our Educational Problem* (Madras: Tagore and Company, 1922), ix.
13. L. L. Rai, "Servants of the People Society and Tilak School of Politics."
14. Moffat, *India's Revolutionary Inheritance Politics*, 48.
15. H. M. Ghodke, *Revolutionary Nationalism in Western India* (New Delhi: Classical Publishing Company, 1990), 31; Arun Chandra Guha, *First Spark of Revolution*, 1st edition (Mumbai: Oriental Longmans, 1971), 221; Stanley A. Wolpert, *Tilak and Gokhale: Revolution and Reform in the Making of Modern India* (New Delhi: S.K. Mookerjee, 1989), 206.
16. Govind Talwalkar, *Gopal Krishna Gokhale: Gandhi's Political Guru* (New Delhi: Pentagon Press, 2015).
17. "From the Archives (June 3, 1919): Mr. Tilak's Service. Mr. Gandhi's Speech," *The Hindu*, https://www.thehindu.com/archives/mr-tilaks-service-mr-gandhis-speech/article27406589.ece, accessed September 27, 2019.
18. Christophe Jaffrelot, *Dr. Ambedkar and Untouchability: Fighting the Indian Caste System* (New York: Columbia University Press, 2005), 177.
19. Parimala V. Rao, "Educating Women and non-Brahmins as 'Loss of Nationality': Bal Gangadhar Tilak and the Nationalist Agenda in Maharashtra," NYU Faculty Digital Archives, Centre for Women's Development Studies (2008), 27.
20. Raghunath Rai, *History* (Faridabad, India: VK Global Publications, 2014), 187.

21. Jawaharlal Nehru, *An Autobiography* (New Delhi: The Bodley Head, 1936), 81.
22. Ibid.
23. Lala Lajpat Rai, "The Clash of Colour," *The People,* May 23, 1926.
24. Durba Ghosh, "The Reforms of 1919: Montagu–Chelmsford, the Rowlatt Act, Jails Commission, and the Royal Amnesty," in *Gentlemanly Terrorists: Political Violence and the Colonial State in India, 1919–1947* (Cambridge: Cambridge University Press, 2017), 27–59; Sashi Tharoor, *Nehru: The Invention of India* (New York: Arcade Publishing, 2003), 41–42.
25. Scott Ellsworth, "Tulsa Race Riot," *The Encyclopedia of Oklahoma History and Culture* (2009), https://www.okhistory.org/publications/enc/entry.php?entry=TU013, accessed September 1, 2019.
26. L. L. Rai, "The Clash of Colour."
27. Ibid.
28. Ibid.
29. J. S. Bains, "Lala Lajpat Rai's Idealism and Indian National Movement," *The Indian Journal of Political Science* 46, no. 4 (1985): 409–410.
30. Lala Lajpat Rai, "Impracticable Idealism," *The People,* January 30, 1927.
31. L. L. Rai, "The Clash of Colour."
32. W. E. B. Du Bois, *The Souls of Black Folk* (New York: Oxford University Press, 2007), 12.
33. L. L. Rai, "The Clash of Colour."
34. Ibid.
35. Lala Lajpat Rai, "Mother India," *The People,* September 8, 1927.
36. *The People,* April 13, 1929.
37. Lala Lajpat Rai, "America in the East," *The People,* July 26, 1925; Sherally Munshi, "Immigration, Imperialism, and the Legacies of Indian Exclusion," *Yale Journal of Law and the Humanities* 28, no.1 (2015): 51–104, 69.
38. L. L. Rai, "America in the East."
39. "World Migration Congress Is Opened in London," June 23, 1926, https://www.jta.org/1926/06/23/archive/world-migration-congress-is-opened-in-london, accessed May 2, 2021.
40. Julius Braunthal, *History of the International: Volume 2: 1914–1943* (1963), trans. John Clark (New York: Frederick A. Praeger, 1967), 264.
41. Lala Lajpat Rai, "World Migration and Colour Question," *The People,* July 25, 1926 (World Migration Conference speech by Lala Lajpat Rai).
42. Ibid.
43. "Tribute from A. Fenner Brockway," *The People,* April 13, 1929.
44. "World Migration Congress," *Manawatu Times* 49, no. 3383 (June 25, 1926): 10.
45. Lala Lajpat Rai, "The Problem of Minorities," *The* People, November 1, 1928.
46. Lala Lajpat Rai, "The World Today," *The People,* September 12, 1926.

47. *The Anti-Slavery Reporter*, August 1, 1865, 187.
48. L. L. Rai, "The World Today."
49. Lala Lajpat Rai, "The Clash of Colour II," *The People*, May 30, 1926.
50. Michael Yudell, *Race Unmasked: Biology and Race in The Twentieth Century* (New York: Columbia University Press, 2014), 41–42.
51. Ian Frazier, "When W.E.B. Du Bois Made a Laughingstock of a White Supremacist," *The New Yorker*, August 19, 2019, N.W. Ayer & Son's American Newspaper Annual Directory, Philadelphia, PA, 1920–1945.
52. L. L. Rai, "The Clash of Colour II."
53. Madison Grant, *The Passing of the Great Race: Or the Racial Basis of European History* (New York: Scribner's Sons, 1922), 70.
54. L. L. Rai, "The Clash of Colour II"; Gerald Horne, *End of Empires: African Americans and India* (Philadelphia: Temple University Press, 2008), 74.
55. Daniel Immerwahr, "Caste or Colony? Indianizing Race in the United States," *Modern Intellectual History* 4, no. 2 (2007): 275–301, 279.
56. Paul Teed, "Race Against Memory: Katherine Mayo, Jabez Sunderland, and Indian Independence," *American Studies* 44, no. 1/2 (2003): 35–57; Mrinalini Sinha, *Specters of Mother India: The Global Restructuring of an Empire* (Durham: Duke University Press, 2006), 6, 68.
57. Teed, "Race Against Memory," 37.
58. Kumari Jayawardena, *The White Woman's Other Burden: Western Women and South Asia during British Colonial Rule* (London: Routledge, 1995), 99; Immerwahr, "Caste or Colony?" 279; Teed, "Race Against Memory," 37.
59. Teed, "Race Against Memory," 37.
60. Bains, "Lala Lajpat Rai's Idealism and Indian National Movement," 405–406.
61. Lala Lajpat Rai, "Reconstruction of Hindu Society," *The People*, October 20, 1927.
62. Susan Bayly, *Caste, Society and Politics in India from the Eighteenth Century to the Modern Age* (New York: Cambridge University Press, 1999), 125–127.
63. Lala Lajpat Rai, "Government Refuses to Help Untouchables," *The People*, March 1, 1928.
64. Ibid.
65. Trina Vithayathil, "Counting Caste: Censuses, Politics, and Castelessness in India," *Politics and Society* 46, no. 4 (2018): 455–484, 459.
66. Bains, "Lala Lajpat Rai's Idealism and Indian National Movement," 405–406.
67. L. L. Rai, "Reconstruction of Hindu Society."
68. Ibid.
69. Ibid.
70. Ibid.
71. Lala Lajpat Rai to W. E. B. Du Bois, October 6, 1927.
72. W. E. B. Du Bois to Lala Lajpat Rai, November 9, 1927.
73. Roland G. Fryer and Steven D. Levitt, "Hatred and Profits: Under the Hood of the Ku Klux Klan," *The Quarterly Journal of Economics* 127, no. 4 (November 1, 2012): 1883–1925.

74. Lala Lajpat Rai, *Unhappy India* (Calcutta: Banna Publishing, 1928), 104.

75. Slate, *Colored Cosmopolitanism*, 61.

76. L. L. Rai, "Government Refuses to Help Untouchables"; Lala Lajpat Rai, "Nationalism and Caste," *The People*, January 16, 1927.

77. L. L. Rai, "Nationalism and Caste."

78. Gail Omvedt, "A Part that Parted," *Outlook India*, August 20, 2012; Andrew Muldoon, *Empire, Politics and the Creation of the 1935 India Act: Last Act of the Raj* (London: Routledge, 2016), 97; Judith Margaret Brown, *Gandhi: Prisoner of Hope* (New Haven: Yale University Press, 1991), 252–257.

79. Mohandas K. Gandhi, *The Collected Works of Mahatma Gandhi*, Vol. XIX (Delhi Publications Division, Ministry of Information and Broadcasting, 1958),174ff.

80. Vanya Bhargav, "Lala Lajpat Rai's Ideas on Caste: Conservative or Radical?" *Studies in Indian Politics* 6, no. 1 (June 2018): 15–26, 18; Rai cited textual traditions of Hinduism such as the Itihasa and Puranas to argue that ancient Hindu society entailed an open, flexible caste system in which even "outsiders," admitted after certain rites, could rise according to "merit" to the highest social positions.

81. Sahadhini Devi to Lala Lajpat Rai, "Congress President on Untouchability," *The People*, February 8, 1927.

82. Mary White Ovington, *The People*, January 3 and 10, 1929.

83. Ibid.

84. W. E. B. Du Bois, "Tribute to Rai from W.E.B Du Bois," *The People*, April 13, 1929.

85. Oswald Garrison Villard, "'NATION' EDITOR'S MESSAGE: Oswald Garrison Villard," *The People*, January 3 and 10, 1929.

86. J. T. Sunderland, *The People*, January 3 and 10, 1929.

87. Ibid.

88. Mohan Lal, "Lalaji and the Depressed Classes," *The People*, April 13, 1929; Mridula Mukherjee, *Peasants in India's Non-Violent Revolution: Practice and Theory* (New Delhi: Sage Publications, 2004), 64.

89. Lal, "Lalaji and the Depressed Classes."

5

W. E. B. Du Bois and the Indian Independence Movement

Between the 1910s and the 1930s, W. E. B. Du Bois attempted to build several alliances with Indians in his quest for transnational racial solidarity. While his "To the Nations of the World" address at the 1900 Pan African Congress was his first major example of internationalizing the Black struggle, his initial impact on Indians came at the First Universal Races in 1911. At the Congress Du Bois's speech entitled "The Negro Race in the United States of America" made a lasting impression on some Indians associated with the Gandhian movement. In his speech he sought to inform the international community about the problems of Black Americans in the hope that he could build international allies to sympathize with the Black American struggle. Du Bois argued that although the Civil War had formally ended slavery, White Americans in the US South were still "determined to deprive the Negroes of political power and force them to occupy the position of a labouring caste."[1] Du Bois came to the meeting armed with a plethora of statistics to prove that Black Americans were relegated to menial labor and were not equally represented in the higher divisions of labor. He gave additional examples of Black Americans being forced to attend underfunded schools and concluded that in addition to racism, a lack of educational funding was the greatest factor for Black Americans being denied the same career paths as their White counterparts.[2]

Du Bois hoped to prove to the Congress that there was no real biological difference between races. White Americans simply chose to subjugate Black Americans to lower socioeconomic positions based on phenotypical features and skin color.[3] He stressed that if Black Americans were offered a more democratic form of government and better educational facilities, they could eventually prove that there were no intellectual deficiencies amongst Black Americans in the US.[4]

Although Gandhi did not attend the Congress, he sent his associate H. S. L. Polak, an English ally from South Africa, in his stead. The event was also attended by Indian National Congress leader Gopal Krishna Gokhale. The following month, Polak published a note in Gandhi's newspaper *Indian Opinion*, stating, "I had the pleasure of hearing Dr. Du Bois.... He is the gifted author of the Souls of Black Folk ... and everyone will rejoice that the negroes have so able and far-seeing a representative; his spirit is co-operation and conciliation."[5] Three weeks after Polak's original article praised Du Bois for his speech at the International Races Congress, the front page of the *Indian Opinion* referred to Du Bois as "one of the best-known authorities on the negro [struggle]."[6] The newspaper specifically focused upon Du Bois because he had drawn similarities between the treatment of Blacks in America and Indians under British rule in an interview with the *Manchester Guardian*. These parts of the interview were quoted in the *Indian Opinion*. The praise given to Du Bois by the *Indian Opinion* showed how Gandhi's associates leaned on Du Bois for understanding the Black American struggle and were drawn to Du Bois's blunt condemnation of British rule in India.[7] Du Bois's solidarity with the Indian people led to a subsequent report in the *Indian Opinion*, which referred to Du Bois as not only a "great man amongst negroes," but also "a great man amongst the world's great men."[8]

In the years after the Universal Races Congress, Du Bois's ideas continued to be circulated by the *Indian Opinion*. Betty Molteno, a White British South African civil rights activist, tried to develop a greater awareness of Du Bois's activism for racial equality amongst the Indian community in South Africa. In January 1914, she spoke at a meeting in Durban attended by Indian leaders in South Africa including Gandhi and referred to Du Bois's vision for solidarity between the "races of colour." She encouraged her Indian audience members to incorporate Indigenous South Africans into their civil rights movement and to "try to comprehend the words of Du Bois – that grand and sympathetic soul: "The 20th century will be the century of colour."[9] While Gandhi's reaction to Molteno's speech is unknown, it was reprinted in the *Indian Opinion* three days later. Gandhi himself became formally acquainted with Du Bois in 1929 when he wrote a motivational letter for the Black American people in the National Association for the Advancement of Colored Peoples (NAACP) magazine, *The Crisis*, at Du Bois's request.

Du Bois's efforts were an integral part of informing Gandhian associates about the plight of Black Americans and sparked early interest in India toward building solidarity with them. The publicity Du Bois generated placed the Black American struggle in a larger global context and helped link it to the discrimination faced by Indians in India and South Africa. Additionally, it played a role in helping him internationalize the Black struggle.

Throughout the 1920s and early 1930s, as the editor of the *The Crisis*, Du Bois used his position and international publicity to foster solidarity between Black Americans and Indians. He observed the Indian independence movement and used it as a source of inspiration for Black Americans, whose lowered socioeconomic status and marginalization he saw as being akin to the experience of a colonial subject rather than a citizen.[10] He energetically sought alliances with other colonized subjects, believing that Black Americans and their White American allies could learn and draw from other anti-colonial struggles to improve their own social status in the US. Du Bois portrayed the Indian struggle to his readers as part of a larger transnational struggle against White supremacy. He understood that Black Americans were a minority in the US, and they needed to contextualize their racial struggle as part of a global movement. To emphasize the relevance of the fight for Indian independence, he printed motivational letters to the Black populace from Rabindranath Tagore and M. K. Gandhi in *The Crisis*, showing that Indian leaders offered moral support from abroad.

Historian Gerald Horne argues that the shared affinity between Black Americans and Indians facilitated natural alliances between them.[11] While in some cases this was true, especially amongst internationalists such as Du Bois and Lala Lajpat Rai, certain roadblocks hindered or strained alliances between the two groups. Utilizing Aryan race theories, some Indians identified themselves as being more racially akin to Europeans or "Aryans" rather than Black Americans and Africans. Hence, they dismissed the latter groups as an inferior race and refused to see the Black American struggle as being relatable to their own. Additionally, since Black Americans and Indians lived on opposite sides of the world, both groups often were not cognizant of each other's struggles.

Aware of some negative Indian attitudes toward Black Americans and Black Africans, Du Bois tried to fight against Indian misconceptions about Black inferiority and "Aryan race" theories by writing in Indian journals such as the *Aryan Path*. He attempted to convince Indian readers to build relationships with Africans, Black Americans, and east Asians on a common basis of racial solidarity to challenge White supremacy and colonialism. Du Bois called upon both Black Americans and Indians to put aside their notions of internal color prejudice or any caste hierarchies and stand together as "representatives of the coloured races," and fight against the "insistent problem of the assumption of the white peoples of Europe that they have a right to dominate the world and especially so to organize it politically and industrially as to make most men their slaves and servants."[12] While Du Bois also criticized India's caste problem, he did not evaluate it as an integral part of the Indian independence movement and dismissed it as a secondary issue which Indians could solve after attaining independence.

Studying the Indian Independence Movement: Du Bois's Aims and Aspirations

During the early 1920s, Du Bois paid close attention to anti-colonial activism in India, and he hoped to inform his readers on the Indian struggle through his writings in *The Crisis*. *The Crisis* was an influential work of journalism for Black Americans. Circulation was at its highest in 1919 because of the coverage of World War I, major race riots in East St. Louis (1917), Chicago (1919), and in other parts of the US, the beginning of the Great Migration (1916–1930), which would take well over one million Black Southerners to northern cities, the suffragist movement, and a significant rise in immigration.[13] American sociologist Arnold Rose has noted that Du Bois and the NAACP were responsible for shaping the attitudes "of a very large proportion of the Negro population." Additionally, historian Elliot M. Rudwick notes that after Booker T. Washington's death in 1915, Du Bois became the "most influential Black man in America."[14] Du Bois took advantage of his popularity and the large readership of *The Crisis* to inform readers about the plight of Indians in hopes that it would create solidarity between Indians and Black Americans.[15]

Du Bois understood that he had to relate India's struggle against the British to the Black American struggle against White supremacy.[16] Du Bois was inspired by fellow NAACP member and Unitarian minister John Haynes Holmes to make Gandhi a centerpiece of his analysis of the Indian independence movement. Du Bois was a frequent attendee to Holmes's New York City–based non-denominational church, "The Community Church." Du Bois noted that while most White-majority churches ignored the issues of Black Americans, Holmes frequently tried to enable discussions among New York Unitarians on the plight of Black American laborers. Du Bois also saw that Holmes, an ardent pacifist, made the Indian anti-colonial struggle a common interest amongst the members of his church and frequently gave sermons on Gandhi.[17] In one of Holmes's 1921 sermons, which Du Bois reprinted in *The Crisis*, he told his Community Church congregation in New York that because of his pacifist strategy to advocate for Indian self-determination, Gandhi was "the greatest man in the world," greater even than Vladimir Lenin and Woodrow Wilson. Holmes remarked, "When I think of Mahatma Gandhi, I think of Jesus Christ."[18]

Du Bois sought to portray Gandhi as a similarly transcendent figure, and called Gandhi's use of non-cooperation "his first and most powerful weapon" because British rule in India depended upon Indian labor. Du Bois argued accurately that the British Raj relied upon Indian labor for providing "imperial necessities," including their armed forces. By the end of 1919, 1.5 million Indians had served in the armed services in either combatant or non-combatant roles during World War I, and India had provided £146 million in revenue for the war.[19] Since the British were dependent on Indian labor for their economy and armed forces in India, if Indians refused to cooperate, the British economy in India would collapse.[20]

Even though Du Bois saw Gandhi as a figure worth educating his readers about, he did not make a judgment on whether Black Americans could draw from Gandhi's methods of protest. However, in noting Gandhi's "powerful weapons," Du Bois showed he was optimistic that Gandhi's methods could lead India toward independence and hence solidify India as a powerful ally for Black Americans.[21] In addition to "non-cooperation," Du Bois noted that Gandhi's second most powerful weapon was his practice of "non-violence." Du Bois believed that this method "killed without striking its adversary" as it prevented the British from having any moral or legal grounds for his arrest or preventing his advocacy.[22] However, Du Bois's theories were incorrect. Gandhi, Lajpat Rai, and Jawaharlal Nehru were all arrested and imprisoned by the British government for their roles in the non-cooperation movement. Gandhi was arrested on March 10, 1922, tried for sedition, and sentenced to six years' imprisonment. He was released in February 1924 for a medical operation, after serving only two years.[23]

Although the non-cooperation movement failed, Du Bois noted that Britain had started to give its subjects in Egypt and India the beginnings of "political autonomy." Furthermore, Du Bois stated that the French had also started openly "catering to the darker races, both yellow and Black." Hence, Du Bois viewed global White supremacy as already in steady decline. He hoped to show his readers that positive movements were occurring in the "colored world" and that Black Americans should support a global movement against White supremacy. In response to the end of the non-cooperation movement, Du Bois referred to India and Africa as "powerful allies," and stated, "We may fail, and they may fail." By making this statement, Du Bois essentially tied the Indian and African movements to that of Black Americans in hopes of creating solidarity between Black Americans, Black Africans, and Indians.[24]

Du Bois's assessment that White supremacy in India had declined was flawed. Although Du Bois expressed optimism that Indians had more "political autonomy," the British maintained strong control over India. Throughout the 1920s, Indians had little governmental or electoral power. The Government of India Act of 1919 had given Indians representation in their government by allowing them to vote if they paid sufficient land tax.[25] The act also created a new diarchal government system, in which the Indian electorate gained more control over areas such as education, agriculture, infrastructure development, and local self-government.[26] However, although a greater number of Indians were enfranchised for voting at the national level, those voting constituted only 10 percent of the total adult male population, many of whom were still illiterate. Furthermore, in the provincial legislatures, the British continued to exercise some control by reserving seats for special interests they considered cooperative or useful. In doing so, the British assigned more seats to rural candidates, who were generally sympathetic to their rule and less confrontational, allowing them to maintain a government where the most powerful Indian figures in it accommodated British imperialism in India. Even though Du Bois was correct that the 1920s gave Indians the most significant opportunity yet for exercising legislative power, he failed to acknowledge the tactics the British used to maintain a stranglehold on the Indian government and suppress Indian political autonomy.[27]

In addition to portraying Gandhi as a symbol of inspiration in *The Crisis*, Du Bois tried to utilize him as a role model for Black children. A December 1921 edition of *The Brownies' Book*, a magazine for African American children edited by Du Bois and Jessie Fauset, introduced Gandhi and the Indian struggle to Black children. Du Bois told his young readers that "[i]n India several hundred millions of brown people are much incensed at the injustice of English rule." At the end of his article on the struggle of the Indian masses, Du Bois noted that Gandhi was the leader of the Indian movement.[28]

Although the Gandhian movement stagnated after the suspension of the non-cooperation movement, Du Bois continued to try and build solidarity between Black Americans and Indians. In 1927, Du Bois published a novella titled *Dark Princess* in which he detailed a fictional love affair between an

African American medical student named Matthew Towns and an Indian princess named Kautilya who was the leader of an international alliance of colored people. In the novel, Matthew and Kautilya work together to unite and liberate the dark world from White supremacy. The novel ends with the birth of their son, who is destined to be the messiah of the darker world.[29] *Dark Princess* represented how Du Bois envisioned unity between Indians and Black Americans, two groups which he believed best represented a shared struggle against White supremacy and colonialism. Du Bois called *Dark Princess* his favorite book.[30] It received mixed reviews. A reviewer for the *New York Times* called its plot "flamboyant and unconvincing" and noted that "the theme of miscegenation is so decidedly controversial that to those who believe in the preservation of racial purity the book will fail to lessen their prejudice." The reviewer criticized Du Bois for dwelling "on social injustices" which the reviewer dismissed as being "inevitable in any period of racial transition and development." Hence, as in the case of this *New York Times* reviewer, some readers were unconvinced that transnational movements against racism could achieve any meaningful change in the US and they believed that the book had little effect toward convincing White supremacists to change their views on interracial relationships.[31] However, some readers understood the symbolism of the book and saw Matthew and Kautilya's relationship as an analogy for Du Bois's own relationship with Lala Lajpat Rai. Four months after Rai's death, an obituary for Rai appeared as a book review of *Dark Princess* in *The Crisis*. The reviewer stated, "Lajpat Rai is dead, a martyr to British intolerance.... Lajpat Rai understood and wrote about the Negro problem in America."[32]

Prior to Rai's death in 1928, Du Bois had sent Rai an unpublished manuscript of *Dark Princess*. His murder mobilized Du Bois, encouraging him to seek out a more active relationship with other leaders of the Indian independence movement and to portray his alliance with Indian leaders in explicit terms. In 1929, Du Bois communicated with Gandhi via a series of letters. In their first contact, Du Bois asked him to write a message for *The Crisis*, hoping that Gandhi could help rally and encourage Black Americans to fight White supremacy. In his letter to Gandhi, Du Bois described Black Americans as "twelve million people who are the grandchildren of slaves, and who amid great difficulties are forging forward in America." Du Bois told Gandhi that he was aware that Gandhi had his "own color problems" in India, where Indians were marginalized by the British Raj. However, Du Bois insisted that "race and color problems [were] world-wide," in hopes that Gandhi would tie the Indian struggle against the British Raj to a global struggle against White supremacy.[33]

Gandhi responded to Du Bois's request in May, writing that he was sending him a "little love message" for Black Americans, rather than a standard article. Gandhi's letter was short, but he emphasized that Black Americans should not feel dishonored in "being slaves," but that the dishonor belongs to those who were "slave-owners." Gandhi encouraged Black Americans to forget the past and focus on the future. While this was a short exchange between Du Bois and Gandhi, it showed that both these men were aware of each other's historical struggles, and that constructive dialogue between these two figures was possible. However, Gandhi's emphasis on slavery rather than Jim Crow was peculiar. Slavery in the US had ended after the Civil War (1861–1865). Gandhi seemed to have a lack of awareness about Jim Crow laws and the current state of race relations in the US. Additionally, he did not give any specific solutions for addressing racial dynamics in the US.[34] His comments suggested that he thought that the abolition of slavery had solved the moral wrongs committed against Black Americans and he underestimated the ongoing struggle for Black civil rights.

It was interesting that Gandhi mentioned slavery in the US. While living in South Africa during the first decade of the twentieth century, Gandhi closely studied the American anti-slavery movement and the methods abolitionists used to protest the institution of slavery. He drew particular inspiration from Henry David Thoreau's 1849 essay, "Resistance to Civil Government" ("Civil Disobedience"). In it, Thoreau referred to "civil disobedience" as "disobedience to the state," and he encouraged citizens to non-violently protest against governments engaged in exploiting human beings. For example, Thoreau suggested that abolitionists who opposed the US government's desire to extend slavery into Texas during the Mexican American war refuse to pay taxes to express their displeasure.[35] Thoreau led by example and he was briefly imprisoned in 1846 for refusing to pay poll tax as part of his "civil disobedience."[36] After closely studying Thoreau, Gandhi modeled his own "satyagraha" (non-violent resistance) campaign on Thoreau's own "civil disobedience" tactics, engaging in boycotts of British goods as his own interpretation of "civil disobedience."[37] In 1907, Gandhi specifically praised Thoreau's essay as being "the chief cause of the abolition of slavery in America."[38] Gandhi envisioned his own actions in a similar way. However, he overestimated the significance of Thoreau's work and ignored the impact Black Americans such as Frederick Douglass had toward advancing the abolitionist cause; Gandhi saw the abolitionist cause through a White savior lens.

Du Bois also reached out to Rabindranath Tagore in 1929. In February, Du Bois sent Tagore a letter, introducing himself as the editor of *The Crisis*. He asked Tagore to contribute a letter to his magazine, believing that Black Americans could learn a great deal from "a great leader of the Indian People."[39] Tagore agreed to Du Bois's request. Shortly before its publication, *The Crisis* sent a statement to readers noting that the great Indian poet Rabindranath Tagore would be writing "another one of the international messages among the colored peoples of the world."[40] In his letter, Tagore spoke of the growing solidarity between Blacks and Indians, stating, "The human races have come out of their enclosures [and] they have gathered together." Tagore presented the lives of both Indians and Black Americans as hindered and repressed by the "fenced seclusion of our racial tradition."[41] Tagore hinted that perhaps both Black people and Indians were trapped within a stagnant class or caste barring them from birthright privileges due to their race.[42] While Tagore did not specifically mention caste or class in his letter, he correctly noted that there was a significant hierarchical difference in social status for Whites and people of colour in both American and Indian societies, based on race. The overwhelming majority of the Indian population was not permitted to vote, and in the US South, Blacks were forced to attend substandard schools, sit in separate train carriages, and use different restrooms and water fountains.

Perhaps the most revealing statement by Tagore in this message which has not been properly acknowledged is that Tagore had an awareness of internal color prejudice, caste discrimination, and colorism in both the Black and Indian communities. Madhumita Lahiri argues that Tagore's letter had an anti-imperialist message and that he believed that race and color prejudice only played a role in differentiating the colonized "Indians" from the colonizer, the "British."[43] Lahiri notes accurately that Tagore believed that race and color differentiated the colonized Indians from British colonizers. However, Tagore also acknowledged that Indians had been convinced of their racial or caste inferiority by members their own communities. Additionally, Nico Slate presents Tagore as an individual who downplayed race and caste frictions within the Indian community and instead chose to criticize primarily the British and White Americans for their treatment of non-White groups.[44] Yet Tagore believed that the colored races of the world had to prove their "worth to the whole world" and to "adhering groups of their own people." Toward the end of his message, Tagore reiterated this point by arguing that "we must justify our existence, we must show, each in our own civilization, that which is universal in the heart of the unique."[45]

Tagore's message represented a strong indication that both Black people and Indians faced a very similar form of racial oppression. However, in Tagore's eyes, the first step was for both of these groups to believe in themselves as being equal to Whites with their own self-worth. Only then would they have the confidence to fight against White supremacy, prove their worth to the entire world, and destroy the racial boundaries of caste and class. Tagore's analysis suggested that in certain cases, Black Americans and Indians had succumbed to the mentality that they were inferior races. Tagore's message was a call for unity between these two groups and a condoning of Du Bois's idea that they should work together in their quest for respect and equality. Through Du Bois's interactions with Gandhi and Tagore, he played a viable role in encouraging intellectual alliance and mutual support between Blacks and Indians, and placed the writings of *The Crisis* into a larger transnational scope.

While Du Bois was able to successfully facilitate meaningful connections with prominent Indians such as Gandhi and Tagore, some Indians attempted to distance themselves from Black people on the basis that Indians were racially superior. In 1930, K. Romola, an Indian immigrant living in Chicago, wrote a letter to the *Chicago Defender*, a Black newspaper, criticizing Black authors such as Du Bois, whom he referred to as a "fourth rate writer" for suggesting that Black Americans and Indians should seek solidarity to fight against White supremacy. Romola wrote, "[W]ho in the hell wants to join the caravan with the Black ones? Our caste system in India excludes those who do not belong to the Aryan race, and we even here exclude any Indians who live and socialize with the Negro." Additionally, Romola wished for Indians to colonize Black Africans in a similar manner as the British, French, and Germans, noting, "If [India] become free in the course of ten or twenty years we are after a slice of Africa too, for the savages there do not have any use for the wealth there."[46]

Romola was condemned by fellow Indian immigrant H. G. Mudgal, a follower of Marcus Garvey and editor of the *Negro World*, as an "out of touch" snob and self-hating "victim of the white propagandists." Mudgal did not mention the "white propagandists" by name, but it was likely that he was referring to eugenicists such as Lothrop Stoddard and Madison Grant who had manipulated the historiography of the Indian caste system to advocate for racial segregation. Furthermore, Mudgal asserted that Romola had "utterly forgotten the political, social, and economical oppression that India has been subjected to under the British." He echoed a viewpoint of Lala Lajpat Rai and suggested that Europeans were trying to create a mythical race term which was symbolized by the so-called Nordic race. According to Mudgal, Romola was an outlier in his racial thinking: "Young India is in the grip of humanism and they care no more for Mr. Romola's caste ideas than they do for his race snobbishness."[47] However, in reality, Romola was not an outlier; Indian immigrants in the US often tried to distance themselves from Black Americans, a trend Du Bois was also aware of.

Du Bois did not offer a direct response to Indians such as Romola, but in 1936, he wrote an article analyzing the difficulties of creating alliances between Black Americans and Indians in the Bombay-based Theosophical journal, the *Aryan Path*. In October 1935, Du Bois received a request from the editors of the *Aryan Path*, asking him to contribute an article. They believed that since both Indians and Black Americans faced oppression in their respective nations, greater knowledge of Black Americans and their culture would help facilitate better cooperation between the two groups.[48] However, instead of trying to simply inform Indians about the culture of Black Americans, Du Bois argued that alliances between the two groups were uncommon and difficult to create because the two groups had very little knowledge of each other, their histories, and their shared struggle against White supremacy. Du Bois blamed this lack of knowledge on Western education (British and American). He claimed that India's history had found absolutely no place in the curriculum of America's schools and these schools had wholly ignored references to the great past Indian civilizations. Because of this lack of education, Du Bois argued that Blacks had "no idea of the great struggle for freedom and self-governance which was going on in India or the deep philosophy of the meaning and end of human life that characterizes the Indian nation."[49] He believed that Black ignorance about the Indian struggle was the result of an "added deliberate and purposeful propaganda" created by American newspapers to make Britain's actions in India appear more benevolent than they were. Likewise, Du Bois argued that educated Indians had a flawed understanding of Black Americans because their knowledge of Black Americans came mainly from the writings of White American and British writers who presented Blacks as being ignorant savages who "were enslaved and made to do physical labour, which was the only thing they could do."[50]

Du Bois was correct that American education portrayed India through a biased British lens, leading to the "false knowledge of Indians" amongst both Black and White Americans. Throughout the early twentieth century, Americans learned more about India from English authors such as Rudyard Kipling than they learned from actual Indians themselves.[51] Kipling was a strong supporter of British imperialism and supported members of the British Raj such as Colonel Reginald Dyer, who was responsible for the 1919 Jallianwala Bagh massacre in Amritsar, Punjab. Since Americans primarily gained knowledge of India and its culture from the viewpoint of authors such as Kipling, they ultimately received a heavily flawed representation of India. Du Bois was also correct that Indians had a poor education regarding Black Americans because British schools primarily informed them of the achievements of White Americans. Additionally, Western racial theories regarding the racial superiority of the "Aryan race" had created a negative representation of Black Americans amongst Indians such as K. Romola and even Gandhi during the 1890s and early 1900s. Gandhi had described Black Africans as "savage," "raw," and living a life of "indolence and nakedness."[52]

Du Bois believed that the issue of "false education" could perhaps be remedied if "Indians and Negroes had the chance to meet one another" and receive a more authentic understanding of one another, rather than the false biased narrative taught to them by supposed Western superiors. Du Bois, however, claimed that creating interactions between the two groups would not be easy because Black Americans and Indians were oppressed groups of people on opposite sides of the world. Therefore, Du Bois believed that the best solution in addressing this issue would be for Indian writers to write articles in Black newspapers, outlining the history and problems of India, and for Black American authors to do the same in Indian newspapers. Du Bois believed that this form of dialogue would help bring these two groups closer together.

"False education" was not the only hurdle Du Bois acknowledged in creating solidarity between Black Americans and Indians. Issues of "color prejudice" in both communities presented a major obstacle. Du Bois attributed "color prejudice" to the pervasive issue of caste. In the *Aryan Path*, he stated, "If India has her castes, American Negroes have their own internal colour lines the plain shadow of a caste system." Therefore, "the problem of the Negroes thus remains part of a worldwide clash of colour. So, too, the problem of the Indians can never be simply a problem of autonomy in the British Commonwealth of nations."[53]

It has been argued that Du Bois failed to "recognize the severity of caste oppression in India."[54] Yet Du Bois was aware of internal caste oppression and did not conceptualize it as a colonial invention. At the end of *The Aryan Path* article, Du Bois sent a stern warning to the colored races to "be sure of their own attitude toward their labouring masses. Otherwise, they will substitute for the exploitation of coloured by white races, an exploitation of coloured races by coloured men."[55] This warning is evidence of his understanding that even in an independent India, a large proportion of its population could still be exploited and marginalized due to its caste hierarchies. However, Du Bois gave this warning to all peoples of color – "Negroes, Indians, Chinese, and Japanese" – suggesting that he saw caste as a widespread problem in both White and non-White communities across the world, not just in India. Nevertheless, Du Bois believed that the caste issue should be solved by Indians themselves and that the cooperation of Indians and Black Americans against White supremacy was more important as "European exploitation desires the Black slave, the Chinese coolie and the Indian laborer for the same ends and the same purposes and calls them all niggers."[56] Du Bois's outlook on caste was akin to that of his friend Lala Lajpat Rai. Rai actively acknowledged and spoke out against caste discrimination, but he insisted that the fight for Indian self-determination was paramount; Indians could then dismantle and annihilate caste within their own culture and society. Du Bois primarily sought solidarity between Indians, Africans, and Black Americans because of their shared marginalization based on race limiting or undervaluing the possibilities of solidarities specifically between low-caste Indians and Black Americans.

Du Bois's March 1936 article in the *Aryan Path* caught the attention of prominent Indians, including the director of public instruction in Mysore, N. S. Subba Rao. In his own article in the *Aryan Path*, in May 1936, Rao agreed with Du Bois's call for Black Americans and Indians to work together to dismantle imperial oppression, but disagreed with his analysis of India's problem of color prejudice. Rao particularly took issue with Du Bois's use of the term "Aryan." Rao argued that Du Bois incorrectly used "Aryan" as a racial rather than a cultural term. In his March article in the *Aryan Path*, Du Bois had stated,

> India has also had the temptation to stand apart from the darker peoples and seek her affinities among whites. She has long wished to regard herself as "Aryan" rather than "colored" and to think of herself as much nearer physically and spiritually to Germany and England than to Africa, China or the South Seas.

Rao, in his response, argued that "Aryanism" in Indian culture was not a racial term, but a term used to describe certain Indian languages, and that

Du Bois had incorrectly associated "race with language."[57] Therefore, Rao argued, much of the lack of solidarity between Indians and other peoples of color stemmed more from language and cultural barriers, rather than racial prejudice. Although Rao correctly noted that the term "Aryan" was a linguistic term rather than a racial one, he ignored the reality that some Indian figures racialized it. Therefore, Du Bois was correct to report that some Indian figures in America such as K. Romola and Bhagat Singh Thind, amongst others, regarded themselves as being "white Aryans" and used the terminology to distance themselves from Black Americans. Racial classifications such as "Aryan" clearly created barriers between Blacks and Indians. The term remained a debated terminology amongst Indians during the 1920s and 1930s.

The racial roadblocks obstructing Black and Indian solidarity have been downplayed by some. Historian Gerald Horne, for example, argues that throughout the 1920s and 1930s there was a "context of ongoing affinity between Black America and India."[58] While in some cases this was true, as exemplified by the relationship between Du Bois and Lala Lajpat Rai, Du Bois accurately admitted in his article in the *Aryan Path* that affinity between the two groups did not always necessarily exist. Certain Indians saw themselves as racially more akin to White Europeans than to Black Americans. For example, Bhagat Singh Thind in his 1923 case for citizenship had attempted to argue that he was "Aryan" and therefore a member of the "white race," distancing himself from any identification as a person of color.[59] In addition to Thind, South Asian immigrants such as Chandra Dharma Sena Gooneratne, a scholar in Chicago during the 1920s, noted that visiting South Asian scholars attempted to distance themselves from Black Americans by wearing turbans. Gooneratne stated, "Any Asiatic [could] evade the whole issue of color in America by winding a few yards of linen around his head." Gooneratne admitted that he himself wore a turban to distance himself from Black Americans. Manan Desai, a board member for the South Asian American Digital Archive, similarly argues, "In mid-20th century America, the turban was a tool that people of color used for confounding the color lines." Both Thind and Gooneratne's attempts to differentiate themselves from Black Americans validated Du Bois's assertion that certain Indians tried to distance themselves from Black Americans to achieve a higher racial status.

While Du Bois warned Indians to modify and reform their caste system, in *The Crisis* Du Bois aggressively criticized British imperialism for the state of the Indian caste system, rather than looking at the ways in which Indians discriminated against each other through caste. He downplayed the internal issues of Indian caste to his American readers to foster as much mutual sympathy as possible; he did not want to turn American opinion against Indians as Katherine Mayo's *Mother India* had done. Du Bois blamed the British for using caste to "divide and conquer" Indians, a perspective consistent with Lala Lajpat Rai's, who argued that the British Raj used "communal compartments for political purposes and out of political motives" to cause friction between the religious and caste groups in India, making Britain a more desirable ruler for India's minority groups than high-caste Hindus such as Gandhi and Nehru.[60]

Du Bois's primary interactions with Indians were with individuals such as Rai and occasionally Tagore and Gandhi. Therefore, he was not sufficiently introduced to the alternative perspectives of Indians such as Dalit activist B. R. Ambedkar. In 1930, Ambedkar began calling for separate electorates for untouchables in India to allow fair representation. Officially labeled the Minorities Act, the act guaranteed representation for Sikhs, Muslims, and untouchables in the newly formed Indian government. The act was supported by British representatives such as Ramsay MacDonald, the British prime minister from 1931 to 1935. Ambedkar and other Dalit activists presented the Minorities Act at the Round Table Conferences, which were a series of discussions organized by the British government and Indian political personalities such as Ambedkar and All-India Muslim League leader Muhammad Ali Jinnah to discuss constitutional reform in India. However, Gandhi was vehemently opposed to the act, warning that it created an unhealthy divide within the Hindu religion. Gandhi believed that the caste system prevented class warfare and competition because it fixed "the duties and occupations of persons" and determined a "man's occupation before he is born.... In the varna system no man has any liberty to choose his occupation."[61]

Although criticized by Ambedkar, Gandhi's opposition to separate electorates and the annihilation of caste did not concern Black Americans such as Du Bois. In a 1932 article in *The Crisis*, Du Bois referred to separate electorates as "the decree of the Raj that the higher caste should constitute an electorate separate from the untouchables."[62] However, he misinterpreted the aims of the Minorities Act and falsely believed that the separate electorates were suggested by the British Raj to increase the power of high-caste Indians.[63] Du Bois was largely unaware that Dalit activists such as Ambedkar supported the Minorities Act, and consistently blamed the race, caste, and religious divisions in India on the British strategy of "divide and rule."

Du Bois either ignored or was unaware of Gandhi's opposition to caste reform for a variety of reasons. He believed that the Gandhian struggle and the Russian Revolution were the two "great events of the modern world" since they were two large mass movements which sought to overthrow imperialism. Thus, he did not want to complicate the Indian independence struggle through the caste narrative and interrogate Gandhi's lack of class consciousness. In Du Bois's eyes, Gandhi had mobilized the Indian people and had created unity through his Salt March, during which thousands of Indians followed Gandhi from his religious retreat near Ahmedabad to the Arabian Sea to protest British laws which forced Indians to buy expensive, heavily taxed salt that often was imported. The march resulted in the arrest of nearly 60,000 people, including Gandhi himself. Du Bois compared Gandhi's leadership to that of a religious figure such as "Buddha, Muhammad, and Jesus Christ."[64] The Salt March forced the British to recognize that their control of India depended entirely on the consent of the Indian masses and ensuring that upper-class Indians supported the British Raj. Gandhi's Salt March was an indicator that the British were gradually losing that consent.[65] It also pressured the British government to renegotiate their ruling terms with Indians and allowed Gandhi to travel to London to discuss these new reforms in the 1931 Round Table Conferences. Du Bois's image of Gandhi as the equivalent of a modern religious prophet and the fact that Gandhi's activism was producing progress toward Indian self-determination blinded him to the ways in which Gandhi was attempting to limit the social and political mobility of untouchables. As he told Gandhi in a 1931 letter, Du Bois's primary vision for the Indian people was independence. Du Bois believed that Indians themselves would solve their various religious and caste differences through the struggle for independence as a new Indian national identity was created liberated from religion and caste.

Another reason why Du Bois may have ignored Gandhi's lack of desire to eradicate caste was because he believed that Indian independence could create "racial balance" in the world. With its large population and immense resources, independent India would become a global power and economy controlled by people of color. Du Bois dreamt of the emergence of global powers in Asia to counteract the hegemony of European powers. In a 1933 article in *The Crisis*, he wrote that the independence of India alongside the unification of Japan and China as one country would lead to a "new era" in the world and "the impossible domination of one mad race will end."[66] Du Bois's desire for the emergence of a pan-Asiatic global power may have caused him to support unconditional Indian independence regardless of whether radical caste and class reforms were integral components of its program. Du Bois believed that Indian independence was paramount to the Black American struggle, noting that regarding the "Black race ... no matter what its destiny in America, its problems will never be settled until the problem of the relation of the white and colored races is settled throughout the world."[67]

Du Bois continued attempting to sow solidarity between Black Americans and Indians in the 1930s, but the readership of *The Crisis* rapidly waned, with monthly circulation numbers regressing to pre-World War I numbers at around thirty thousand by 1930. Du Bois blamed the declining readership on higher production costs. Additionally, although readership began to decline throughout the 1920s, by 1930 the US had entered the Great Depression and Americans did not have as much disposable income as they did in the 1920s.[68]

Throughout the early 1930s, NAACP board members made Du Bois a scapegoat for the financial issues of *The Crisis* and he gradually lost control of the magazine to assistant secretary Roy Wilkins. Frustrated by the economic and organizational problems of the NAACP and *The Crisis*, Du Bois began to advocate more radical views and suggested that Black Americans replace White NAACP leaders and some Black leaders such as Walter White, whom Du Bois referred to as being more like a White man than a "Negro" because of his predominantly European ancestry, and his light skin, hair, and eyes.[69] Because of his ability to pass as a White man, DuBois believed that White could not understand the Black experience the same way as most Black Americans. Additionally, Du Bois suggested that a racially segregated economy for Black Americans would lead to greater progress for them. His opinions contradicted those of the NAACP, which advocated for Black civil rights, not Black separatism.[70] Du Bois's radical views were condemned by other Black newspapers such as the *Chicago Defender* and the *Philadelphia Tribune*. They bombarded the NAACP with questions about whether Du Bois's plan for Black separatism was part of its platform. In response, in April 1934, NAACP board members decided to censor Du Bois's ideas to limit any criticism of the organization's civil rights program. The association also pressured Du Bois to retract his endorsement of voluntary Black segregation, but he refused and resigned in June.[71] Du Bois hoped his resignation would lead the Black masses away from the organization under his leadership. However, he ultimately overestimated his influence, and failure to actively recruit disciples left him with few followers.[72]

Du Bois's frustration and anger toward White allies and White liberals was readily apparent in his *Aryan Path* article in October 1936. A response to N. S. Subba Rao's article in May, Du Bois's article scoffed at the idea of collaborating with White Americans and Europeans to address civil rights because both groups had never hesitated to look at "their own destiny and of their work and future without reference to the rest of the world." Du Bois criticized the hesitancy of Indians, other Asian groups, Black Americans, and Black Africans in seeking a destiny that was independent of White Europeans. Du Bois saw Rao's plan of peoples of color working with the White races to better their status as unfeasible. He no longer sought cooperation with White allies through organizations such as the NAACP as a method for overthrowing White supremacy. According to Du Bois, the only way the "colored world" would have bargaining power with the "white world" would be to "establish a real union of colours and all races" which would have to have its own inner organizations and be "strong in its power of thought and defense." Du Bois argued that on the surface "peoples of colour" were faced with two options, either they declare war to achieve equal status or face continued humiliation.[73] Du Bois did not advocate a violent war and he still maintained a belief in India's "economic war" through Gandhi's methods of boycotting British products. Du Bois asserted that the teachings of Gandhi and Japanese Christian pacifist Toyohiko Kagawa would encourage non-White consumers to be less dependent on White exploitation. Du Bois would not condemn a potential race war if the "advancement of coloured folk" was suppressed by White people, although a race war was unlikely and imprudent as it could lead to the "hegemony of the white race to be replaced by tyranny from people of colour."[74]

While Du Bois asserted that he wanted all of mankind to work together, his *Aryan Path* article proved that he no longer trusted White allies and was fully committed to unconditionally supporting the anticolonial struggle of India even if it meant a new world war. Additionally, the issue of caste amongst the Hindu community was secondary for Du Bois. He believed that the "incubus of colour caste" which White supremacists used to marginalize the "children of India, Africa, and Negro America" was far more pervasive than any internal caste system in India. To destroy "colour caste," in the aftermath of his NAACP departure, Du Bois sought non-White allies outside the US as a necessity for advancing the Black struggle. International dialogue became an integral part of his activism. While he was restricted from traveling to India because the British would not give him a visa unless he promised to "limit [his] words and activities" supporting Indian independence, he managed to travel to China, Japan, and Manchuria in 1936.[75]

Although Du Bois criticized White European colonialism, he defended Japanese colonialism in Manchuria as benevolent, noting that "colonial enterprise by a colored nation need not imply the caste, exploitation and subjection which is always implied in the case of white Europe."[76] Hence, by the mid-1930s, Du Bois was fully committed to overthrowing White supremacy even if it meant supporting Asian colonial nations such as Japan and minimalizing India's internal caste issue. Du Bois saw an ascendent Japanese Empire and an independent India as an opportunity to break the monopoly that White nations had on international affairs.[77] To achieve these aims, Du Bois expressed loyalty toward both Japan and India. In addition to drawing interest in India to write for the *Aryan Path*, his influence in Asia was exemplified by the Japanese ambassador arranging a trip to Japan for Du Bois and a small group of academics.[78] The interest Du Bois drew from Indians and the Japanese signified that although his influence in the US had dwindled, he was still a respected transnational figure.

Notes

1. W. E. B. Du Bois, "The Negro Race in the United States" (speech, London: UK, June 1911), in *Papers on Inter-racial Problems, Communicated to the First Universal Races Congress, Held at the University of London, July 26–29, 1911*, ed. G. Spiller, 349–364 (London: P.S. King and Son, 1911).
2. Ibid.
3. Ibid.
4. Ibid.
5. *Indian Opinion* 9, no. 31 (August 5, 1911): 303.
6. *Indian Opinion* 9, no. 34 (August 26, 1911).
7. Ibid.
8. *Indian Opinion* 9, no. 36 (September 9, 1911): 350.
9. E. S. Reddy, "Some Remarkable European Women Who Helped Gandhiji in South Africa," in *Gandhiji's Vision of a Free South Africa*, 1–61 (New Delhi: Sachar Publishing House: 1995), 27.
10. Daniel Immerwahr, *How to Hide an Empire: A History of the Greater United States* (New York: Picador, Farrar, Straus, and Giroux, 2019), 8.
11. Gerald Horne, *End of Empires: African Americans and India* (Philadelphia: Temple University Press 2008), 74.
12. Ibid.
13. Lamia Dzanouni, Hélène Le Dantec-Lowry, and Claire Parfait, "From One Crisis to the Other: History and Literature in The Crisis from 1910 to the Early 1920s," *European Journal of American Studies* (online) (2016), 2.
14. Elliott M. Rudwick, "W.E.B. Du Bois in the Role of Crisis Editor," *The Journal of Negro History* 43, no. 3 (1958): 214–240, 228.

15. Ibid., 214, 229; Amy Tikkanen, "*The Crisis* American Magazine," in *Encyclopedia Britannica*, https://www.britannica.com/topic/The-Crisis-American-magazine, accessed September 27, 2019.

16. W. E. B. Du Bois, "The Woes of India," *The Crisis* 22, no. 1 (May 1921), 27.

17. W. E. B. Du Bois, "Dr. Holmes, the Community Church, and World Brotherhood" (1948), https://credo.library.umass.edu/view/full/mums312-b229-i073, accessed March 3, 2021; Leonard A. Gordon, "Mahatma Gandhi's Dialogues with Americans," *Economic and Political Weekly* 37, no. 4 (2002): 337–352, 338.

18. Lloyd I. Rudolph, "Gandhi in the Mind of America," *Economic and Political Weekly* 45, no. 47 (2010): 23–26; Nico Slate, *Colored Cosmopolitanism: The Shared Struggle for Freedom in the United States and India* (Cambridge: Harvard University Press, 2012), 37.

19. Judith M. Brown, *Modern India: The Origins of an Asian Democracy* (Oxford: Oxford University Press, 1994), 195–196.

20. W. E. B. Du Bois, "Gandhi and India," *The Crisis* 23, no. 5 (March 1922): 207.

21. Ibid., 207; Payal K. Patel, "On the Path of the Maharajah of Bwodpur: The Global Problem of the Color Line in W.E.B. Du Bois's Dark Princess," *CR: The New Centennial Review* 15, no. 2 (2015): 119–156, 122.

22. Slate, *Colored Cosmopolitanism*, 44.

23. Ashwin Desai and Goolam Vahed, *The South African Gandhi: Stretcher-Bearer of Empire* (Redwood City: Stanford University Press, 2015), 131.

24. W. E. B. Du Bois, "The World and Us," *The Crisis* 23, no. 6 (April 1922): 247; W.E.B. Du Bois, "Again Africa," *The Crisis* 23, no. 6 (April 1922): 251.

25. Sir Courtenay Peregrine Ilbert, *The Government of India* (Oxford: Clarendon Press, 1922), 125.

26. J. M. Brown, *Modern India*, 205–207.

27. Ibid.

28. Slate, *Colored Cosmopolitanism*, 43.

29. Horne, *End of Empires*, 79; Slate, *Colored Cosmopolitanism*, 75; Patel, "On the Path of the Maharajah of Bwodpur," 127.

30. Horne, *End of Empires*, 79.

31. "Race Discrimination," *New York Times*, May 13, 1928.

32. Dohra Ahmad, "'More than Romance': Genre and Geography in 'Dark Princess,'" *ELH* 69, no. 3 (2002): 775–803, 790.

33. W. E. B. Du Bois to Mohandas K. Gandhi, February 19, 1929.

34. M. K. Gandhi, "Message to the American Negro," May 1, 1929.

35. Henry David Thoreau, "Resistance to Civil Government," in Elizabeth Palmer Peabody, *Aesthetic Papers*, 189–213 (New York: G.P. Putnam, 1849).

36. Ibid., para 33

37. M. K. Gandhi, "Non-Violent Resistance," in Lawrence A. Rosenwald, "The Theory, Practice, and Influence of Thoreau's Civil Disobedience," in *A Historical Guide to Henry David Thoreau*, ed. William E. Cain, 153–180

(New York, NY, 2000; online edn, Oxford Academic, October 31, 2023), https://doi.org/10.1093/oso/9780195138627.003.0006, accessed April 22, 2024.

38. M. K. Gandhi, "For Passive Resisters," *Indian Opinion*, October 26, 1907.

39. W. E. B. Du Bois to Rabindranath Tagore, February 19, 1929.

40. Announcement of Tagore statement in *The Crisis*, ca. 1929.

41. Rabindranath Tagore, "A Message to the American Negro from Rabindranath Tagore," ca. July 1929.

42. Ibid.

43. Madhumita Lahiri, "World Romance: Genre, Internationalism, and W.E.B. Du Bois," *Callaloo* 33, no. 2 (2010): 537–552, 538.

44. Nico Slate, *Colored Cosmopolitanism: The Shared Struggle for Freedom in the United States and India* (Cambridge, MA: Harvard University Press, 2012) 61.

45. A message to the American Negro from Rabindranath Tagore, ca. July 1929.

46. "A Hindu Speaks His Mind about Us," *The Chicago Defender*, November 29, 1930, 14; Slate, *Colored Cosmopolitanism*, 88.

47. "Another Hindu Writes," *The Chicago Defender*, December 13, 1930, 12.

48. W. E. B. Du Bois Papers (MS 312) Special Collections and University Archives, University of Massachusetts Amherst Libraries, Letter from *The Aryan Path* to W. E. B. Du Bois, October 10, 1935.

49. W. E. B. Du Bois, "The Clash of Colour," *The Aryan Path* 7, no. 3 (March 1936): 112.

50. Ibid., 111.

51. Harold R. Isaacs, *Scratches on Our Minds: American Views of China and India* (Armonk, NY: M.E Sharpe, 1980), 241.

52. Desai and Vahed, *The South African Gandhi*.

53. Du Bois, "The Clash of Colour," 114.

54. Slate, *Colored Cosmopolitanism*, 78.

55. Du Bois, "The Clash of Colour," 115.

56. Ibid.

57. N. S. Subba Rao, "The Union of Colour," *The Aryan Path* 7, no. 3 (May 1936): 216.

58. Horne, *End of Empires*, 74.

59. Ian Haney-López, *White by Law: The Legal Construction of Race* (New York: New York University Press, 1996), 149. See also Georgia Warnke, *After Identity: Rethinking Race, Sex, and Gender* (Cambridge: Cambridge University Press, 2007).

60. Lala Lajpat Rai, "Supplement to '*The People*' for December 3, 1925," *The People*, December 6, 1925.

61. Bhimrao Ambedkar, *Writings and Speeches*, 12 vols. (Bombay 1979–1993), ix, 277.

62. W .E. B. Du Bois, "Foreign News," *The Crisis* 39 (1932): 351.

63. Ibid.

64. Slate, *Colored Cosmopolitanism*, 109.

65. Richard L. Johnson, *Gandhi's Experiments with Truth: Essential Writings by and about Mahatma Gandhi* (Washington, DC: Lexington Books, 2006), 32; Peter Ackerman and Jack DuVall, *A Force More Powerful: A Century of Nonviolent Conflict* (New York: St Martin's Press, 2000), 109.

66. Horne, *The End of Empires*, 129.

67. W. E. B. Du Bois, "India," originally published in *Freedomways* 5, no. 1 (Winter 1965), reprinted in *Against Racism: Unpublished Essays, Papers, Addresses, 1887–1961*, ed. Herbert Aptheker, 115–117 (Amherst: University of Massachusetts Press, 1985); Bill V. Mullen and Cathryn Watson, *W.E.B. Du Bois on Asia: Crossing the World Color Line* (Jackson: University Press of Mississippi, 2005), 24–25. According to Mullen and Watson, Du Bois's "India" essay was a personal essay written in 1936 or 1937, but it was only published after his death in 1963.

68. David Levering Lewis, *W.E.B. Du Bois: A Biography* (New York: Henry Holt and Company, 2009), 544; Rudwick, "W.E.B. Du Bois in the Role of Crisis Editor," 234–236.

69. Gerald Horne, *W.E.B. Du Bois: A Biography* (Westport, CT: Greenwood Press, 2010), 143–144; Lewis, *W.E.B. Du Bois*, 535, 547; Rudwick, "W.E.B. Du Bois in the Role of Crisis Editor," 234–240.

70. Lewis, *W.E.B. Du Bois*, 569–570.

71. Ibid., 573.

72. Rudwick, "W.E.B. Du Bois in the Role of Crisis Editor," 237–240.

73. W. E. B. Du Bois, "The Union of Colour," *The Aryan Path* 7, no. 10 (October 1936). This is a correspondence between Du Bois and N.S. Subba Rao.

74. Ibid.

75. Horne, *End of Empires*, 10, 124.

76. W. E. B. Du Bois, *Newspaper Columns*, Vol. 1, ed. Herbert Aptheker, 167–168 (White Plains, NY: Kraus-Thomson, 1986) (column from the *Pittsburg Courier* in February 1937); Reginald Kearney, "The Pro-Japanese Utterances of W.E.B. Du Bois," *Contributions in Black Studies* 13, no. 7 (1995): 201–217, 205.

77. Kearney, "The Pro-Japanese Utterances of W.E.B. Du Bois."

78. Ibid., 204.

6

W. E. B. Du Bois, Walter White, and B. R. Ambedkar's Quest to Address Race, Caste, and Class

India finally achieved independence in 1947. Afterwards, W. E.B. Du Bois sought to utilize the newly free country to put pressure on the US to address its racism. His strategy was to build publicity and awareness of White supremacy in the US amongst the international community. His primary means for doing so was by drafting a petition for the United Nations (UN) in collaboration with the National Association for the Advancement of Colored Peoples (NAACP), hoping that the UN could mandate a resolution for Black civil rights. Du Bois's efforts caught the attention of B. R. Ambedkar who saw parallels between the Black American struggle and Indian untouchability. Using Du Bois as a source of inspiration, Ambedkar sought to create his own UN petition to solve India's caste problem. Du Bois's petition did not reach the floor of the UN, however. Prominent NAACP members such as Eleanor Roosevelt refused to present it, fearing that it could tarnish the international reputation of the US. Ambedkar also did not follow through on his UN petition and instead tried to address caste by working with the Nehru government.

One of the most significant aspects of Du Bois's work during the 1950s was his generation and harnessing of negative Indian sentiment toward the US to apply pressure upon the US government to address Black civil rights. In 1951, Du Bois collaborated with fellow Black Americans Paul Robeson and William Patterson to draft a second UN petition. While the petition again stopped short of the floor of the UN, it tarnished America's image amongst some Indians and the Indian media and increased Indian awareness of American racism. As a result, it prompted Supreme Court Justice William O. Douglas to urgently repair the image of the US abroad. Indian public opinion played a part in pressuring the US Supreme Court to desegregate public schools through the 1954 *Brown v. Board of Education* decision. Douglas along with fellow justice Earl Warren acknowledged it as an influential factor, although international concerns were not cited explicitly in the ruling's text.

The Activism of W. E. B. Du Bois, Walter White, and B. R. Ambedkar after Indian Independence

In 1945, the British granted India terms for self-government. After World War II, a new Labour Party government came to power in Britain under Prime Minister Clement Atlee. Its election manifesto called for "the advancement of India to responsible self-government."[1] Attlee was more sympathetic to Indian independence than his predecessor Winston Churchill, although he still preferred Dominion status for India. Britain had also become more reliant on American opinion after the war, making the US's pressure to decolonize in the aftermath of the war more pressing. America emerged as an important economically for a post-war Britain that no longer had the economic means to rule India single-handedly.[2]

Although India had achieved independence, the question of caste remained an urgent concern for B. R. Ambedkar, particularly the civil rights of untouchables. Ambedkar saw caste as a local issue in many rural communities and it was difficult for many who did not live there to truly comprehend its pervasiveness. Ambedkar described India's villages as "caste ridden," representing "a sink of localism, a den of ignorance, narrow-mindedness and communalism."[3]

He believed that caste was a central part of Hinduism and could not imagine that Indians would remedy the caste system themselves even when given independence. Ambedkar saw Hindu Brahmins, not the British, as the main culprit responsible for the marginalization of Dalits, accurately acknowledging that caste discrimination had been occurring for centuries even before the British arrived.[4] Ambedkar concluded that the inherently flawed, Brahmin-controlled Hindu teachings and scriptures were the primary reason why the discriminatory caste system was so heavily defended in India and why Dalits were forced to live on the fringes of society. He theorized that endogamy was the root of caste distinctions in Hindu society. To codify this integral element of caste, he noted that Brahmins stressed the superior "position of endogamy" over "exogamy," which led to the "creation of caste."[5] Furthermore, Ambedkar asserted that other problematic elements of caste such as child marriage stemmed from the Brahmin practice of endogamy. Brahmin elites saw unmarried adult women with a free sexual agency as a threat to "endogamous caste." Child marriage prevented the possibility of girls breaking caste norms because marriage prevented them from having sexual relations outside of caste lines.[6]

Because Ambedkar believed that privileged Hindus were unwilling to annihilate the caste system or reform it, he sought out international parallels to understand how other societies addressed similar social problems. Like Lala Lajpat Rai and Taraknath Das, Ambedkar investigated the Black American struggle and used American slavery as a comparative base for caste in India. Ambedkar had studied at Columbia University in New York between 1913 and 1916 and obtained a PhD in economics. Unlike Rai, he did not come to America to learn specifically about the Black struggle, but he too understood that the experience of a Black American was comparable to that of an Indian untouchable; both groups were relegated to a lower socioeconomic class. Ambedkar credited Rai's 1928 book *Unhappy India* for drawing his attention to the parallels between low-caste Indians and Black Americans. However, Ambedkar was disappointed that Rai believed that American slavery was a greater evil than Indian untouchability. Unlike Rai, Ambedkar had personally experienced what it was like to live in India as an untouchable. Although Rai was an ally of low-caste Indians, his privileged background prevented him from fully understanding the plight of Dalits. Nevertheless, Ambedkar acknowledged that Rai throughout his life was "great a friend of the untouchables," and noted that Rai even bringing up the comparison signified that the parallels between the lived experiences of Black Americans and Indian untouchables needed to be studied further.[7]

Even though Ambedkar showed an interest in pursuing connections between American racism and the Indian caste system, his solidarity with Black Americans was limited. He denied a racial basis for untouchability and he did not think that the identity and place of low-caste Indians in India society was determined by their supposed racial inferiority. Therefore, he did not condone an absolute analogy between caste in India and American racism, and he saw different pathways to equality for Black Americans and low-caste Indians. Ambedkar conceptualized caste as solely a cultural issue in India, not one that was "fixed or hereditary." He therefore theorized that caste discrimination could be eradicated by improving the "environment" which untouchables were forced to live in, changing the "psychology" of Indians who saw caste hierarchies as true, and modifying the "language" Indian Brahmins used to argue that untouchables were inferior. Ambedkar saw "environment, psychology, and language" as "elements that were key in the construction of [Indian] identities and societies."[8]

Because Ambedkar denied a racial element to caste and saw different pathways to equality for Black Americans and Dalits, unlike Lala Lajpat Rai, he did not actively seek out alliances with Black Americans during his stay in the US between 1913 and 1916.[9] The divergent attitudes of Rai and Ambedkar regarding their eagerness to form alliances with Black Americans was likely a result of their opposing backgrounds and lived experiences. Since Rai primarily thought his marginalization in India under British rule was due to his skin color, he saw a natural alliance with African Americans because like himself, Black Americans were active in a struggle against White supremacy. Conversely, Ambedkar was victimized by other Indians through the caste system, and he did not see his Indian oppressors as being racially distinct from himself. Additionally, Ambedkar thought that the marginalization of Black Americans had ended after the abolition of slavery. He inaptly noted that after abolition Black Americans had become a "part and a parcel of the great [American] Society," overlooking contemporary American racism.[10]

While Ambedkar did not energetically seek out alliances with Black Americans, many Black Americans failed to see their own struggle as parallel to Ambedkar's anti-caste movement too. Since prominent Black Americans such as W. E. B. Du Bois and Walter White as well as White liberals such as Oswald Garrison Villard were allied to Gandhi's movement and unconditional Indian independence, Ambedkar did not draw much attention from American civil rights activists. Black Americans and White liberals found Gandhi's racial solidarity between the entire Indian population and Black Americans more appealing and convincing, and thus Gandhi became a more natural ally than Ambedkar for American figures. Ambedkar received some sympathy from right-wing Americans such as Katherine Mayo. Yet Mayo only supported Ambedkar because she wanted to use India's caste system as an excuse for India's lack of fitness for self-rule.[11] Due to a lack of support and interest from progressive internationalists, Ambedkar's primary method for challenging caste discrimination was to find an international solution through the League of Nations.[12] Ambedkar elaborated on his desire for assistance from the League of Nations in a 1930 *New York Times* article. He framed caste as an international moral issue similar to the slave trade, noting that the Indian caste system affected "the economic and social welfare of the entire world," and it was "a case for the League of Nations just as slavery or the drug traffic." The organization did not, however, have the effect he desired; many powerful nations, including the US, did not join it and the organization had very limited influence on global politics.[13]

By the 1940s, Ambedkar had come to see clear analogies between the contemporary lived experiences of Black Americans and Dalits. Although he concluded that untouchables were in a worse position than slaves in his 1944 pamphlet *Which Is Worse? Slavery or Untouchability?* in his 1945 book *What Congress and Gandhi Have Done to the Untouchables,* Ambedkar compared the situation of Indian untouchables to the treatment of Black Americans in the immediate aftermath of the American Civil War. Ambedkar theorized that India's independence struggle in many ways mirrored the American Civil War because both events were a struggle for freedom for groups marginalized by White supremacy. Ambedkar, however, noted that, although the Civil War was intended by Northern Radical Republicans to grant freedom and equality to Black Americans, their economic, political, and social status remained secondary to that of White Americans even though the Union won the war. Ambedkar feared India's post-independence caste situation could resemble American Jim Crow and many Indian localities could subject Indian untouchables to a similar second-class status as Black Americans. Ambedkar concluded that "[t]he Untouchables cannot forget the fate of the Negroes. It is to prevent such treachery [Jim Crow laws in India] that the Untouchables have taken the attitude they have with regard to this 'Fight for Freedom' [Indian independence]."[14]

The commonality that Ambedkar now saw between the Black American and Indian Dalit lived experience led him to enthusiastically seek out Black American allies to find solutions to address India's caste problem. In 1946, he sought out Du Bois for ideas about how to address the issues faced by Black Americans and untouchables. Ambedkar was intrigued by Du Bois's decision to present a petition to the UN. After a ten-year hiatus, Du Bois had rejoined the NAACP in 1944 as the director of special research.[15] Ambedkar requested copies of the petition from Du Bois as he sought to model his own proposal in a similar manner. Particularly inspired by Du Bois's methods of informing the international community of the problems faced by Black Americans and drawing their sympathy, Ambedkar believed he could use these same techniques to improve the social status of untouchables in the newly formed Indian nation-state. Du Bois agreed to Ambedkar's request but cautioned him that only the National Negro Congress had approved the petition. Du Bois also noted that he was aware of Ambedkar's activism and gave his full support to Ambedkar's cause, pledging that he was willing to provide any service he required.[16] Du Bois and Ambedkar did not have the same bond and relationship that Du Bois had with Lala Lajpat Rai, but nevertheless the two men considered each other to be a valuable ally in their shared struggle for human rights.

Du Bois received approval from the NAACP and sent a petition titled "An Appeal to the World" to the UN on October 23, 1947. In the petition, Du Bois highlighted how American racism marginalized several groups of color, including Indians. He placed the petition in a global context, claiming that saving democracy abroad required saving it at home. He demanded a world hearing to persuade the US "to be just to its own people." During the preliminary presentation to persuade the UN to advance the petition to the floor of the UN, Walter White also pressed the international community to recognize the urgency of Black civil rights. He asserted that "injustice against Black men in America" had repercussions for the "brown men of India, yellow men of China, and Black men of Africa."[17] White and Du Bois understood that Indians were people of color and therefore interested in the Black American struggle. Du Bois tied the Black American experience to British and Belgian colonial subjects as well as South African apartheid and White supremacy in Australia to pressure the UN to address racial discrimination on a global scale. He stated,

[The] treatment in America is not merely an internal question of the United States. It is a basic problem of humanity; of democracy; of discrimination because of race and color; and as such it demands your attention and action. No nation is so great that the world can afford to let it continue to be deliberately unjust, cruel and unfair toward its own citizens.[18]

Despite Du Bois and White's efforts, the petition never reached the floor of the UN. The NAACP and Du Bois wanted former first lady Eleanor Roosevelt to introduce the petition, but she refused to endorse it out of concern that it would harm the international reputation of the US.[19] According to Du Bois, the American delegation had "refused to bring the curtailment of our civil rights to the attention of the General Assembly [and] refused willingly to allow any other nation to bring this matter up." Additionally, Du Bois affirmed that Mrs Roosevelt declared that she would "probably resign from the UN delegation" if the petition reached the floor of the UN. The Soviet Union, a nation that had emerged as the second leading superpower behind the US, attempted to back the NAACP's petition. However, on December 4, 1947, the UN Commission on Human Rights rejected that proposal, and the UN took no action on the petition.[20] The UN believed that its role was to defend national sovereignty rather than fighting systems of oppression within nations. Although there was no concrete action from the UN regarding the petition, it nevertheless brought knowledge of American racism to the world stage and focused both domestic and foreign attention on racial discrimination in the US. The publicity from the failed petition played a role toward compelling President Harry Truman in a February 1948 congressional address to make the case that tackling civil rights for people of color was especially urgent to validate America's role as a global leader for freedom and democracy.[21]

Because the UN was primarily concerned with preserving national sovereignty rather than fighting systems of oppression within nations, both Du Bois and Ambedkar were unable to utilize the organization to internationalize their struggles and obtain reform. Ambedkar made plans to submit his own petition to the UN with the aid of the British Foreign Office. However, the latter wanted positive relations with India and did not back Ambedkar's petition. The British Foreign Office argued that Dalits were a political faction, not a minority group marginalized by the Government of India as there were no legal sanctions against untouchables. Therefore, the UN had no grounds to intervene since untouchability was a form of de facto discrimination, not de jure discrimination. Thus, Ambedkar's only option was to work within the Indian government and Nehru's administration to produce caste reform. Consequently, Ambedkar never submitted his petition to the UN.[22]

While the NAACP approved Du Bois's petition, the association forced him to step down from the organization because he had tried to work with the UN and asked India's new UN delegate, Vijaya Lakshmi Pandit, to get a hearing for the petition. The NAACP did not support Du Bois directly working with nations such as India that were not US allies. By 1948, Du Bois's nemesis, Walter White, had reached the pinnacle of his control and influence over the NAACP. Under White's leadership, the organization wanted to work with the US government to address the Black struggle. White believed that working with other nations could embarrass the US on an international stage and working with foreign nations to address internal American issues could push the NAACP out of favor with the US government.

White and Du Bois had different approaches toward using India as an ally for Black Americans. Du Bois wanted to bring the plight of Black Americans before the international community with assistance from other nations of color such as India, even if that meant destroying America's image on the international stage. White, on the other hand, desired to maintain a cordial relationship between India and the US government and sought to bring the two nations together. He planned to use the "colored solidarity" between Black Americans and Indians to pressure the US government to grant Black Americans protection against racial discrimination because Indians such as Prime Minister Jawaharlal Nehru were disturbed by the lynching and socioeconomic exclusion of Black Americans.[23]

Although Du Bois's UN petition failed, he believed that the independence of India was a significant moment toward ending White supremacy globally. Du Bois stated that Indian independence marked the moment "the sun of the colored man ha[d] arisen in Asia as it will yet rise in Africa and America and the West Indies."[24] Prior to Indian independence, Du Bois had formed a friendship with Nehru. Both men shared a mutual admiration for one another; Nehru had written to Du Bois in 1940 that he was "greatly interested in the future of the American Negroes." He told Du Bois that his books had left a "powerful impression" on his understanding of the discrimination and violence Black Americans faced.[25] In 1946, Nehru had sent Du Bois a book about Gandhi. Du Bois responded that Nehru and Gandhi had the "sympathy of myself and my people in the great work that you are attempting to do for India."[26] Likewise, Du Bois commented that reading Nehru's autobiography helped him understand that the violence against the Indian people by the British was similar to the violence inflicted upon Black Americans by White supremacists in America and through reading Nehru's autobiography he learned that "the so-called race problems of the modern world [were] essentially one."[27]

Because Du Bois and Nehru had a personal relationship and Nehru had expressed interest and solidarity with Black Americans, Du Bois saw Nehru as a powerful ally as well as an individual who would reform the capitalist exploitation of India's masses. However, Du Bois was underwhelmed and disappointed by Nehru's early leadership. In an October 1949 open letter to Nehru, Du Bois decried the imprisonment of trade union members, peasants, and political leaders and noted that India's jails "held more political prisoners than they did under the British Raj."[28] Du Bois's open criticism of Nehru showed that he prioritized the civil liberties of Indians even if that meant diminishing the public image of India as well as the image of Nehru whom he greatly admired. Despite their friendship, Du Bois was so disturbed by the number of political prisoners in India that he did not attempt to contact or set up a meeting with Nehru when he visited the US the following week.[29]

Furthermore, Du Bois's actions suggested that he had come to question Nehru's suitability as an ally for achieving class consciousness.

Both Du Bois and Nehru had bonded over their shared affinity for socialism. However, Du Bois acknowledged that Nehru could not or was not willing to "carry out socialism" against Indian capitalist elites and American capitalists. Instead, Nehru favored forming an alliance with them. Thus, the newly formed Indian state was catering to the White supremacist capitalists whom Du Bois had hoped independent India and China would fight against.[30] Nehru disappointed Du Bois when he and his administration took several steps to maintain relations with Britain and other British commonwealth nations after independence. In 1950, Nehru's government accepted the British monarch as the Head of the Commonwealth, a symbol of the free association of its independent member nations.[31] India's decision to become a member of the British Commonwealth, along with the Nehru's administration's decision to limit criticizing American racism, signified that India was prioritizing maintaining positive relations with capitalist nations. These decisions counteracted Du Bois's hopes that India would challenge the hegemony of European and American nations.[32]

The decision of the Nehru government to align itself with the British government showed the limits of utilizing race as grounds for solidarity between Indians and African Americans. The Nehru government prioritized building alliances with wealthy countries to aid India's economic development and urban industrialization and feared that aggressive lobbying for Black civil rights could hinder diplomatic and economic alliances with the US government. Nehru's decision proved that wealthy nations such as the US and the United Kingdom (UK) maintained economic leverage over the nations in Asia that they had granted independence to. The global economic influence of the US, UK, and other wealthy European nations served as a significant roadblock for Du Bois and his vision for newly independent nations to be economically self-sufficient and not be under the economic and political influence of their former colonizers.

Just as Du Bois hoped to work with the Nehru government to attain Black civil rights, Ambedkar also tried to mobilize the Indian government to achieve caste reform. On August 29, 1947, Ambedkar was appointed chairman of the Constitution Drafting Committee by the newly elected Congress government and chosen by the Constituent Assembly of India to write India's new Constitution.[33] Through his new appointment, Ambedkar was able to get many civil liberties and human rights enshrined in the Constitution of

India, including freedom of religion, the abolition of untouchability, and the outlawing of all forms of discrimination. He additionally won the Assembly's support for introducing a system of reservation of jobs in the civil services, schools, and colleges for members of Scheduled Castes and Tribes, a system akin to affirmative action. India's lawmakers and Ambedkar hoped these new measures would eradicate socioeconomic inequalities and the lack of opportunities for India's depressed classes.[34]

In practice, the reforms did little to change the socioeconomic status of untouchables; the stigma surrounding low-caste Indians remained strong in Hindu circles. In 1951, Ambedkar regretted his decision to cancel his plans to present his petition to the UN. He was hopeful that the Constituent Assembly of India would solve the problem of untouchability, but he noted that within the Indian community the condition of untouchables was the "same as before. The same old tyranny, the same old oppression, the same old discrimination which existed before, exists now, and perhaps in a worse form."[35] In his writings, Ambedkar criticized Nehru for his lack of vigilance safeguarding Indian minority groups, aside from Indian Muslims. Ambedkar additionally shifted from his earlier exchange with Du Bois in which he asserted that the plight of untouchables and Black Americans was "similar" to highlighting the uniqueness of the treatment of untouchables and noting that he could find no other "parallel in the world to the condition of Scheduled Castes in India."[36] Because Ambedkar was convinced that the problem of Indian untouchables and Scheduled Castes was exceptionally violent and discriminatory, he did not seek out further alliances and input from Black Americans to address the plight of low-caste Indians.

While Du Bois and Ambedkar were disappointed with the Nehru administration's lack of assertiveness in supporting American civil rights as well as class and caste reform in India, Walter White saw the Nehru administration as a viable ally for Black Americans. White believed that if Black Americans had a powerful leader like Nehru as an ally, he could encourage the US to grant Black civil rights in exchange for a positive relationship with India. Likewise, White tried to pitch himself to the US government as a conduit between the US and India, urging the Truman administration to accept that he could strengthen ties between the two nations and prevent India from forming an alliance with communist Soviet Union. Hence, White tried to align Black America as both an ally of the US government as well as the Indian people.

White visited India in early 1949 and met with Nehru. During the meeting, they planned for Nehru to meet with Black leaders in the US to show that he was an ally of the Black struggle. White publicly tried to paint an image that the US was in danger of losing India to the Soviet Union because of America's racial discrimination against people of color. In a 1949 recorded appearance with the Cooper Union Forum in New York City, White asserted that America's race problem undermined its efforts to build overseas allies with non-White nations such as India. White spoke of his meeting with Nehru and stressed that America was in danger of losing India to the Soviet because the population was naturally horrified at reported discrimination against people of color.[37] Rather than convince the American people to support Black civil rights due to moral reasons, White hoped to capitalize on American fears during the Second Red Scare that had started in the immediate aftermath of World War II. After the war, the Soviet Union had emerged as the US's primary competitor regarding global influence, and some Americans, including the US federal government, feared the prospect of newly created nations in Asia aligning with the Soviet Union, which might lead to communism spreading throughout the world. Thus, White believed that American support for Black civil rights would increase if it encouraged India to align with the US rather than the Soviet Union.[38]

White was relatively successful at drawing the ear of the US federal government. In a letter to American businessman Fowler McCormick, White noted that a "high official" in the US government had reached out to him asking him for advice on what was needed to steer India away from aligning with communist Russia. In another letter to Vijaya Lakshmi Pandit, White told her that President Truman had asked him if he believed there was any "prospect of India and Pakistan solving the Kashmir Problem." Thus, White, in the eyes of the US government, did become a channel between India and the US. The Truman administration saw him as somebody who had a strong relationship with Nehru.

White and Nehru tried to exploit the Truman administration's perception of their relationship by attempting to set up a meeting between Nehru and leading Black Americans during his trip to the US in October 1949. However, the plan was quickly thwarted by the US State Department because it did not want Black Americans and Indians conducting their own foreign policy discussions.[39] President Truman feared that some Black Americans had an affinity for Paul Robeson's more aggressive tactics to gain civil rights. Robeson had met with Truman in 1946 lobbying for immediate anti-lynching legislation.[40] When Truman refused Robeson's demands, Robeson publicly called upon all Americans to demand that Congress pass civil rights legislation and founded the organization the American Crusade Against Lynching (ACAL). The NAACP initially withheld support from ACAL because they perceived the organization to be a competitor, but Robeson gained support from Du Bois since Du Bois believed that "the fight against mob law is the monopoly of no one person, no one organization."[41] Other members and supporters of the organization included Max Yergan, Joseph Curran, Canada Lee, Jack Kroll, Lena Horne, Oscar Hammerstein II, and Albert Einstein.[42] However, the Federal Bureau of Investigation (FBI) designated Robeson's organization as a "communist front" because they believed that Robeson was part of the Communist Party of the United States of America and a Soviet sympathizer.[43] Robeson and the ACAL were thus both investigated by the FBI.[44]

The US government and its intelligence agencies worried about Black Americans colluding with men such as Robeson and tried to restrict them from having the liberty of forming their own political alliances with Indians such as Nehru. However, only a small fraction of Black Americans sought alliances with the Soviet Union like Robeson did. White himself supported the ostracization of Robeson and did not plan for Nehru to meet with Black Americans who were followers of him. Nevertheless, "Red scare" fears amongst American intelligence agencies pressured them to interfere with any plans for meetings with Black leaders. Nehru, who was no longer an anti-colonial figure but the leader of a nation state, had the responsibility of forming amicable ties with the US and thus accepted the State Department's scheduled itinerary for his visit.

Nehru's lack of meetings with Black leaders and the Black community disappointed some Black Americans such as Langston Hughes. Hughes believed that Nehru had missed an opportunity as speaking with Black Americans would have helped him to better understand the Black experience and relate it to his own experiences during the "colonial days of British India." Hughes's comments suggested that Indians could not understand the Black experience without being fully immersed in it. Although Nehru at times declared himself to be an unwavering ally of Black Americans, without spending time in southern American cities such as "Nashville; Jackson, Mississippi, and Dallas, Texas," Hughes believed Nehru could not truly feel the despair of Black Americans.[45] Hughes's remarks suggested that Nehru did not fully understand that the US was just as much a White supremacist nation as the British Empire. Had he done so, Nehru might have looked at an alliance with the US with caution.

As the leader of India, Nehru believed that he had a responsibility to form amicable relationships with the governments of other nations, including the US. On November 5, 1949, Nehru and Vijaya Lakshmi Pandit attended a private meeting arranged by White and the NAACP in New York City to discuss how the Nehru government could assist Black Americans. At the meeting Nehru admitted that as prime minister of India, he could only pursue the questions of race and color in India and noted that he "felt it would have been highly improper for him to come into another country, especially on an official visit and venture to criticize the internal policies of that country."[46] Hence, White's plan to use India as a bargaining chip for Black civil rights was no longer a reality. He had to search for other ways to advance Black civil rights. India, which was a country with religious division and border disputes with Pakistan, needed amicable relationships with the West to prosper. While Nehru was a fervent supporter of Black Americans in their struggle for civil rights and was presented with a lifetime membership of the NAACP by White the following day, he was not willing to risk India's relationship with the US to help advance the goals of the NAACP.[47]

Since Nehru was not willing to advocate for civil rights on the behalf of Black Americans as the leader of India, his administration in the early 1950s avoided making public statements endorsing the civil rights struggle while in the US. The Nehru administration's lack of public support strained the relationship between Du Bois and Nehru and Lakshmi Pandit. In 1950, Du Bois noted that while Pandit was willing to condemn the treatment of Blacks and Indians in South Africa she refrained from criticizing the treatment of Black Americans in the US. He mentioned a recent speech that Pandit gave in San Francisco in front of a "colored sorority" in which she declared that "patience and waiting" was needed for Black civil rights. Because Du Bois had worked with Pandit to get Indian support for his UN petition and he thought of her and Nehru as allies of the Black American cause, he felt betrayed by the lack of urgency Pandit expressed regarding Black civil rights. Du Bois accused Pandit of being "flattered and dined" by high-ranking White officials in Washington D.C., yet he was also sympathetic toward India's position. He acknowledged that both Nehru and Pandit needed foreign money to address the "poverty and illiteracy" in their country. Du Bois understood that the Government of India could no longer assist him in bringing the Black human rights struggle in the US to international attention.[48]

While Du Bois was disappointed with the Nehru administration's lack of assertiveness toward supporting American civil rights, the Black press sided with Walter White and praised Nehru's kinship with Black Americans. In March 1950, a front-page article in the *Pittsburgh Courier* showcased an interview with Nehru in which Nehru suggested that he would "welcome" a Black ambassador to India. *Courier* interpreted Nehru's comments as proof that "The Indian people [were] very proud of their color and [felt] closer to the darker people [of America]." However, the writer exaggerated Nehru's comments since Nehru noted that he would not specifically ask for a Black ambassador to India and would be satisfied with any American diplomat. Nehru similarly refrained from making any statements criticizing American racism and instead highlighted the firm and unequivocal stand his own country had taken against racism and the moral support India was willing to provide.[49] Although the Nehru administration was only willing to provide moral support to Black Americans, the *Courier* still presented Nehru as a strong ally in order to emphasize continued solidarity between Indians and African Americans.

Even though Nehru did not try and pressure America to end racial segregation, in 1949, the US government sent an African American UN delegate, Edith Sampson, to India to gauge Indian sentiment regarding Black American civil rights. In the aftermath of the NAACP's 1947 'An Appeal to the World' petition for Black American civil rights, racism in the US was brought to international attention. Hence, the US government under the Truman administration needed to rehabilitate America's international image to stop countries such as India from favoring a relationship with communist Soviet Union. Working on behalf of the Truman administration, Sampson took part in multiple public appearances in India. Her goal was to ease Indian concerns regarding Jim Crow segregation to present a positive image of the US. Although Sampson decried slavery, she noted that the socioeconomic status of Black Americans was improving rapidly. She stated, "[T]he Negro has advanced further in this period than any similar group in the entire world. You here get considerable misinformation about American Negroes and hear little or nothing that is constructive."[50] She similarly tried to reassure Indians that America was a great nation by stating, "I would rather be a Negro in America than a citizen in any other land." While Sampson received a positive response from Americans such as US Supreme Court Justice William O. Douglas who stated that her actions "created more good will and understanding in India than any other single act by any American," in reality,

Indian opinion toward the US was far from positive. Sampson reported back to the US State Department that Indian audiences at her meetings were still very much concerned about the treatment of Black Americans. She regarded the "Negro problem" as the "Number one problem" discussed by town hall audiences during her overseas tour.[51]

American public figures who traveled to India during the late 1940s and 1950s faced similar questions from the Indian press and audiences regarding America's race problem, indicating that it was an important issue for Indians. When Supreme Court Justice William O. Douglas traveled to India in 1950, the first question he faced at a press conference in New Delhi was: "Why does America tolerate the lynching of Negroes?" After Douglas was hounded with questions about Black civil rights, he understood that the attitude of the US toward its minorities of color had a striking bearing on whether it could have amicable foreign relations with nations such as India.[52]

In some cases, Du Bois and his Black American associates raised Indian concern for Black Americans. After the failed "An Appeal to the World" petition by the NAACP, the more radical left-wing organization the Civil Rights Congress (CRC) lead by William Patterson attempted to elevate the Black struggle to the international stage by creating its own UN petition. The CRC had been formed in Detroit in 1946 as an alternative civil rights organization to the NAACP. It had over ten thousand members primarily in the left-wing coastal areas of the US, but its support was weaker in more conservative areas of the south.[53] The CDC's petition titled "We Charge Genocide" alleged that every branch of the US government used systematic oppression and violent White supremacy against African Americans which amounted to genocide.[54] On December 17, 1951, the organization led by Patterson and Paul Robeson presented its petition to the UN at two separate venues. Robeson gave the petition to a UN official in New York and Patterson delivered the petition to Paris. Du Bois was slated to join Patterson in Paris but had been barred from traveling abroad by the US State Department as an "unregistered foreign agent."[55]

Eager to protect its image amongst the international community, the US government made attempts to stop the CRC's petition from being distributed globally. It allegedly intercepted the 125 copies Patterson sought to disseminate. However, Patterson distributed other copies, which he had shipped separately in small packages to individual homes. The petition spread internationally and had a strong impact on Indian sentiment toward the US. When Black American author Saunders Redding visited India in 1953, he noted several accounts of Indians questioning him on the CRC's petition. He recounted that during his lecture, which in Patterson's words "had nothing to do with race relations," a student asked him about the validity of the petition. When Redding told the students that it was an exaggeration, a student responded stating that he did not find Redding's statements convincing and continued to hold up the petition.[56]

Like Redding, when she traveled to India in 1952, Eleanor Roosevelt faced similar questions regarding why the US tolerated "discrimination, color prejudice and Negro lynching[s]." Roosevelt acknowledged that Indians were cognizant and conscious of racism in the US, and White supremacy was "never out of [Indian] minds." In a 1953 book titled *India and the Awakening East*, Roosevelt mentioned that Indians "always asked her pointedly … [about] the treatment of minorities" in America. She understood that there was a growing color solidarity between Indians and Black Americans, and that there was a growing feeling in Asia that White Americans looked down upon all people whose skins were "yellow, Black, or brown."[57] Indian opinion demonstrated to Sampson, Douglas, Redding, and Roosevelt that American racism was no longer just a local problem, but an issue which had expanded transnationally to countries such as India.

While Du Bois, Patterson, and Robeson failed to get the UN or the Indian government to engage in any concrete action on the petition, the publicity it generated made Indians, notably the young, more aware of America's race problem. Indian students frequently referred to the CRC's petition as a banner for America's violent racism toward its Black citizens.[58] Even though both the 1947 "An Appeal to the World" and the 1951 "We Charge Genocide" petitions did not reach the floor of the UN, they effectively besmirched America's reputation amongst Indians due to its treatment of racial minorities. Roosevelt, Douglas, Redding, and Sampson's trips to India reflected how attaining Black civil rights was necessary to rehabilitate America's image abroad. Redding suggested that everywhere he went in India, the feeling he got was that the Indian people saw America as a nation clouded by problems regarding "racial discrimination and injustice" and believed that American policy was "opposed to the 'liberation and rise' of the colored people of the world."[59]

As people of color, Indians displayed solidarity with Black Americans. They saw themselves as being part of a common marginalized community that the US disparaged as being racially inferior to White Americans and Europeans. During Redding's trip to India, Indians explicitly asked him if he would join them in an allied fight against White supremacy. Redding noted that he "was asked more than once whether the Negro community of America would join with the colored peoples of the world in a war against the white man."[60] Redding being a centrist and a moderate was horrified at the prospect of such radical ideas, but they nevertheless proved how some left-wing Indians were at a crossroads, forced to decide whether to follow the Nehru government's policy to allow America to solve its race problems internally or to join Black Americans in solidarity.

In some ways, after the "We Charge Genocide" petition, Du Bois and Robeson had greater publicity in India than ever before and thus the petition had a tremendous influence on how ordinary Indians understood the Black American experience. Robeson in particular was well known in India due to his successful singing career as well as his friendship with Jawaharlal Nehru.[61] While Redding was being interviewed by the assistant director of the All-India Radio station in Gauhati (Guwahati), the director mentioned how he was surprised that Redding, a "Black American," was permitted by the US government to travel to India. The director noted how "[t]he American government confiscated Paul Robeson's wealth … and refused Du Bois a passport" as examples of how the US government ruthlessly targeted Black Americans who sought Black civil rights.[62] Redding, Sampson, Douglas, and Roosevelt's trips to India provided them with insight as to how America's image had tarnished in India due to a greater awareness of American racism amongst the Indian population.

Black Americans were able to benefit from negative Indian opinion regarding US race relations. After Sampson, Douglas, and Roosevelt's trips to India, the US government realized that Black civil rights were essential in order to maintain friendly ties with India and rehabilitate Indian confidence in the US. In 1954, the US Supreme Court issued the landmark *Brown v. Board of Education* decision which labeled racial segregation in public schools as unconstitutional, even if the segregated schools were otherwise equal in quality. Indian influence was a factor in the decision. Supreme Court Justices William O. Douglas and Earl Warren sought to use the *Brown v. Board of Education* decision as an example of goodwill to colored nations such as India by showing that the highest judicial office in America was actively addressing the question of race. After Justice Douglas traveled to India in 1950, he wrote that he had learned from his travels that "the attitude of the United States toward its colored minorities is a powerful factor in our relations with India." In a 1954 speech to the American Bar Association, Chief Justice Earl Warren, nominated to the Supreme Court by President Dwight Eisenhower, similarly asserted that international opinion directly impacted his decision to vote in favor of the decision proclaiming,

> Our American system like all others is on trial both at home and abroad, ... the extent to which we maintain the spirit of our constitution with its Bill of Rights, will in the long run do more to make it both secure and the object of adulation than the number of hydrogen bombs we stockpile.[63]

Trapped in a Cold War, Douglas and Warren did not want to lose a large powerful nation such as India to the Soviet Union. Douglas remarked that the US had to do everything in its power to prevent Asia from becoming "the great staging ground for Russian imperialistic designs." He cited Asia's large population and immense resources as examples of why ensuring that Asian nations aligned with the US rather than the Soviet Union was imperative.[64] During his travels to India in 1950, Douglas noted that Soviet Radio was much more popular amongst Indians while the "Voice of America" was "ranked somewhere near the bottom."[65] Through his travels Douglas saw that "the world [was] choosing sides America or Russia." Thus, India needed to be "wooed" by the US to prevent Indians from becoming communists.[66] Both Douglas and Warren believed that the most expedient way to prevent communist sympathy in India was to show the country America's moral superiority over the Soviet Union, and that the US federal government was committed to ending racial discrimination. Douglas understood the solidarity between Indians and Black Americans as people of color, and realized that the manner in which citizens of color were treated in the US had tremendous impact on how Indians saw the country.

It is important to note that improving foreign relations was only one aspect of the *Brown* decision and international concerns were not cited in the ruling's text. However, as British barrister Anthony Lester notes, "[A]lthough the Court's opinion in *Brown* made no reference to these considerations of foreign policy, there is no doubt that they significantly influenced the decision."[67] Additional evidence that illustrated the impact of foreign relations on the *Brown* decision included the Court's citation of Gunnar Myrdal's 1944 book, *An American Dilemma: The Negro Problem and Modern Democracy*, in which Myrdal argued, "The treatment of the Negro in America has not made good propaganda for America abroad and particularly not among the coloured nations."[68]

The *Brown v. Board of Education* decision had some success in fostering positive publicity amongst the Indian media. Indian newspapers such as the *Hindustan Times*, which had a circulation around 59,000, called *Brown* "A Great Decision," noting "American democracy stands to gain in strength and prestige from the unanimous ruling ... the practice of racial segregation in schools ... has been a long-standing blot on American life and civilization."[69] The *Brown* decision represented a tangible example of how Black Americans and Indians could work together in encouraging the US government to take an active step toward civil rights legislation. Furthermore, it proved just how powerful Du Bois's "Agitation and Publicity" strategy was toward fighting White supremacy. Historian Mary Dudziak notes that "in no other country was the focus on American race relations of greater importance than in India."[70] Indian opinion became a focal point of the US government because Du Bois, Robeson, Patterson, and to a lesser degree Walter White brought publicity to American racism in India.

Overall, between 1947 and 1954, Black Americans and Indians produced mixed results in their fight against White supremacy. Although the *Brown* decision was an example of how foreign pressure from nations had the potential to influence the US government to address racial segregation, the Nehru government's eagerness to create diplomatic relations and solidify an economic alliance with the US limited his solidarity with Du Bois and Black Americans. Nevertheless, Du Bois and Black Americans showed that they did not necessarily need the Nehru government to lobby for civil rights; the *Brown* case proved the strength of Indian support for Black Americans. The impact of *Brown* was limited though; southern segregationists refused to comply with the decision and desegregation in schools remained inadequate until the late 1960s and early 1970s.

Notes

1. F.W.S. Craig, ed., *British General Election Manifestos: 1918–1966* (Chichester, UK: Political Reference Publications, 1970), 105.
2. Andrew N. Buchanan, "The War Crisis and the Decolonization of India, December 1941–September 1942: A Political and Military Dilemma," *Global War Studies* 8, no. 2 (2011): 5–31.
3. Narender Kumar, "Ambedkar Villages: An Alternative to Village Development – Case Studies from Lucknow," *Contemporary Voice of Dalit* 6, no. 1 (January 2013): 9–24, 9.
4. Babasaheb Ambedkar, "India and the Pre-requisites of Communism," in *Dr. Babasaheb Ambedkar, Writings, Debates, Interviews, Handwriting, Photos, Voice, Video*, ed. Anand Teltumbde (Mumbai, 2004), 8; B. R. Ambedkar, *The Untouchables: Who They Were and Why they Became Untouchables* (1948; reprint Shravasti, India: Bharatiya Bauddha Shiksha Parishad, 1977), 204.

5. Durba Mitra, "'Surplus Woman': Female Sexuality and the Concept of Endogamy," *Journal of Asian Studies* 80, no. 1 (2021): 3–26, 15–17.

6. Ibid., 17–18.

7. B. R. Ambedkar, "Which Is Worse? Slavery or Untouchability?" in *Dr. Babasaheb Ambedkar: Writings and Speeches* 12, https://archive.org/stream/Ambedkar_CompleteWorks/62.Which%20is%20Worse_Slavery%20or%20Untouchability_djvu.txt, accessed September 15, 2020.

8. Jesús Francisco Cháirez-Garza, "B.R. Ambedkar, Franz Boas and the Rejection of Racial Theories of Untouchability," *South Asia: Journal of South Asian Studies* 41, no. 2 (2018): 281–296, 281–282.

9. Eleanor Zelliot, "Dr. Ambedkar and America" (paper presented at the Columbia University Ambedkar Centenary, 1991), http://www.columbia.edu/itc/mealac/pritchett/00ambedkar/timeline/graphics/txt_zelliot1991.html, accessed September 30, 2020.

10. Nico Slate, *Colored Cosmopolitanism: The Shared Struggle for Freedom in the United States and India* (Cambridge: Harvard University Press, 2012), 62; B. R. Ambedkar, "Negroes and Slavery," in *Dr. Babasaheb Ambedkar: Writings and Speeches* 5: 80–88 (Bombay: Education Department, Government of Maharashtra, April, 14, 1989; reprinted by Dr. Ambedkar Foundation, January 2014).

11. Ibid.

12. Daniel Immerwahr, "Caste or Colony? Indianizing Race in the United States," *Modern Intellectual History* 4, no. 2 (2007): 275–301, 291.

13. Thomas J. Knock, *To End All Wars: Woodrow Wilson and the Quest for a New World Order* (Princeton: Princeton University Press, 1995), 263.

14. B. R. Ambedkar, *What Congress and Gandhi Have Done to the Untouchables* (Bombay: Thacker & Co., 1945), 176, 185, 270–271; Talat Ahmed, *Mohandas Gandhi: Experiments in Civil Disobedience* (London: Pluto Press, 2019), 68.

15. David Levering Lewis, *W.E.B. Du Bois: A Biography* (New York: Henry Holt and Company, 2009), 648.

16. Letter from W. E. B. Du Bois to B. R. Ambedkar, July 31, 1946.

17. Jamil Dakwar, "W.E.B. Du Bois's Historic U.N. Petition Continues to Inspire Human Rights Advocacy," *ACLU Blog of Rights* (October 25, 2017), https://www.aclu.org/blog/human-rights/human-rights-and-racial-justice/web-du-boiss-historic-un-petition-continues, accessed September 22, 2020.

18. W. E. B. Du Bois, "An Appeal to the World: A Statement of Denial of Human Rights to Minorities," *Blackpast* (1947), https://www.Blackpast.org/global-african-history/primary-documents-global-african-history/1947-w-e-b-DuBois-appeal-world-statement-denial-human-rights-minorities-case-citizens-n/, accessed March 1, 2021.

19. Mary L. Dudziak, *Cold War Civil Rights: Race and the Image of American Democracy* (Princeton: Princeton University Press, 2000), 45; David Helps,

"'We Charge Genocide': Revisiting Black Radicals' Appeals to the World Community," *Radical Americas* 3, no. 9 (2018): 2–24, 9, 5.

20. Dudziak, *Cold War Civil Rights*, 45.
21. Dakwar, "W.E.B. Du Bois's Historic U.N. Petition Continues to Inspire Human Rights Advocacy."
22. Jesús Francisco Cháirez-Garza, "'Bound Hand and Foot and Handed Over to the Caste Hindus': Ambedkar, Untouchability and the Politics of Partition," *The Indian Economic and Social History Review* 55, no. 1 (2018): 1–28, 2, 18.
23. Gerald Horne, *The End of Empires: African Americans and India* (Philadelphia: Temple University Press, 2008), 193–194.
24. Bill V. Mullen and Catheryn Watson, *W.E.B. Du Bois on Asia: Crossing the World Color Line* (Jackson: University Press of Mississippi, 2005), 53, 54, 154.
25. Slate, *Colored Cosmopolitanism*, 141.
26. Ibid., 196.
27. Mullen and Watson, *W.E.B. Du Bois on Asia*, 144.
28. W.E.B. Du Bois, "Open letter to Pandit Jawaharlal Nehru, Prime Minister of India," October 10, 1949, Special Collections and University Archives, University of Massachusetts Amherst Libraries, https://www.digitalcommonwealth.org/search/commonwealth-oai:9s1695924, accessed September 21, 2020.
29. Slate, *Colored Cosmopolitanism*, 197.
30. W. E. B. Du Bois, "As the Crow Flies," August 4, 1950, http://credo.library.umass.edu/view/full/mums312-b216-i250, accessed September 21, 2020.
31. Robert Barnes, "Between the Blocs: India, the United Nations, and Ending the Korean War," *Journal of Korean Studies* 18, no. 2 (2013): 263–286, 265.
32. Horne, *End of Empires*, 79, 185.
33. "Some Facts of Constituent Assembly," *Parliament of India*, National Informatics Centre, https://web.archive.org/web/20110511104514/http://parliamentofindia.nic.in/ls/debates/facts.htm, accessed September 18, 2020.
34. D. L. Sheth, "Reservations Policy Revisited," *Economic and Political Weekly* 22, no. 46 (1987): 1957–1962.
35. B. R. Ambedkar, *Dr. Babasaheb Ambedkar: Writings and Speeches* 14, no. 2 (1979): 1317–1327, https://ambedkarism.wordpress.com/2011/03/10/dr-ambedkars-resignation-speech/, accessed September 18, 2020.
36. Ibid.
37. 1949 Walter White interview at the Cooper Union Forum, recording available at https://www.wnyc.org/story/216859-walter-white, accessed September 22, 2020. The Cooper Union Forum was an arts and culture venue that was made famous when Abraham Lincoln gave a historic address regarding the end of slavery.
38. Ibid.
39. Horne, *The End of Empires*, 195–196.

40. Martin B. Duberman, *Paul Robeson* (London: Bodley Head, 1989), 307; Horne, *The End of Empires*, 200.

41. Lindsey R. Swindall, *Paul Robeson: A Life of Activism and Art* (Landham, MD: Rowman and Littlefield Publishers, Inc, 2013), 113–114.

42. "American Crusade against Lynching to See President," *The Chicago Defender (National Edition) (1921–1967)*, September 28, 1946, ProQuest Historical Newspapers, *Chicago Defender* 2, https://search.proquest.com/docview/492741205, accessed September 23, 2020.

43. Horne, *The End of Empires*, 200.

44. Paul Finkelman, *Encyclopedia of African American History, 1896 to the Present: From the Age of Segregation to the Twenty-first Century, Five-Volume Set* (Oxford: Oxford University Press, 2009), 81.

45. Langston Hughes, "To Understand America, Nehru Should Visit Negro Ghettos Too," *Chicago Defender*, November 5, 1949, 6.

46. Slate, *Colored Cosmopolitanism*,180.

47. Brenda Gayle Plummer, *Rising Wind Black Americans and U.S. Foreign Affairs, 1935–1960* (Chapel Hill: University of North Carolina Press, 1996), 219; "Nehru Presented Life Membership in NAACP," *The Atlanta Daily World*, November 11, 1949, 2; "Jawaharlal Nehru Joins the NAACP," *New York Amsterdam News*, November 12, 1949, 1.

48. Du Bois, "As the Crow Flies."

49. Dunbar S. McLaurin, "India Would Welcome Negro Ambassador," *The Pittsburgh Courier*, March 4, 1950, 1. Note: The circulation of *The Pittsburgh Courier* reached an all-time high of 357,000 in 1947 but declined to 250,000 by 1953. George Swetnam, *The Bicentennial History of Pittsburgh and Allegheny County* (Pittsburgh: University of Pittsburgh Digital Research Library, 1956), 357; Lois Mulkearn and Edwin V. Pugh, *A Traveler's Guide to Historic Western Pennsylvania* (Pittsburgh: University of Pittsburgh Press, 1954), 38.

50. Oliver C. Cox, "The Programs of Negro Civil Rights Organizations," *Journal of Negro Education* 20, no. 3 (1951): 354–366, 362.

51. William O. Douglas, *Strange Lands and Friendly People* (New York: Iarper & Brothers Publishers, 1951), 296; Mary L. Dudziak, "Josephine Baker, Racial Protest, and the Cold War," *Journal of American History* 81, no. 2 (1994): 543–570, 567; Horne, *The End of Empires*, 207.

52. Dudziak, *Cold War Civil Rights*, 42,105.

53. Charles H. Martin, "The Civil Rights Congress and Southern Black Defendants," *The Georgia Historical Quarterly* 71, no. 1 (1987): 25–52, 25; Kwame Anthony Appia and Henry Louis Gates Jr., "Civil Rights Congress," in *Civil Rights: An A–Z Reference of the Movement That Changed America*, 187–189 (Philadelphia: Running Press, 2004).

54. João H. Costa Vargas, "Genocide in the African Diaspora: United States, Brazil, and the Need for a Holistic Research and Political Method," *Cultural*

Dynamics 17, no. 3 (November 2005): 267–290, 269–270; Charles H. Martin, "Internationalizing 'The American Dilemma': The Civil Rights Congress and the 1951 Genocide Petition to the United Nation," *Journal of American Ethnic History* 16, no. 4 (1997): 35–61, 44–45.

55. John Docker, "Raphaël Lemkin, Creator of the Concept of Genocide: A World History Perspective," *Humanities Research* 16, no. 2 (2010): 49–74; Carol Elaine Anderson, *Eyes Off the Prize: African-Americans, the United Nations, and the Struggle for Human Rights, 1944–1952* (Columbus: The Ohio State University, 1995), 169.

56. Saunders Redding, "A Report from India," *The American Scholar* 22, no. 4 (1953): 441–449, 444.

57. Eleanor Roosevelt, *India and the Awakening East* (New York: Harper and Row, 1953), 115, 189; Horne, *The End of Empires*, 206.

58. Gerald Horne, *Black Revolutionary: William Patterson and the Globalization of the African American Freedom Struggle* (Urbana, Chicago, and Springfield: University of Illinois Press, 2013), 10.

59. Saunders Redding, *An American in India: A Personal Report on the India Dilemma and Her Conflicts* (New York: The Bobbs-Merrill Co., Inc, 1954), 47; Redding, "A Report from India," 443.

60. Horne, *Black Revolutionary*, 142.

61. Slate, *Colored Cosmopolitanism*, 163, 169.

62. Redding, "A Report from India," 444.

63. Mary L. Dudziak, "Brown as a Cold War Case," *Journal of American History* 91, no. 1 (2004): 32–42, 37.

64. Douglas, *Strange Lands and Friendly People*, Foreword, xi.

65. Ibid., 75–76.

66. Ibid., 294.

67. Anthony Lester, "Brown v. Board of Education Overseas," *Proceedings of the American Philosophical Society* 148, no. 4 (2004): 455–463, 459.

68. Ibid., 456; Clayborne Carson, "Two Cheers for Brown v. Board of Education," *Journal of American History* 91, no. 1 (2004): 26–31, 26.

69. Dudziak, "Brown as a Cold War Case," 35. Sources estimate the *Hindustan Times* as achieving a ciriculation of 58,693 copies in 1950s, http://asu.thehoot.org/media-watch/media-business/ht-media-a-business-in-flux-10124, accessed January 2022.

70. Dudziak, *Cold War Civil Rights*, 33; Horne, *End of Empires*, 206.

Epilogue

While there are many vital words at the heart of Indo-American histories, *Indian, caste,* and *thug* are all uniquely connected to Indo-American relations – and to the struggle for democracy in both countries.
                                                                    —Nico Slate

Black Americans and Indians built many connections to combat White supremacy and they positioned the Black American and Indian struggle as part of a global movement for equality, as W. E. B. Du Bois and Lala Lajpat Rai commonly emphasized. They utilized each other to modify their aspirations for their respective societies and achieve a meaningful social impact, particularly in the US. However, this impact largely occurred after Indian independence through the efforts of Black radicals such as Du Bois, Paul Robeson, and William Patterson who identified India as a source of sympathy for the Black American cause because Indians were similarly victimized by White supremacy under the British Raj.

Caste was not a colonial invention and, therefore, the end of British colonialism did not result in its annihilation and some caste elements of British colonialism have remained in India. One of the most striking parallels regarding how African Americans and Dalits remain marginalized is the persistence of "criminal castes." Although some low-caste Indians could access education, land, and better jobs during the British Raj, occupational specialization was generally accepted as a defining characteristic of castes and tribes, even to the extent of defining certain tribal communities as "habitually" criminal under the Criminal Tribes Act. Originally passed by the British government in 1871, the British used the act to categorize some communities across the country as "born criminals," irrespective of their criminal precedents. The act required adult male members of such groups to have weekly meetings with the local police and they were not allowed to leave their villages without permission.[1] The categorizations had no basis in criminal evidence and were merely based upon racial and caste stereotypes.[2] The British government initially proposed the act to reform "born criminals" through labor. However, when these "born criminals" attempted to make a living like members from other castes, they struggled to find work outside the settlement because of public prejudice and marginalization. Additionally, there was no end date to their government-prescribed labor. It could be for life, with no hope of returning to their home villages.[3]

In India, although the Criminal Tribes Act was fully repealed by the legislature of India in 1952, historian Rachel Tolen argues that "the notion of criminal caste has been internalized by the [previously] colonized."[4] Tolen argues that much of the Indian population continued to believe stereotypes about low-caste groups as "born criminals." More importantly, according to Tolen, the official methodology of the Indian police, even after the repeal of the act, often reflected many elements of it, and certain tribes, primarily those of low-caste status, continued to be closely watched, studied, and documented. "Justifications" by the police and other privileged Indians for labeling lower-caste Indians as "born criminals" are contrived based on a false perception that these groups have a natural "disinclination to 'self-improvement,'" and have a "lack of work-discipline," which provides a natural explanation for "their poverty, their poor standards of hygiene, their nomadic tendencies," all of which are "tokens signifying their criminality."[5] Suraj Yengde also illustrates how low-caste Indians are often falsely perceived as criminals, noting that "any Dalit who voids the codes of caste order is declared rowdy, deceitful, in some cases criminal or even a rapist. Dalits who try to break the mold of caste are time and again reminded of their lower status."[6]

Similarly in the US, civil rights advocate Michelle Alexander argues that a large majority of Black men in some urban areas, as high as 80 percent in areas such as Chicago, are considered by mainstream American society to be "felons for life." Alexander notes that these men are part of a growing "undercaste – not class, caste," because they are "permanently relegated by law to a second-class status." She uses the term "caste" rather than "class" to describe the experience of Black men labeled "felons for life" because they are denied basic human rights and, much like in a caste system, they are awarded little to no opportunity to regain those rights within their lifetimes. They can be "denied the right to vote" and they can be "automatically excluded from juries, legally discriminated against in employment, housing, access to education, and public benefits, much as their grandparents and great-grandparents were during the Jim Crow Era."[7]

Alexander refutes the notion that rising incarceration rates are a result of a rise in crime by noting that crime rates in 2010 were at a historical low but imprisonment rates had quadrupled. Alexander argues that incarceration rates have primarily increased due to the "War on Drugs" which was "waged [by law enforcement and the US government] almost exclusively in poor communities of color." In "some states, African Americans comprise 80 to 90 percent of all drug offenders sent to prison."[8] The sentencing report by the Bureau of Justice Statistics supports Alexander's arguments and attests that

> [r]acial minorities are more likely than white Americans to be arrested; once arrested, they are more likely to be convicted; and once convicted, they are more likely to face stiff sentences for the same offenses. African American males are six times more likely to be incarcerated than white males and 2.5 times more likely than Hispanic males.[9]

Furthermore, if the statistics remain unchanged, one of every three Black American males born today will go to prison during his lifetime, and so will one of every six Latino males, whereas for White males that number is one of every seventeen.[10] The American Civil Liberties Union affirms that "[o]f the 8.2 million marijuana arrests between 2001 and 2010, 88 percent were for simply having possession of marijuana. Despite roughly equal usage rates, Blacks are 3.73 times more likely than whites to be arrested for marijuana."[11] The specific targeting of African Americans for drug crimes by the US penal and judicial system mirrors the way in which the Criminal Tribes Act in India marginalized many Scheduled Tribes and Caste groups.

Another linkage between the "criminalization" of low-caste Indians and Black Americans includes the terminology and rhetoric White Americans and British colonial administrators used to stereotype these groups as being prone to criminality. The term "thug" stems from the Hindi word "thag," meaning "swindler" or "deceiver" and was used by Indians as early as the fourteenth century. However, the British broadened and sensationalized the term during the early nineteenth century through stories about Indian criminals committing robberies and ritual murders in India. The book *Confessions of a Thug* written by colonial official Philip Meadows Taylor in 1839 became a bestseller throughout England and was one of Queen Victoria's favorite books. Much of the material in the British books about thugs committing ritual mass murders was largely fictional and exaggerated by the British to justify the need for British colonial rule in India and a "tough on crime" approach with Indians, especially those without high-caste privileges or those that were hostile to British rule. Furthermore, the portrayal of thugs being dangerous and violent murderers helped the British justify the need for the Criminal Tribes Act. As colonial administrator James Fitzjames Stephens noted while describing the act,

> When we speak of professional criminals, we ... [mean] a tribe whose ancestors were criminals from time immemorial, who are themselves destined by the usage of caste to commit crime, and whose descendants will be offenders against the law, until the whole tribe is exterminated or accounted for in manner of thugs.[12]

Nico Slate notes that the mobility of the term "thug justified the expansion of surveillance regimes, as authorities from California to Calcutta used the threat of the radical criminal to bolster the police state." This terminology was transported to the US to some extent by Indians themselves. In a series of lectures in New York City in 1895, Swami Vivekananda noted, "In the last century ... there were notorious bands of robbers in India called thugs; they thought it their duty to kill any man they could." However, the term became common knowledge to Americans through the entertainment and film industry. Films like *Gunga Din* (1939) and *Indiana Jones and the Temple of Doom* (1984) assimilated the term "thug" into the American mainstream vernacular. Tough-on-crime Americans began applying this term more frequently to describe Black Americans and their perceived "criminal behavoir." Black American musicians like Tupac Shakur fought back against stereotypes framing his fellow Black citizens as thugs and sought to inform White Americans of the nihilism and dejection many Black men faced in America due to their marginalization. Tupac argued that social and economic exclusion pushed young Black men into gangs and created violent communities. Tupac, whose parents were part of the Black Panthers, further insinuated that many Black men framed as "thugs" were simply defending themselves from police brutality and trying to survive. To Tupac, Black Americans were not "thugs" prone to criminality; they were engaged in a struggle to liberate themselves from the political and economic structures that treated them as second-class citizens. It is likely that Tupac, like many Americans in the late twentieth century, did not understand the linkages between the term "thug" in the US and India, but it was nevertheless a common example that framed Black Americans and marginalized Indians as "born criminals."

Because of the commonality between discrimination in the criminal justice system for racial minorities in the US and low-caste Indians, future work for drawing out race and caste linkages between the US and India could include comparing the links between the criminalization or "born criminality" stereotypes of Dalits in India and the mass incarceration of Black Americans in the US. Although the US elected Barack Obama, its first Black president, in 2008, discrimination against Black Americans and other minority groups still exists in multiple facets of social and judicial life. Throughout the 2010s, the Black Lives Matter movement has served as a vital reminder that Black lives, even in the twenty-first century, are too often undervalued or ignored in America. The marginalization of Black lives and the lives of other racial minorities in the US is perhaps seen most prominently in the criminal justice system and the disproportionate number of Blacks and Hispanics arrested and convicted compared to Whites.

Predicated on the differences in social outcomes due to race in the US, particularly in the criminal justice system, the disparity in criminal justice outcomes in the US is a form of apartheid. Although apartheid was condemned as an international crime by the 2002 Rome Statute of the International Criminal Court and it does not classify the US as an apartheid society, Michelle Alexander suggests that the US criminal justice system is a "a form of apartheid unlike any the world has ever seen," since it puts the victims behind bars rather than "merely shunting Black people to the other side of town or corralling them in ghettos."[13] However, the issue of apartheid cannot just be studied by isolating the US. The lived experience of marginalized Black Americans must be contextualized as a larger part of the construction of modern "nation-states." Gyanendra Pandey notes that "nations, and nationalisms, are established by defining boundaries. However, these are not always – or perhaps, ever – sharply or easily defined. Nationalisms have therefore commonly moved along the path of identifying the core or mainstream of the nation. Alongside this emerge notions of minorities, marginal communities, or elements."[14] Groups such as African Americans, Indian Muslims, and Dalits exist outside the respective mainstream national identities of their respective "nations" and dominant groups consequently see them as a threat to the mainstream identity of their societies. Hence, the power structures of both the US and India seek to keep African Americans, Indian Muslims, Dalits, and Indigenous Americans on the fringes of society to maintain the social order that favors the mainstream groups, which are White Americans in the US and upper-caste Hindus in India.

Particularly in India, divisive forms of nationalism based on race, ethnicity, and religion continued in the aftermath of the 1947 partition. Among the negative legacies of British colonialism, the partition of British India sustained modern Hindu and Muslim identities which were a result of the British "divide-and-rule" policy to drive apart religious communities. Historian John Docker states, "[P]artition establishes new social formations which create minorities where there had once been a mosaic of communities."[15] Thus, although British colonialism ended with partition and the creation of nation-states, India and Pakistan, the partition further reinforced national identities based on caste, ethnicity, and religion, and thus India became a state in which the dominant religious group, Hindus, became the mainstream of India's identity and Muslims and Dalits remained as minority groups on the fringes of society. Because of the exclusion of lower castes and classes by Hindu society, many of them converted to Islam and Christianity and, therefore, the "othering" of Muslims and Christians as existing outside the national identity of India is another element that illustrates how religious differences equate to caste differences in modern-day Indian society.[16] Gyanendra Pandey offers a similar assertion as Docker, noting that, since partition, within the

> conception of the Indian nation … Muslims had an unenviable place, the Dalits and other oppressed castes and classes were invisible or only symbolically present [in India's national identity], and other religious minorities and marginal nationalities had to work in collaboration with, and willy-nilly in subordination to, that other invisible category, the "mainstream, Hindu majority."[17]

Just as Muslims and Dalits in India must work "in subordination" to the Hindu majority to uplift their social groups, Black Americans have to work "in subordination" to the mainstream groups, which are White Americans. According to Pandey, it was "whiteness that came to be constructed as the core" of American nationhood.[18] The progress of social groups such as Black Americans threatened White American nationhood. Michelle Alexander notes that Black progress such as increased Black voter influence threatened the dominance of White voters as America's silent majority and mainstream group. Hence, beginning in 1971, the War on Drugs and mass incarceration was a reaction to Black progress, and it was used by the US government as a counter to policies such as "civil rights enforcement, and affirmative action."[19] The mass incarceration of Black Americans gave White Americans a position of advantage, power, and control over African Americans, limiting their opportunities to benefit from the Civil Rights Act of 1964, which allowed Black Americans and other racial minorities access to the same economic, social, and educational opportunities as their White counterparts. Like Alexander, Pandey argues that marginalized groups such as Black Americans and Dalits face further "denigration, castigation, and even expulsion at times when they are seen as challenging the existing order of caste and race, Black and White."[20]

It is important to study how both African Americans and Dalits are marginalized because they exist outside the mainstream identities of their respective nations in the contemporary age. Since Indians and Black Americans were able to transnationally bind their struggles to achieve social change, analyzing Indian and Black American relations, particularly those created between Indians from marginalized groups and the Black American "underclass," might help facilitate the social advancement of both groups. Searching for examples of caste systems in transnational contexts outside of India and the US and tying the struggles of the underclass in those nations to the struggles of Dalits and Black Americans would only build on the research contained in this study. For example, Dwaipayan Sen ponders why Dalits have not more regularly tied their struggle to the plight of Palestinians and other marginalized groups.[21] Sen's question is difficult to answer, but most Indian Dalits, like Black Americans, primarily want to integrate with the mainstream, and have representation and equality in their respective nations, whereas the Palestinians are fighting for an independent state. Hence, connecting the Dalit struggle to the African American struggle is a more logical parallel than comparing it to a self-determination movement such as the Palestinian cause. Nevertheless, broadening the ideas of caste into a global context may lead to a greater understanding of how such systems are created.[22]

However, while the aspirations of Indian Dalits and Black Americans differ from those of Palestinians, there is a parallel between how the Palestinians' lack of "whiteness" has caused White Americans and Europeans to see Palestinian freedom fighters as "criminals" or terrorists while they hail Ukrainian fighters against the Russian invasion of their country, which is underway as I write in March 2024, as heroes. The Russian invasion of Ukraine is arguably comparable to Israel occupying the West Bank and displacing its inhabitants. Both the Palestinians and Ukrainians are fighting for their right to self-determination. However, the boycott, divestment, and sanctions movement against Israel lacks support from many who quickly condoned imposing economic sanctions on Russia. This includes US president Joe Biden, former UK prime minister Boris Johnson and Labour Party leader Keir Starmer, organizations such as the International Federation of Association Football (FIFA) and UEFA Champions League, and companies such as Visa, Mastercard, and Airbnb. Palestinian writer and researcher Mariam Barghouti points out the "inherent racism" displayed by Western news outlets in terms of how they paint the Palestinian cause as being a "criminal" or "terrorist" movement and do not provide them with the same legitimacy as the Ukrainian struggle for self-determination and sovereignty. The same attitude applies to refugees. Muslim refugees and African migrants are seen by some White Europeans and media sources as potential terrorists or criminals but concerns about Ukrainian refugees potentially being neo-Nazis do not gain the same traction among most White Europeans. Hence, in addition to there being dominant and mainstream groups within sovereign nations, there is a broader international dominant group which is defined by White "Europeanness."

The closer one is to being a White European (preferably a Christian one), the more likely Western media outlets are to provide sympathy, legitimize their struggles, and accept their refugee status. Less questions are asked in the media about their ability to assimilate and provide value to society. The situation in Poland exemplifies these biases. In November 2021, Poland deployed security forces to prevent some 4,000 refugees and migrants from entering their country, resulting in thousands, including women and children, spending weeks outdoors in freezing conditions. Conversely, in the aftermath of the Russian invasion of Ukraine, Poland has taken in 575,000 Ukrainian refugees. Even in the context of accepting Ukrainian refugees, there have been reports of non-White Ukrainian residents such as African migrants and Indian students facing more difficulty gaining safe passage than White Ukrainians. It would be naïve to simply assume that this bias is simply restricted to refugees and migrants.

The biases that frame refugees of color as being less "civilized" than White refugees directly relate to those which dehumanize Black Americans in the US on the basis that they are less "civilized" than White Americans. Privileged White Americans and White supremacists utilize these biases to question the ability of Black Americans to be an integrative part of the mainstream "civilized" American identity. They believe that Black Americans are more prone to violence and provide less value to society than White Americans. These problematic stereotypes afford Black Americans less empathy during crises that disproportionately affect them. For example, during the crack epidemic in the late 1980s, the media frequently used terminology that criminalized Black Americans for their addictions. Yet, during the opioid crisis in the 2010s which primarily affected White Americans, the media instead responded with medical terminology and called for medical and social help for the addicts rather than treating them as criminals. Race clearly influences public responses to substance-use epidemics.[23]

Double standards define how Black Americans were treated during the crack epidemic and how refugees of color are not as welcome in Europe as White victims of war. Nations in the Global North, such as the US and Canada – which is also now being interrogated for its mistreatment of Indigenous schoolchildren – and those of Europe, all prioritize "whiteness" in their cultures. Some elements of multiculturalism may permeate their societies, but ultimately groups that are non-White are seen as a threat to their nationhood. The postulation that "Blackness" is often considered to be outside the mainstream identity of America was exemplified by the words of US Senator Mitch McConnell in January 2022. McConnell expressed concern over the high Black voter turnout in recent elections, stating disapprovingly that "African American voters are voting in just as high a percentage as Americans," obliquely suggesting that being Black makes one less American than a White person.

Nationhood that prioritizes the dominant mainstream social or ethnic group at the expense of minorities occurs in many contexts across the world. Aside from the US and India, the downtrodden experience of Arabs in Israel or the social exclusion of the Aborigines in Australia is a result of the idea that the national identities of Israel and Australia consider Arabs and Aborigines to be outside the mainstream culture of their nation-states. Hence, their lives are deemed as being less valuable than Israeli Jews or White Australians. Like the double standards in criminal justice in the US for Black and White Americans, Arabs in Israel face a similar disparity in their criminal justice system. A preliminary report commissioned by Israel's Courts Administration and the Israel Bar Association found in 2011 that Israeli Arabs are more likely than Israeli Jews to be convicted of crimes after being charged, more likely to be given custodial sentences, and to receive longer sentences.[24] Hence, according to John Docker, although nations such as India, Israel, Australia, and the US refer to themselves as free democracies, the "formation [of] democracy is a privilege maintained only for a select group to be considered equals amongst themselves."[25]

Rabindranath Tagore warned American audiences about the flaws of forming a national identity based on a mainstream social and ethnic group and ignoring the plight of the "Negro" and "Red Indian" (Native Americans) in his essays and lectures on nationalism.[26] Tagore stressed the importance of racial and religious harmony. He emphasized the same message to Indian audiences, asserting that India belonged not just to "Aryans" or north Indian upper-caste Hindus but also the "Dravidian civilizations" of India as well as Indian Muslims. Tagore called for an "undivided" version of Indian history and an Indian identity that incorporated and synchronized the histories of all groups in India to create unity and to avoid a nation-state that prioritized the Hindu mainstream.[27] Similarly, Lala Lajpat Rai regularly warned Indians that if they did not address caste discrimination and solve religious communalism, India would never be a functional democracy that serves all its people.[28]

In contemporary society, we often hear rhetoric about "nations" having the right to exist. At the outbreak of the Israel–Hamas war in October 2023, many asserted Israel's right to exist and unconditionally defend itself as a nation-state even in situations where the Israeli government's actions have resulted in the mass displacement, killing, and imprisonment of Palestinian civilians, including women and young children. However, an important question to ask is: should we be focused on a "nation" having the right to exist or do all the people who inhabit those lands have a right to exist and live in harmony? Often when a "national identity" is utilized as a mechanism of self-defense, groups which live in those lands that are excluded from that "national identity" remain marginalized, ostracized, or imprisoned. Dalits, Black Americans, and Palestinians are regularly excluded from the national identities of the lands they currently reside in and are reduced to second-class citizens who face state-sponsored violence as a result of their inferior place in those societies.

With his critiques of nationalism, Tagore sought to send a unifying message that societies should be focused on protecting all human life rather than just those that fit within the mainstream national identities of their countries. In many ways Israel, India (with its treatment of Dalits and Muslims), and the US have not lived up to Tagore's important message and, as a result of ethnic nationalism, societies and nations continue to be divided based on race, religion, and ethnicity. "Caste" in many ways, according to Tagore, arose in India from ethnic nationalism. He noted that a similar form of racially influenced American ethnic nationalism marginalized African Americans, Native Americans, and Asian Americans because of America's mainstream identity as a White Christian nation. "Caste" to both Tagore and Rai was a transnational concept that could be applied to any system of hereditary marginalization. Cognizant of this, Tagore accused White Americans of creating a racial caste system to exclude non-White racial and ethnic groups from their national identity. In many ways, Tagore's criticisms could be applied to America as I write in December 2023, especially through the evidence we see in the criminal justice system and the significant wealth gap between Black and White Americans.

The continued marginalization of Black Americans in the criminal justice system and the secondary status of Dalits in India exemplify how the ideas of Tagore and Rai still hold relevance in contemporary times and how both Americans and Indians can learn from their message. Although the US has in theory legislated racial equality through the Civil Rights Act, Black leaders such as Malcolm X questioned the practical impact of the law. Malcolm X supported voting rights for Black Americans, noting that they had the ability to "determine who's going to sit in the White House and who's going to be in the doghouse."[29] However, he was skeptical that voting would bring about full equality for African Americans and he doubted that police departments would actually enforce laws that provided racial equality. The US government, he contended, cannot solve the race problem and legislating equality achieves little as friction between races has existed since the beginning of time.[30] Racism, according to Malcolm X, was "not just an American problem but a world problem."[31]

Although Black Americans have gained both economically and educationally since the 1960s, wealth disparities, housing discrimination, mass incarceration, and racial profiling by law enforcement has limited full racial equality. The lack of legislative impact on erasing caste inequality is also seen in India. Due to the deep cultural embedment of casteism, the annihilation of caste may appear to be a distant fantasy. However, while it is important to recognize the reality of the status quo, it is imperative to actively try and assess how race, caste, and class issues can be solved. As Martin Luther King rightly said, "Change does not roll in on the wheels of inevitability, but comes through continuous struggle. And so we must straighten our backs and work for our freedom. A man can't ride you unless your back is bent."[32]

Notes

1. Jessica Hinchy, "Gender, Family, and the Policing of the 'Criminal Tribes' in Nineteenth-Century North India," *Modern Asian Studies* 54, no. 5 (2021): 1669–1711, 1670; Crispin Bates, "Race, Caste and Tribe in Central India'," *Edinburgh Papers in South Asian Studies* no. 3 (1995): 1–35, 10, 23, 26.

2. Hinchy, "Gender, Family, and the Policing of the 'Criminal Tribes' in Nineteenth-Century North India," 1681.
3. Meena Radhakrishna, "The Criminal Tribes Act in the Madras Presidency Implications for Itinerant Trading Communities," *The Indian Economic and Social History Review* 26, no. 3 (1989): 269–295, 277. See also Meena Radhakrishna, *Dishonoured by History: 'Criminal Tribes' and British Colonial Policy* (Hyderabad, India: Orient Blackswan, 2001).
4. Rachel J. Tolen, "Colonizing and Transforming the Criminal Tribesman," in *Deviant Bodies: Critical Perspectives on Difference in Science and Popular Culture*, ed. Jennifer Terry and Jacqueline Urla, 78–108 (Indiana University Press, 1995), 100.
5. Rachel J. Tolen, "Colonizing and Transforming the Criminal Tribesman: The Salvation Army in British India," *American Ethnologist* 18, no. 1 (1991): 106–125, 112.
6. Suraj Yengde, "Castes of Mind: On the Intersection of Race and Caste," review of *Caste: The Origins of our Discontents*, by Isabel Wilkerson, *The Baffler* no. 56, March 24, 2021.
7. Michelle Alexander, "The War on Drugs and the New Jim Crow," *Race, Poverty and the Environment* 17, no. 1 (2010): 75–77.
8. Ibid.
9. U.S. Bureau of Justice Statistics, "Prisoners in 2011," 8 tbl. 8 (December 2012), https://bjs.ojp.gov/content/pub/pdf/p11.pdf, accessed April 18, 2024.
10. Marc Mauer, "Addressing Racial Disparities in Incarceration," *The Prison Journal* 91, no. 3 suppl. (September, 2011): 87S–88S.
11. "The War on Marijuana in Black and White," American Civil Liberties Union, https://www.aclu.org/feature/war-marijuana-Black-and-white, accessed May 2, 2021.
12. Louis A. Knafla, *Raj and Born Criminals Crime, Gender, and Sexuality in Criminal Prosecutions* (Greenwood Publishing Group, 2002).
13. Michelle Alexander, *The New Jim Crow: Mass Incarceration in the Age of Color Blindness* (New York: The New Press, 2010).
14. Gyanendra Pandey, "Can a Muslim Be an Indian?" *Comparative Studies in Society and History* 41, no. 4 (1999): 608–629, 608.
15. John Docker, "The Two-State Solution and Partition: World History Perspectives on Palestine and India," *Journal of Holy Land and Palestine Studies* 9, no. 2 (2010): 146–168, 153.
16. Pandey, "Can a Muslim Be an Indian?" 621–622.
17. Ibid., 625.
18. Ibid.
19. Alexander, *The New Jim Crow*, 246.
20. Pandey, "Racialization of Subaltern Populations across the Globe," 98.
21. Dwaipayan Sen, "Uncanny Juxtapositions: Conditions of Possibility for the Comparison of Race and Caste" (lecture, *Race and Racism in the Global South* from King's College London. June 1, 2021).

22. Arjun Appadurai, "Comparing Race to Caste Is an Interesting Idea, but There Are Crucial Differences between Both," review of *Caste: The Origins of Our Discontents*, by Isabel Wilkerson, *The Wire*, September 12, 2020.

23. C. Shachar, T. Wise, G. Katznelson, and A. L. Campbell, "Criminal Justice or Public Health: A Comparison of the Representation of the Crack Cocaine and Opioid Epidemics in the Media," *J Health Polit Policy Law* 45, no. 2 (2020): 211–239.

24. Tomer Zarchin, "Israeli Arabs More Likely to Be Convicted for Crimes Than Their Jewish Counterparts, Study Shows," *Haaretz*, August 2, 2011, https://www.haaretz.com/1.5039052, accessed May 26, 2020.

25. Docker, "The Two-State Solution and Partition," 153.

26. Rabindranath Tagore, "Nationalism in India" (1917), in *Indian Philosophy in English: From Renaissance to Independence*, ed. Nalini Bhushan and Jay L. Garfield, 22–36 (New York: Oxford University Press, 2011), 23.

27. Mohit Chakrabarti, *Rabindranath Tagore: Diverse Dimensions* (New Delhi: Atlantic Publishers and Distributers, 1990), 134–135.

28. Lala Lajpat Rai, "Reconstruction of Hindu Society," *The People*, October 20, 1927.

29. Malcolm X, *Malcolm X Speaks: Selected Speeches and Statements*, ed. George Breitman (New York: Grove Weidenfeld, 1990), 33–38.

30. Malcolm X, "Not Just an American Problem, but a World Problem" (speech delivered in the Corn Hill Methodist Church, Rochester, New York, February 16, 1965), in *Malcolm X: The Last Speeches*, ed. Bruce Perry, 151–181 (New York: Pathfinder Press, 1989).

31. Ibid., 1.

32. Martin Luther King, Jr., "The Death of Evil upon the Seashore" (speech at the Cathedral of St. John the Divine, New York City, May 17, 1956), "Martin Luther King, Jr. Black History Quotes," *Birmingham Times*, July 15, 2015.

Bibliography

Primary Sources

1949 Walter White interview at the Cooper Union Forum. Recording available at https://www.wnyc.org/story/216859-walter-white. Accessed September 22, 2020.

Ambedkar, B. R. *Dr. Babasaheb Ambedkar: Writings and Speeches* 14, no. 2 (1979): 1317–1327. https://ambedkarism.wordpress.com/2011/03/10/dr-ambedkars-resignation-speech/. Accessed September,18, 2020.

———. "India and the Pre-requisites of Communism." In *Dr. Babasaheb Ambedkar, Writings, Debates, Interviews, Handwriting, Photos, Voice, Video*, edited by Anand Teltumbde. Mumbai, 2004.

———. "Negroes and Slavery." In *Dr. Babasaheb Ambedkar: Writings and Speeches* 5: 80–88. Bombay: Education Department, Government of Maharashtra, April, 14, 1989; reprinted by Dr. Ambedkar Foundation, January 2014.

———. *The Untouchables: Who They Were and Why They Became Untouchables.* 1948; reprint Shravasti, India: Bharatiya Bauddha Shiksha Parishad, 1977.

———. "Waiting for a Visa." In *Dr. Babasaheb Ambedkar: Writings and Speeches*, Vol. 12, edited by Vasant Moon, 661–692. Bombay: Education Department, Government of Maharashtra, 1993.

———. *What Congress and Gandhi Have Done to the Untouchables.* Bombay: Thacker & Co., 1945.

———. "Which Is Worse? Slavery or Untouchability?" In *Dr. Babasaheb Ambedkar: Writings and Speeches* Vol. 12, edited by Vasant Moon, 741–759. Bombay: Education Department, Government of Maharashtra, 1993. https://archive.org/stream/Ambedkar_CompleteWorks/62.Which%20is%20Worse_Slavery%20or%20Untouchability_djvu.txt. Accessed September 15, 2020.

———. *Who Were the Shudras? How They Came to Be the Fourth Varna in the Indo-Aryan Society.* Bombay: Thackers, 1970.

———. *Writings and Speeches*, 12 vols. Bombay: Education Department, Government of Maharashtra, 1979–1993.

Birmingham Times. "Martin Luther King, Jr. Black History Quotes." July 15, 2015.

Bose, Sudhindra. "Sir Rabindranath Tagore at the State University of Iowa." *Modern Review* 21, no. 2 (February 1917): 216–220.

Chatterjee, Ramananda. "Rabindranath Tagore in America." *Modern Review* 21 (June 1917).

Craig, F. W. S., ed., *British General Election Manifestos: 1918–1966.* Chichester, UK: Political Reference Publications, 1970.

Daily Iowa Capitol. "Swami Vivekananda Tells of Ancient Faith Speaks Again Tonight." November 28, 1893.

Das, Taraknath. "International Aspects of the Indian Question." *The Independent Hindustan* 1, no. 6 (February 1921): 130–131.

———. "Review of Beasts, Men and Gods." *The People*, March 7, 1926. NMML, New Delhi.

———. "Young Asia and World Peace." *The People*, August 8, 1926. NMML, New Delhi.

———. Taraknath Das to Lala Lajpat Rai. *The People*, August 2, 1927 (featured in the October 6, 1927, edition of *The People*). NMML, New Delhi.

———. "Young Asia and World Peace." *The People*, August 8, 1926. NMML, New Delhi.

———. "American Policies Today." *The People*, January 16, 1927. NMML, New Delhi.

———. *Is Japan a Menace to Asia?* Shanghai, 1917.

———. Taraknath Das to J. T. Sunderland. June 17, 1925. In Tapan K. Mukherjee, *Taraknath Das: Life and Letters of a Revolutionary in Exile.* Jadavpur: National Council of Education, 1998.

———. "Our National Life Is at Stake." *Free Hindusthan* 1, no. 1 (April 1908).

De Valera, Eamonn. "Address Delivered at the India Freedom dinner of the Friends of Freedom for India, on February 28, 1920, at the Central Opera House, New York City." *India & Ireland.* Friends of Freedom for India, New York, 1920.

Devi, Sahadhini. Sahadhini Devi to Lala Lajpat Rai, "Congress President on Untouchability." *The People.* February 8, 1927. NMML, New Delhi.

Dixie. "Our First Anniversary Dinner." *Young India* 1 (December 1918).

Douglas, William O. *Strange Lands and Friendly People.* New York: Harper & Brothers Publishers, 1951.

Du Bois, W. E. B. "To the Nations of the World." Speech, London, July 25, 1900. In *My Life and Work*, edited by Alexander Walters, 257–260. New York: Fleming H. Revell Company, 1917.

———. "An Appeal to the World: A Statement of Denial of Human Rights to Minorities" (1947). https://www.Blackpast.org/global-african-history/primary-documents-global-african-history/1947-w-e-b-DuBois-appeal-world-statement-denial-human-rights-minorities-case-citizens-n/. Accessed March 1, 2021.

———. "As the Crow Flies." August 4, 1950. http://credo.library.umass.edu/view/full/mums312-b216-i250. Accessed September 21, 2020.

———. "Doubts Gandhi's Plan." *Amsterdam News*, March 13, 1943. In *W.E.B. Du Bois: A Reader*, edited by David Levering Lewis, 409–410. New York: Henry Holt and Company, 1995.

———. "Dr. Holmes, the Community Church, and World Brotherhood" (1948). https://credo.library.umass.edu/view/full/mums312-b229-i073. Accessed March 3, 2021.

———. "Gandhi and the American Negro." *Gandhi Marg* (July 1957).

———. *The Souls of Black Folk.* New York: New American Library, 1903.

———. *The Souls of Black Folk.* New York: Oxford University Press, 2007.

———. *Dusk of Dawn: An Essay toward an Autobiography of a Race Concept.* New Brunswick, NJ: Transaction, 1984 (originally published 1940).

———. "India." Originally published in *Freedomways* 5, no. 1 (Winter 1965). Reprinted in *Against Racism: Unpublished Essays, Papers, Addresses, 1887–1961*, edited by Herbert Aptheker, 115–117. Amherst: University of Massachusetts Press, 1985.

———. *Newspaper Columns,* Vol. 1, edited by Herbert Aptheker, 167–168. White Plains, NY: Kraus-Thomson, 1986. (Column from the *Pittsburg Courier* in February 1937.)

———. "Open Letter to Pandit Jawaharlal Nehru, Prime Minister of India." October 10, 1949, Special Collections and University Archives, University of Massachusetts Amherst Libraries. https://www.digitalcommonwealth.org/search/commonwealth-oai:9s1695924. Accessed September 21, 2020.

———. "The Woes of India." *The Crisis* 22 (May 1921).

———. "Triumph." *The Crisis* 2 (September 1911).

———. "The World in Council." *The Crisis* 2 (September 1911).

———. "Gandhi and India." *The Crisis* 23, no. 5 (March 1922): 203–207.

———. "Again Africa." *The Crisis* 23, no. 6 (April 1922): 247–252.

———. "The World and Us." *The Crisis* 23, no. 6 (April 1922).

———. "Foreign News." *The Crisis* 39 (1932).

———. "The Clash of Colour." *The Aryan Path* 7, no. 3 (March 1936).

———. "The Union of Colour." *The Aryan Path* 7, no. 10 (October 1936).

———. "The First Universal Races Congress." In *The Oxford W.E.B. Du Bois Reader*, edited by Eric J. Sundquist, ch. 1. New York: Oxford University Press, 1996.

———. "Tribute to Rai from W.E.B Du Bois." *The People*, April 13, 1929. NMML, New Delhi.

———. Letter from W. E. B. Du Bois to B. R. Ambedkar, July 31, 1946.

———. W. E. B. Du Bois to Mohandas K. Gandhi, February 19, 1929.

———. W. E. B. Du Bois to Lala Lajpat Rai, November 9, 1927.

———. W. E. B. Du Bois to Rabindranath Tagore, February 19, 1929.

———. Du Bois to White, May 2, 1942, Reel 54, Du Bois Papers.

Du Bois, W. E. B. and David L. Lewis. *W.E.B. Du Bois: A Reader*. New York: Macmillan, 1995.

Evening Tribune. "Swami Vivekananda Tells about the Religion of High Caste Indians." Lawrence, Massachusetts, May 16, 1894.

Franklin, George. "Philadelphia Rings the Liberty Bell of India." *Independent Hindustan*, October 1920.

Friends of Freedom for India Pamphlet (1916), Slide 403, Reel 5, W.E.B. Du Bois Papers.

Gandhi, M. K. *Collected Works of Mahatma Gandhi*, Vol. 1 (July 4, 1888–November 30, 1896). Delhi: Publications Division, Ministry of Information and Broadcasting, 1958.

———. *The Collected Works of Mahatma Gandhi*, Vol. XIX. Delhi Publications Division, Ministry of Information and Broadcasting, 1958.

———. "For Passive Resisters." *Indian Opinion*, October 26, 1907.

———. "Message to the American Negro." May 1, 1929. W. E. B. Du Bois Papers (MS 312). Special Collections and University Archives, University of Massachusetts Amherst Libraries.

———. "Non-Violent Resistance." In Lawrence A. Rosenwald, "The Theory, Practice, and Influence of Thoreau's Civil Disobedience," in *A Historical Guide to Henry David Thoreau*, edited by William E. Cain, 153–180. New York, NY, 2000; online edn, Oxford Academic, October 31, 2023. https://doi.org/10.1093/oso/9780195138627.003.0006. Accessed April 22, 2024.

Grant, Madison. *The Passing of the Great Race: Or the Racial Basis of European History*. New York: Scribner's Sons, 1922.

Hardayal, Lala. "The Social Conquest of the Hindu Race and the Meaning of Equality." San Francisco: Hindustan Ghadar Party, December 1913, p. 5. Folder 3, box 2, South Asians in North America Collection.

———. "Social Conquest of the Hindu Race." Reprinted from December 1909 article in *The Modern Review Calcutta* in *The Independent Hindustan* 1, no. 8 (April 1921). https://www.saada.org/item/20120807-1030. Accessed April 22, 2024.

———. *Forty-four Months in Germany and Turkey*. 1920.

Hindustan Ghadar Party. "An Open Letter to the People at Large." San Francisco, CA, USA.

Hughes, Langston. "To Understand America, Nehru Should Visit Negro Ghettos Too." *The Chicago Defender,* November 5, 1949.

Independent Hindustan. "California Labor Stands for Freedom of India." September 1920, 72.

Indian Opinion 9, no. 31 (August 5, 1911).

Indian Opinion 9, no. 34 (August 26, 1911).

Indian Opinion 9, no. 36 (September 9, 1911).

Jewish Telegraphic Agency. "World Migration Congress Is Opened in London." June 23, 1926. https://www.jta.org/1926/06/23/archive/world-migration-congress-is-opened-in-london. Accessed May 2, 2021.

King, Jr., Martin Luther. "The Death of Evil upon the Seashore." Speech at the Cathedral of St. John the Divine, New York City, May 17, 1956.

Lal, Mohan. "Lalaji and the Depressed Classes." *The People,* April 13, 1929. NMML, New Delhi.

Letter from *The Aryan Path* to W.E.B. Du Bois, October 10, 1935. W. E. B. Du Bois Papers (MS 312) Special Collections and University Archives, University of Massachusetts Amherst Libraries.

Lewis, E. H. *The Work of Tagore.* Chicago: Chicago Literary Club, 1917.

Lincoln, Abraham. "House Divided." Illinois Republican State Convention. Springfield, Illinois, June 16, 1858.

———. "Peoria Speech." Speech, Peoria, Illinois, October 16, 1894.

Malcolm X. "Not Just an American Problem, but a World Problem" (Speech delivered in the Corn Hill Methodist Church, Rochester, New York, February 16, 1965). In *Malcolm X: The Last Speeches,* edited by Bruce Perry, 151–181. New York: Pathfinder Press, 1989.

———. *Malcolm X Speaks: Selected Speeches and Statements.* Edited by George Breitman, 33–38. New York: Grove Weidenfeld, 1990.

Manawatu Times. "World Migration Congress." 49, no. 3383 (June 25, 1926).

McKinley, William (President). "Benevolent Assimilation Proclamation." December 21, 1898.

McLaurin, Dunbar S. "India Would Welcome Negro Ambassador." *The Pittsburgh Courier,* March 4, 1950.

Müller, F. Max. *Biographies of Words and the Home of the Aryas.* New York: Longmans, Green, and Co., 1888).

National Association for the Advancement of Colored People. "NAACP Timeline." https://web.archive.org/web/20100617133445/http:/www.naacp.org/about/history/timeline/. Accessed on January 17, 2020.

Nehru, Jawaharlal. *An Autobiography.* New Delhi: The Bodley Head, 1936.

New York Evening Post. "Explosion of Asia as Menace to Peace." September 22, 1917.

New York Times. November 14, 1913.

———. November 15, 1913.

———. "Race Discrimination." May 13, 1928.

New York Tribune. November 14, 1913.

Ovington, Mary White. *The People*, January 3 and 10, 1929. NMML, New Delhi.

Plessy v. Ferguson, 163 U.S. 559 (1896).

Rai, Lala Lajpat. "Introduction." In Lala Har Dayal, *Our Educational Problem*. Madras: Tagore and Company, 1922.

———. Lala Lajpat Rai to W. E. B. Du Bois, October 6, 1927.

———. "Supplement to '*The People*' for December 3, 1925." *The People*, December 6, 1925. Nehru Memorial Museum and Library (NMML), New Delhi.

———. "Servants of the People Society and Tilak School of Politics." *The People*, March 7, 1926. NMML, New Delhi.

———. "Reconstruction of Hindu Society." *The People*, October 20, 1927. NMML, New Delhi.

———. *The Arya Samaj: Aan Account of Its Aims, Doctrine and Activities, with a Biographical Sketch of the Founder.* London: Longman Publishing, 1915.

———. "The Clash of Colour." *The People*, May 23, 1926. NMML, New Delhi.

———. "The Clash of Colour II." *The People*, May 30, 1926. NMML, New Delhi.

———. "Impracticable Idealism." *The People*, January 30, 1927. NMML, New Delhi.

———. "Mother India." *The People*, September 8, 1927. NMML, New Delhi.

———. "America in the East." *The People*, July 26, 1925. NMML, New Delhi.

———. "World Migration and Colour Question." *The People*, July 25, 1926 (World Migration Conference speech by Lala Lajpat Rai). NMML, New Delhi.

———. "The Problem of Minorities." *The* People, November 1, 1928. NMML, New Delhi.

———. "The World Today." *The People*, September 12, 1926. NMML, New Delhi.

———. "Nationalism and Caste." *The People*, January 16, 1927. NMML, New Delhi.

———. "Government Refuses to Help Untouchables." *The* People, March 1, 1928. NMML, New Delhi.

———. *The Problem of National Education in India.* London: George Allen & Unwin Ltd, 1920.

———. *The United States of America: A Hindu's Impressions and a Study*. Calcutta: Brahmo Mission Press, 1916.

———. *Unhappy India*. Calcutta: Banna Publishing, 1928.

———. *Young India*, January 1918.

Rao, N. S. Subba. "The Union of Colour." *The Aryan Path* 7, no. 3 (May 1936): 111–115.

Redding, Saunders. "A Report from India." *The American Scholar* 22, no. 4 (1953): 441–449.

———. *An American in India: A Personal Report on the India Dilemma and her Conflicts*. New York: The Bobbs-Merrill Co., Inc, 1954.

Roosevelt, Eleanor. *India and the Awakening East*. New York: Harper and Row, 1953.

San Francisco Examiner. October 5, 1916.

Seal, Brajendranath. "Meaning of Race, Tribe, Nation." Speech, London, UK, June 1911. https://archive.org/stream/papersoninterrac00univiala/papersoninterrac00univiala_djvu.txt. Accessed April 1, 2021.

Sunderland, J. T. *The People*, January 3 and 10, 1929. NMML, New Delhi.

——— "Communications: India's Need of Foreign Propaganda." *The People*, May 16, 1926. NMML, New Delhi.

Tagore, Rabindranath. "A Message to the American Negro from Rabindranath Tagore." Ca. July 1929. https://credo.library.umass.edu/view/collection/mums312. Accessed April 19, 2024.

———. "A Monotony of Multitudes" (1924). In *From the Outer World*, edited by Oscar Handlin and Lilian Handlin, 57–64. Cambridge, MA: Harvard University Press, 1997.

———. "Bharatbarser Itihas: Hemlata Devi" (1903). British Library, London.

———. "Safalatar Sadupay." In *Rabindra Rachanabali*, Vol. 13. Kolkata: West Bengal Government, 1990.

———. *Selected Letters of Rabindranath Tagore*. Edited by Krishna Dutta and Andrew Robinson. Cambridge: Cambridge University Press, 1997.

———. "Nationalism in the West." In *Nationalism*, 11–62. New York: Macmillan, 1917.

———. "Nationalism in India" (1917). In *Indian Philosophy in English: From Renaissance to Independence*, edited by Nalini Bhushan and Jay L. Garfield, 22–36. New York: Oxford University Press, 2011.

———. Rabindranath Tagore to Somendrachandra Devbarma, October 12, 1913.

———. *Selected Poems of Rabindranath Tagore*. Edited by William Radice. London: Penguin Classics, 2005.

———. *The English Writings of Rabindranath Tagore*. Edited by Sisir Kumar Das, 3 vols. New Delhi: Sahitya Akademi, 1994–1996.

The Anti-Slavery Reporter. August 1, 1865.

The Atlanta Daily World. "Nehru Presented Life Membership in NAACP." November 11, 1949.

The Chicago Defender. "A Hindu Speaks His Mind about Us." November 29, 1930.

———. "American Crusade against Lynching to See President." *The Chicago Defender (National Edition) (1921–1967)*, September 28, 1946: ProQuest Historical Newspapers, *Chicago Defender*, 2. https://search.proquest.com/docview/492741205. Accessed September 23, 2020.

———. "Another Hindu Writes." December 13, 1930, 12.

The Crisis. 19, no. 2 (November 1919).

———. Announcement of Tagore statement, ca. 1929.

The Hindu. "From the Archives (June 3, 1919): Mr. Tilak's Service. Mr. Gandhi's Speech." June 3, 2019. https://www.thehindu.com/archives/mr-tilaks-service-mr-gandhis-speech/article27406589.ece. Accessed September 27, 2019.

The Independent. "The First Universal Races Congress." 70, August 24, 1911.

The People. April 13, 1929.

The New York Amsterdam News. "Jawaharlal Nehru Joins the NAACP." November 12, 1949.

The People. "Tribute from A. Fenner Brockway." April 13, 1929. NMML, New Delhi.

———. "Tribute from Roger Nash Baldwin." April 13, 1929. NMML, New Delhi.

The Times-Democrat. "Springfield's Riot Bill." New Orleans, Louisiana, September 19, 1908.

Thoreau, Henry David. "Resistance to Civil Government." In Elizabeth Palmer Peabody, *Aesthetic Papers*, 189–213. New York: G.P. Putnam, 1849.

U.S. Bureau of Justice Statistics. "Prisoners in 2011," 8 tbl. 8 (December 2012). https://bjs.ojp.gov/content/pub/pdf/p11.pdf. Accessed April 18, 2024.

Villard, Oswald Garrison. "'NATION' EDITOR'S MESSAGE: Oswald Garrison Villard." *The People,* January 3 and 10, 1929. NMML, New Delhi.

Vivekananda, Swami. "Response to Welcome" Speech, Chicago, September 11, 1893. Belur Math. https://belurmath.org/swami-vivekananda-speeches-at-the-parliament-of-religions-chicago-1893/.

———. "The Future of India." *The Complete Works of Swami Vivekananda,* Vol. 3. Mayavati: Advaita Ashrama, 1927.

———. "The Great Teachers of the World" (Delivered at the Shakespeare Club, Pasadena, California, February 3, 1900). In *Complete Works of Swami Vivekananda,* Vol. 4. Mayavati: Advaita Ashrama, 1927.

————. "The Way to the Realisation of a Universal Religion" (Delivered in the Universalist Church, Pasadena, California, January 28, 1900). In *Complete Works of Swami Vivekananda*, Vol. 2. Mayavati: Advaita Ashrama, 1927.

Weatherly, Ulysses G. "The First Universal Races Congress." *The American Journal of Sociology* 17, no. 3 (1911): 315–328.

Wilson, Woodrow. "State of the Union 1913." December 2, 1913.

Young India. "Farewell Dinners." 3, no.1, (January 1920): 11–14.

Secondary Sources

Books

Ackerman, Peter, and Jack DuVall. *A Force More Powerful: A Century of Nonviolent Conflict*. New York: St Martin's Press, 2000.

Ahmed, Talat. *Mohandas Gandhi: Experiments in Civil Disobedience*. London: Pluto Press, 2019.

Airriess, Christopher A. *Contemporary Ethnic Geographies in America*. Lanham, MD: Rowman and Littlefield, 2006.

Alexander, Michelle. *The New Jim Crow: Mass Incarceration in the Age of Color Blindness*. New York: The New Press, 2010.

Anderson, Carol Elaine. *Eyes Off the Prize: African-Americans, the United Nations, and the Struggle for Human Rights, 1944–1952* (Columbus: The Ohio State University, 1995).

Arnold, K. R. *Anti-Immigration in the United States: A Historical Encyclopedia*. Westport, CT: Greenwood Press, 2011.

Aufderheide, Arthur C., Conrado Rodríguez-Martín, and Odin Langsjoen. *The Cambridge Encyclopedia of Human Paleopathology*. Cambridge: Cambridge University Press, 1998.

Bayly, C. A. *Empire and Information: Intelligence Gathering and Social Communication in India, 1780–1870*. New York: Cambridge University Press, 1996.

Bayly, Susan. *Caste, Society and Politics in India from the Eighteenth Century to the Modern Age*. New York: Cambridge University Press, 1999.

Berreman, Gerald D. "Caste in India and the United States." *The American Journal of Sociology* 66, no. 2 (1960): 120–127.

Beteille, Andre. *Caste, Class and Power: Changing Patterns of Stratification in a Tanjore Village*. Berkeley: University of California, 1965.

Bhole, L. M. *Essays on Gandhian Socio-Economics*. Delhi: Shipra Publications, 2000.

Braunthal, Julius. *History of the International: Volume 2: 1914–1943* [1963]. Translated by John Clark. New York: Frederick A. Praeger, 1967.

Brown, Emily C. *Har Dayal: Dalit Revolutionary and Rationalist*. Tucson: University of Arizona Press, 1975.

Brown, Judith Margaret. *Gandhi: Prisoner of Hope*. New Haven: Yale University Press, 1991.

————. *Modern India: The Origins of an Asian Democracy*. Oxford: Oxford University Press, 1994.

Bruner, Robert, and Sean Carr. *The Panic of 1907: Lessons Learned from the Market's Perfect Storm*. Hoboken, NJ: John Wiley and Sons, 2007.

Bryant, Edwin F., and Laurie L. Patton. *The Indo-Aryan Controversy: Evidence and Inference in Indian History*. London: Routledge, 2005.

Chakrabarti, Mohit. *Rabindranath Tagore: Diverse Dimensions*. New Delhi: Atlantic Publishers and Distributers, 1990.

Chakravorty, C. Sanjoy, Devesh Kapur, and Nirvikar Singh. *The Other One Percent: Indians in America*. New York, NY: Oxford University Press, 2017.

Chaturvedi, Vinayak. "Cosmopolitan Thought Zones: South Asia and the Global Circulation of Ideas." *Journal of Global History* 6, no. 3 (November 2011): 538–539.

Chunder, Rajarshi. "Tagore and Caste: From Brahmacharyasram to Swadeshi Movement (1901–07)." *Sahapedia* (September 19, 2018).

Cooper Jr., John Milton. *Woodrow Wilson*. New York: Knopf Doubleday Publishing Group, 2009.

Desai, Ashwin, and Goolam Vahed. *The South African Gandhi: Stretcher-Bearer of Empire*. Redwood City: Stanford University Press, 2015.

Dirks, Nicholas. *Castes of Mind: Colonialism and the Making of Modern India*. Princeton, NJ: Princeton University Press, 2001.

Duberman, Martin B. *Paul Robeson*. London: Bodley Head, 1989.

Dudziak, Mary L. *Cold War Civil Rights: Race and the Image of American Democracy*. Princeton: Princeton University Press, 2000.

Dumont, Louis. *Homo Hierarchicus: The Caste System and its Implications*. Chicago: Chicago University Press, 1970.

Dutta, K., and A. Robinson. *Rabindranath Tagore: An Anthology*. Saint Martin: Saint Martin's Press, 1997.

————. *Rabindranath Tagore: The Myriad-Minded Man*. Saint Martin: Saint Martin's Press, 1995.

Edwards, Linda. *A Brief Guide to Beliefs: Ideas, Theologies, Mysteries, and Movements*. Louisville: Westminster John Knox Press, 2001.

Finkelman, Paul. *Encyclopedia of African American History, 1896 to the Present: From the Age of Segregation to the Twenty-first Century, Five-volume Set*. Oxford: Oxford University Press, 2009.

Fox, Richard G. *Kin, Clan, Raja and Rule! State–Hinterland Relations in Pre-industrial India*. Berkeley: University of California Press, 1971.

Ghodke, H. M. *Revolutionary Nationalism in Western India*. New Delhi: Classical Publishing Company, 1990.

Ghurye, G. S. *Caste and Race in India*. Bombay: Popular Prakashan, 1969.

Guha, Arun Chandra. *First Spark of Revolution*. Mumbai: Oriental Longmans, 1971.

Guha, Sumit. *Beyond Caste: Identity and Power in South Asia, Past and Present*. Leiden: Brill, 2013.

Gupta, Dipankar. *Interrogating Caste: Understanding Hierarchy and Difference in Indian Society*. New Delhi: Penguin, 2000.

Gupta, Jugal Kishore. *History of Sirsa Town*. New Delhi: Atlantic Publishers & Distributors, 1991.

Gupta, Om. *Encyclopedia of India, Pakistan and Bangladesh*. Delhi: Gyan Books, 2006.

Haney-López, I. F. *White by Law: The Legal Construction of Race*. New York and London: New York University Press, 1996.

Hill, Robert A. *Marcus Garvey and UNIA Papers, Vol. 1* (1826–August 1919). Los Angeles: University of California Press, 1983.

Hitchens, Christopher. *Blood, Class, and Empire: The Enduring Anglo–American Relationship*. New York: Nation Books, 2004.

Horne, Gerald. *Black Revolutionary: William Patterson and the Globalization of the African American Freedom Struggle*. Urbana, Chicago, and Springfield: University of Illinois Press, 2013.

———. *End of Empires: African Americans and India*. Philadelphia: Temple University Press, 2008.

———. *W.E.B. Du Bois: A Biography*. Westport, CT: Greenwood Press, 2010.

Ilbert, Sir Courtenay Peregrine. *The Government of India*. Oxford: Clarendon Press, 1922.

Immerwahr, Daniel. *How to Hide an Empire: A History of the Greater United States*. New York: Picador, Farrar, Straus, and Giroux, 2019.

Isaacs, Harold R. *Scratches on Our Minds: American Views of China and India*. Armonk, NY: M.E Sharpe, 1980.

Jaffrelot, Christopher. *Dr. Ambedkar and Untouchability: Fighting the Indian Caste System*. New York: Columbia University Press, 2005.

Jayawardena, Kumari. *The White Woman's Other Burden: Western Women and South Asia during British Colonial Rule*. London: Routledge, 1995.

Johnson, Richard L. *Gandhi's Experiments with Truth: Essential Writings by and about Mahatma Gandhi*. Washington, DC: Lexington Books, 2006.

Kennedy, Malcolm D. *The Estrangement of Great Britain and Japan.* Los Angeles: University of California Press, 1969.

Knafla, Louis A. *Raj and Born Criminals Crime, Gender, and Sexuality in Criminal Prosecutions.* Westport, CT: Greenwood Publishing Group, 2002.

Knock, Thomas J. *To End All Wars: Woodrow Wilson and the Quest for a New World Order.* Princeton: Princeton University Press, 1995.

Kopf, David. *The Brahmo Samaj and the Shaping of the Modern Indian Mind.* Princeton, NJ: Princeton University Press, 1979.

Lal, Mohan. *Encyclopaedia of Indian Literature: Sasay to Zorgot.* New Delhi: Sahitya Akademi, 1992.

Lewis, David Levering. *W.E.B. Du Bois: Biography of a Race 1868–1919.* New York: Henry Holt and Company, 1993.

———. *W.E.B. Du Bois: A Biography.* New York: Henry Holt and Company, 2009.

Lorca, Arnulf Becker. *Mestizo International Law: A Global Intellectual History 1842–1933*, Cambridge Studies in International and Comparative Law. Cambridge: Cambridge University Press, 2015.

Macdonell, Arthur Anthony, and Arthur Barriedale Keith. *Vedic Index of Names and Subjects, Vol. 2.* London: John Murray, 1912.

Manela, Erez. *The Wilsonian Moment: Self-Determination and the International Origins of Anticolonial Nationalism.* Oxford: Oxford University Press, 2007.

Manjapra, Kris. *Age of Entanglement.* Cambridge, MA: Harvard University Press, 2014.

Marshall, Gordon. "Caste." In *A Dictionary of Sociology*, edited by John Scott. Oxford, UK; New York, NY: Oxford University Press, 2005.

Moffat, Chris. *India's Revolutionary Inheritance Politics and the Promise of Bhagat Singh.* Cambridge: Cambridge University Press, 2019.

Mukherjee, Mridula. *Peasants in India's Non-Violent Revolution: Practice and Theory.* New Delhi: Sage Publications, 2004.

Muldoon, Andrew. *Empire, Politics and the Creation of the 1935 India Act: Last Act of the Raj.* London: Routledge, 2016.

Mulkearn, Lois and Edwin V. Pugh. *A Traveler's Guide to Historic Western Pennsylvania.* Pittsburgh: University of Pittsburgh Press, 1954.

Mullen, Bill V., and Cathryn Watson. *W.E.B. Du Bois on Asia: Crossing the World Color Line.* Jackson: University Press of Mississippi, 2005.

Myrdal, Gunnar. *An American Dilemma, Volume I: The Negro in a White Nation.* New York: McGraw Hill, 1964 (originally published 1944).

Nauriya, Anil. *The African Element in Gandhi.* Delhi: Gyan Publishing House, 2006.

Pandey, Gyanendra. *A History of Prejudice: Race, Caste, and Difference in India and the United States.* New Delhi: University of Cambridge Press, 2013.

Pathak, Sushil Madhava. *American Missionaries and Hinduism: A Study of Their Contacts from 1813 to 1910*. Delhi: Munshiram Manoharlal, 1967.

Peers, Douglas. *India and the British Empire*. New York: Oxford University Press, 2012.

Plummer, Brenda Gayle. *Rising Wind Black Americans and U.S. Foreign Affairs, 1935–1960*. Chapel Hill: University of North Carolina Press, 1996.

Price, Ruth. *The Lives of Agnes Smedley*. Oxford: Oxford University Press, 2005.

Radhakrishna, Meena. *Dishonoured by History: 'Criminal Tribes' and British Colonial Policy*. Hyderabad, India: Orient Blackswan, 2001.

Rafter, Kevin. *Sinn Féin, 1905–2005: In the Shadow of Gunmen*. Dublin: Gill & Macmillan, 2005.

Rai, Raghunath. *History*. Faridabad, India: VK Global Publications, 2014.

Rangaswamy, Padma. *Namasté America: Indian Immigrants in an American Metropolis*. University Park: Pennsylvania State University Press, 2000.

Sinha, Mrinalini. *Specters of Mother India: The Global Restructuring of an Empire*. Durham: Duke University Press, 2006.

Slate, Nico. *Colored Cosmopolitanism: The Shared Struggle for Freedom in the United States and India*. Cambridge, MA: Harvard University Press, 2012.

———. *Lord Cornwallis Is Dead: The Struggle for Democracy in the United States and India*. Cambridge, MA: Harvard University Press, 2019.

Sohi, Seema. *Echoes of Mutiny: Race, Surveillance, and Indian Anticolonialism in North America*. New York: Oxford University Press, 2014.

Stanton, Andrea. *An Encyclopedia of Cultural Sociology of the Middle East, Asia, and Africa*. New York: Sage Publications, 2012.

Swetnam, George. *The Bicentennial history of Pittsburgh and Allegheny County*. Pittsburgh: University of Pittsburgh Digital Research Library, 1956.

Swindall, Lindsey R. *Paul Robeson: A Life of Activism and Art*. Landham, MD: Rowman and Littlefield Publishers, Inc, 2013.

Talwalkar, Govind. *Gopal Krishna Gokhale: Gandhi's Political Guru*. New Delhi: Pentagon Press, 2015.

Tharoor, Shashi. *Nehru: The Invention of India*. New York: Arcade Publishing, 2003.

The Oxford Companion to English Literature, 6th edition. Oxford: Oxford University Press, 2006.

Trautmann, Thomas R. *Aryans and British India*. New Delhi: Vistaar Publications, 1997.

Versluis, Arthur. *The Esoteric Origins of the American Renaissance*. Oxford: Oxford University Press, 2001.

Vertovec, S. *The Hindu Diaspora: Comparative Patterns*. London: Routledge, 2000.

Warnke, Georgia. *After Identity: Rethinking Race, Sex, and Gender.* Cambridge: Cambridge University Press, 2007.

Wilkerson, Isabel. *Caste: The Origins of Our Discontents.* New York, Random House, 2020.

Winthrop, Robert H. *Dictionary of Concepts in Cultural Anthropology.* Santa Barbara, CA: ABC-CLIO, 1991.

Wolpert, Stanley. *Gandhi's Passion: The Life and Legacy of Mahatma Gandhi.* Oxford: Oxford University Press, 2002.

———. *Tilak and Gokhale: Revolution and Reform in the Making of Modern India.* New Delhi: S.K. Mookerjee, 1989.

Yudell, Michael. *Race Unmasked: Biology and Race in The Twentieth Century.* New York: Columbia University Press, 2014.

Zhao, X. and Park, E. J. W. *Asian Americans: An Encyclopedia of Social, Cultural, Economic, and Political History*. Westport: Greenwood, 2013.

Articles and Essays

"A Timeline of Tagore's Life and Work." http://www.rabindratirtha-wbhidcoltd.co.in/Rabisarani/event/VZlSXRFWwJlUsRmdT1WNXJ1aKVVVB1TP. Accessed January 30, 2021.

Ahmad, Dohra. "'More Than Romance': Genre and Geography in 'Dark Princess.'" *ELH* 69, no. 3 (2002): 775–803.

Alexander, Michelle. "The War on Drugs and the New Jim Crow." *Race, Poverty and the Environment* 17, no. 1 (2010): 75–77.

American Civil Liberties Union. "The War on Marijuana in Black and White." https://www.aclu.org/feature/war-marijuana-Black-and-white. Accessed May 2, 2021.

Appadurai, Arjun. "Comparing Race to Caste Is an Interesting Idea, but There Are Crucial Differences Between Both." Review of *Caste: The Origins of Our Discontents,* by Isabel Wilkerson. *The Wire.* September 12, 2020.

Appia, Kwame Anthony and Henry Louis Gates Jr. "Civil Rights Congress." In *Civil Rights: An A–Z Reference of the Movement That Changed America,* 187–189. Philadelphia: Running Press, 2004.

Bains, J. S. "Lala Lajpat Rai's Idealism and Indian National Movement." *The Indian Journal of Political Science* 46, no. 4 (1985): 401–420.

Balaji, Murali. "Indian Independence and the African American Struggle." *Little India: Overseas Indian, NRI, Asian Indian, Indian American,* August 14, 2007. https://littleindia.com/indian-independence-and-the-african-american-struggle/. Accessed August 1, 2020.

Barnes, Robert. "Between the Blocs: India, the United Nations, and Ending the Korean War." *The Journal of Korean Studies* 18, no. 2 (2013): 263–286.

Bates, Crispin. "Race, Caste and Tribe in Central India: The Early Origins of Indian Anthropometry." *Edinburgh Papers in South Asian Studies* no. 3 (1995): 1–35.

———. "Race, Caste and Tribe in Central India: The Early Origins of Indian Anthropometry." In *The Concept of Race in South Asia*, edited by P. Robb, 219–259. New Delhi: Oxford University Press, 1995.

Bhargav, Vanya. "Lala Lajpat Rai's Ideas on Caste: Conservative or Radical?" *Studies in Indian Politics* 6, no. 1 (June 2018): 15–26.

Bose, Neilesh. "Taraknath Das (1884–1958), British Columbia, and the Anti-Colonial Borderlands." *BC Studies* 204 (2020): 67–88.

Brown, Emily. "Book Reviews; South Asia." *The Journal of Asian Studies* 32, no. 3 (May 1973): 522–523.

Buchanan, Andrew N. "The War Crisis and the Decolonization of India, December 1941–September 1942: A Political and Military Dilemma." *Global War Studies* 8, no. 2 (2011): 5–31.

Burden-Stelly, Charisse. "Caste Does Not Explain Race." Review of *Caste: The Origins of Our Discontents*, by Isabel Wilkerson. *Boston Review*, December 15, 2020.

Carby, Hazel V. "The Limits of Caste." Review of *Caste: The Origins of Our Discontents* by Isabel Wilkerson. *London Review of Books* 43, no. 2, January 21, 2021.

Carby, Hazel V. and Adam Shatz. "The Colour Line in the Americas." *London Review of Books Conversations*, podcast audio, January 21, 2020.

Carson, Clayborne. "Two Cheers for Brown v. Board of Education." *The Journal of American History* 91, no. 1 (2004): 26–31.

Cháirez-Garza, Jesús Francisco. "Bound Hand and Foot and Handed Over to the Caste Hindus: Ambedkar, Untouchability and the Politics of Partition." *The Indian Economic and Social History Review* 55, no. 1 (2018): 1–28.

———. "B.R. Ambedkar, Franz Boas and the Rejection of Racial Theories of Untouchability." *South Asia: Journal of South Asian Studies* 41, no. 2 (2018): 281–296.

Chakrabarty, Dipesh. "Friendships in the Shadow of Empire: Tagore's Reception in Chicago, circa 1913–1932." *Modern Asian Studies* 48, no. 5 (2014): 1161–1187.

Coates, Ta-Nehisi. "The Case for Reparations." *The Atlantic*, June 2014.

Cox, Oliver C. "The Programs of Negro Civil Rights Organizations." *The Journal of Negro Education* 20, no. 3 (1951): 354–366.

Dakwar, Jamil. "W.E.B. Du Bois's Historic U.N. Petition Continues to Inspire Human Rights Advocacy." *ACLU Blog of Rights*, October 25, 2017. https://www.aclu.org/blog/human-rights/human-rights-and-racial-justice/web-du-boiss-historic-un-petition-continues. Accessed September 22, 2020.

Das, Subrata Kumar. "Tagore's Crisis in America: An Overview." https://www.academia.edu/9554036/Tagore_s_Crisis_in_America_An_Overview. Accessed November 15, 2020.

Desai, Manan. "*Oh Niagara!* Lala Lajpat Rai at Niagara Falls in 1905." September 1, 2017. https://www.saada.org/tides/article/oh-niagara. Accessed March 1, 2021.

Docker, John. "Raphaël Lemkin, Creator of the Concept of Genocide: A World History Perspective." *Humanities Research* 16, no. 2 (2010): 49–74.

———. "The Two-State Solution and Partition: World History Perspectives on Palestine and India." *Journal of Holy Land and Palestine Studies* 9, no. 2 (2010): 146–168.

Dirks, Nicholas B. "Discriminating Difference: The Postcolonial Politics of Caste in India." In *The Construction of Minorities: Cases for Comparison Across Time and Around the World*, edited by André Burguière and Raymond Grew, 593–620. Ann Arbor: University of Michigan Press, 2001.

Dudziak, Mary L. "Brown as a Cold War Case." *The Journal of American History* 91, no. 1 (2004): 32–42.

———. "Josephine Baker, Racial Protest, and the Cold War." *The Journal of American History* 81, no. 2 (1994): 543–570.

Dutt, Yashica. "Feeling Like an Outcast." *Foreign Policy*, September 17, 2020.

Dzanouni, Lamia, Hélène Le Dantec-Lowry, and Claire Parfait. "From One Crisis to the Other: History and Literature in The Crisis from 1910 to the Early 1920s." *European Journal of American Studies* [online] (November 1, 2016). http://journals.openedition.org/ejas/11432. Accessed July 15, 2021.

Ellsworth, Scott. "Tulsa Race Riot." *The Encyclopedia of Oklahoma History and Culture* (2009). https://www.okhistory.org/publications/enc/entry.php?entry=TU013. Accessed September 1, 2019.

Finseth, Ian Frederick. "The Emergence of Transcendentalism." In *American Studies and The University of Virginia*. Charlottesville, VA: The University of Virginia Press, 1995. http://xroads.virginia.edu/~MA95/finseth/trans.html. Accessed August 6, 2020.

Fischer-Tiné, Harald. "Indian Nationalism and the 'World Forces': Transnational and Diasporic Dimensions of the Indian Freedom Movement on the Eve of the First World War." *Journal of Global History* 2, no. 3 (2007): 325–344.

Frazier, Ian. "When W.E.B. Du Bois Made a Laughingstock of a White Supremacist." *The New Yorker*, August 19, 2019. https://www.newyorker.com/

magazine/2019/08/26/when-w-e-b-du-bois-made-a-laughingstock-of-a-white-supremacist. Accessed March 1, 2021.

Frederick, Norris. "William James and Swami Vivekananda: Religious Experience and Vendata/Yoga in America." *William James Studies* 9, no. 1 (2012): 37–55.

Fryer, Roland G. and Steven D. Levitt. "Hatred and Profits: Under the Hood of the Ku Klux Klan." *The Quarterly Journal of Economics* 127, no. 4 (November 1, 2012): 1883–1925.

Ganachari, Arvind Gururao. "Myron H. Phelps (1856–1916): An Early American Advocate of India's Freedom." *Proceedings of the Indian History Congress* 52 (1991): 650–657.

———. "Two Indian Revolutionary Associations Abroad: Some New Light on the Pan-Aryan Association and the Indo-Japanese Association." *Proceedings of the Indian History Congress* 57 (1996): 789–798.

Ganguly, Sumit. "Review of *Lord Cornwallis Is Dead: The Struggle for Democracy in the United States and India* by Nico Slate." *The Journal of Asian Studies* 79, no. 1 (2020): 219–220.

Ghosh, Durba. "The Reforms of 1919: Montagu–Chelmsford, the Rowlatt Act, Jails Commission, and the Royal Amnesty." In *Gentlemanly Terrorists: Political Violence and the Colonial State in India, 1919–1947*, 27–59. Cambridge: Cambridge University Press, 2017.

Gordon, Leonard A. "Mahatma Gandhi's Dialogues with Americans." *Economic and Political Weekly* 37, no. 4 (2002): 337–352.

Gowen, Robert Joseph. "British Legerdemain at the 1911 Imperial Conference: The Dominions, Defense Planning, and the Renewal of the Anglo-Japanese Alliance." *Journal of Modern History* 52, no. 3 (1980): 385–413.

Guha, Ramachandra. "Traveling with Tagore." In Rabindranath Tagore, *Nationalism* (London: Penguin Classics, 2010).

Hallberg, Gerald N. "Bellingham, Washington's Anti-Hindu Riot." *Journal of the West* 12 (January 1973): 163–175.

Hay, Stephen N. "Rabindranath Tagore in America." *American Quarterly* 14, no. 3 (1962): 439–463.

Helps, David. "'We Charge Genocide': Revisiting Black Radicals' Appeals to the World Community." *Radical Americas* 3, no. 9 (2018): 2–24.

Hinchy, Jessica. "Gender, Family, and the Policing of the 'Criminal Tribes' in Nineteenth-Century North India." *Modern Asian Studies* 54, no. 5 (2021): 1669–1711.

Immerwahr, Daniel. "Caste or Colony? Indianizing Race in the United States." *Modern Intellectual History* 4, no. 2 (2007): 275–301.

————. "Review of *Colored Cosmopolitanism: The Shared Struggle for Freedom in the United States and India* by Nico Slate." *Journal of Social History* 47, no. 2 (2013): 547–549.

Kämpchen, Martin. "Rabindranath Tagore and Germany." *Indian Literature* 33, no. 3 (May–June 1990): 109–140.

Karuka, Manu. "Black and Native Visions of Self-Determination." *Critical Ethnic Studies* 3, no. 2 (2017): 77–98.

Kearney, Reginald. "The Pro-Japanese Utterances of W.E.B. Du Bois." *Contributions in Black Studies* 13, no. 7 (1995): 201–217. https://scholarworks.umass.edu/cgi/viewcontent.cgi?article=1128&context=cibs. Accessed April 18, 2024.

Kishwar, Madhu. "Arya Samaj and Women's Education: Kanya Mahavidyalaya, Jalandhar." *Economic and Political Weekly* 21, no. 17 (1986): WS9–24.

Kumar, Ajay. "Sexual Violence against Dalit Women: An Analytical Study of Intersectionality of Gender, Caste, and Class in India." *Journal of International Women's Studies* 22, no. 10 (2021): 123–134.

Kumar, Narender. "Ambedkar Villages: An Alternative to Village Development – Case Studies from Lucknow." *Contemporary Voice of Dalit* 6, no. 1 (January 2013): 9–24.

Lahiri, Madhumita. "World Romance: Genre, Internationalism, and W.E.B. Du Bois." *Callaloo* 33, no. 2 (2010): 537–552.

Lee, Erika. "Hemispheric Orientalism and the 1907 Pacific Coast Race Riots." *Amerasia Journal* 33, no. 2 (2007): 19–48.

————. "The 'Yellow Peril' and Asian Exclusion in the Americas." *Pacific Historical Review* 76, no. 4 (November 2007): 537–562.

Lester, Anthony. "Brown v. Board of Education Overseas." *Proceedings of the American Philosophical Society* 148, no. 4 (2004): 455–463.

Manela, Erez. "Imagining Woodrow Wilson in Asia: Dreams of East–West Harmony and the Revolt against Empire in 1919." *The American Historical Review* 111, no. 5 (2006): 1327–1351.

Martin, Charles H. "Internationalizing 'The American Dilemma': The Civil Rights Congress and the 1951 Genocide Petition to the United Nation." *Journal of American Ethnic History* 16, no. 4 (1997): 35–61.

————. "The Civil Rights Congress and Southern Black Defendants." *The Georgia Historical Quarterly* 71, no. 1 (1987): 25–52.

Mauer, Marc. "Addressing Racial Disparities in Incarceration." *The Prison Journal* 91, no. 3 suppl. (September 2011): 87S–88S.

McIntosh, Kriston, Emily Moss, Ryan Nunn, and Jay Shambaugh. "Examining the Black–White Wealth Gap." *Brookings Institute*, February 27, 2020.

https://www.brookings.edu/blog/up-front/2020/02/27/examining-the-Black-white-wealth-gap/. Accessed May 31, 2021.

McPhee, Michelle. "Obama Called Cop Who Arrested Gates, Still Sees 'Overreaction' in Gates' Arrest." ABC News, July 24, 2009.

Meier, August, and Elliott Rudwick. "The Rise of Segregation in the Federal Bureaucracy, 1900–1930." *Phylon (1960–)* 28, no. 2 (1967): 178–184.

Mitra, Durba. "'Surplus Woman': Female Sexuality and the Concept of Endogamy." *The Journal of Asian Studies* 80, no. 1 (2021): 3–26.

Mukharji, Projit Bihari. "From Serosocial to Sanguinary Identities: Caste, Transnational Race Science and the Shifting Metonymies of Blood Group B, India c. 1918–1960." *Indian Economic and Social History Review* 51, no. 2 (June 2014): 143–176.

Mukherjee, Sujit. "Early American Images of India." *India Quarterly* 20, no. 1 (1964): 43–50.

Munshi, Sherally. "Immigration, Imperialism, and the Legacies of Indian Exclusion." *Yale Journal of Law and the Humanities* 28, no. 1 (2015): 51–104.

Naidis, Mark. "Propaganda of the Gadar Party." *Pacific Historical Review* 20, no. 3 (1951): 251–260.

National Indo-American Museum. "Indian Freedom Fighters in the United States." https://www.niam.org/galleries/the-right-to-liberty/across-the-nation/. Accessed May 1, 2021.

Oberwittler, Dietrich and Julia Kasselt. "Honor Killings." In *The Oxford Handbook of Gender, Sex, and Crime*, edited by Rosemary Gartner and Bill McCarthy, 652–670. New York: Oxford University Press, 2014.

Omvedt, Gail. "A Part That Parted." *Outlook India*, August 20, 2012. https://www.outlookindia.com/magazine/story/a-part-that-parted/281929. Accessed September 1, 2019.

Oxford Dictionary of National Biography. "Sir Herbert Hope Risley." Oxford: Oxford University Press, 2004.

Pandey, Gyanendra. "Can a Muslim Be an Indian?" *Comparative Studies in Society and History* 41, no. 4 (1999): 608–629.

———. "Racialization of Subaltern Populations across the Globe: The Politics of Difference." *The Review of Black Political Economy* 43, no. 2 (January 2016): 87–99.

Patel, Payal K. "On the Path of the Maharajah of Bwodpur: The Global Problem of the Color Line in W.E.B. Du Bois's Dark Princess." *CR: The New Centennial Review* 15, no. 2 (2015): 119–156.

Pathak, Sushmita, and Lauren Frayer. "Child Marriages Are Up in the Pandemic: Here's How India Tries to Stop Them." *National Public Radio*, November 5, 2020. https://www.npr.org/sections/goatsandsoda/2020/11/05/931274119/

child-marriages-are-up-in-the-pandemic-heres-how-india-tries-to-stop-them. Accessed March 1, 2022.

Perl, Jeffry M. and Andrew P. Tuck. "The Hidden Advantage of Tradition: On the Significance of T. S. Eliot's Indic Studies." *Philosophy East and West* 35, no. 2 (April 1985): 115–131.

Prashad, Vijay. "Black Gandhi." *Social Scientist* 37, no. 1/2 (2009): 3–20.

———. "The Wretchedness of Caste – Ambedkar, Fanon, and the Blocked Indian Revolution." *Leftword*. https://mayday.leftword.com/blog/post/the-wretchedness-of-caste-part-one. Accessed October 16, 2024.

Puri, Harish K. "Lajpat Rai in USA 1914–1919: Life and Work of a Political Exile." https://theprg.files.wordpress.com/2009/07/puri-lala-lajpat-rai.pdf. Accessed May 1, 2021.

Rabindra Smaraka Grantha. "Rabindranath in America – Cincinnati, Ohio & Detroit, Michigan." Rabindranath Tagore – A Search for Creativity of Rabindranath (Blog), March 3, 2012. http://sesquicentinnial.blogspot.com/2012/03/rabindranath-in-america-cincinnati-ohio.html. Accessed August 2021.

Radhakrishna, Meena. "The Criminal Tribes Act in the Madras Presidency Implications for Itinerant Trading Communities." *The Indian Economic and Social History Review* 26, no. 3 (1989): 269–295.

Rao, Parimala V. "Educating Women and non-Brahmins as 'Loss of Nationality': Bal Gangadhar Tilak and the Nationalist Agenda in Maharashtra." *NYU Faculty Digital Archives*, Centre for Women's Development Studies (2008). https://archive.nyu.edu/handle/2451/34236. Accessed June 27, 2021.

Raucher, Alan. "American Anti-Imperialists and the Pro-India Movement, 1900–1932." *Pacific Historical Review* 43, no. 1 (1974): 83–110.

Reddy, E. S. "Some Remarkable European Women Who Helped Gandhiji in South Africa." In *Gandhiji's Vision of a Free South Africa*, 1–61. New Delhi: Sachar Publishing House: 1995.

Reuter, William C. "The Anatomy of Political Anglophobia in the United States, 1865–1900." *Mid America* 61, no. 2 (1979): 117–132.

Risley, H. H. "The Study of Ethnology in India." *Journal of the Anthropological Institute of Great Britain and Ireland* 20 (1891): 235–263.

Rudolph, Lloyd I. "Gandhi in the Mind of America." *Economic and Political Weekly* 45, no. 47 (2010): 23–26.

Rudwick, Elliott M. "W.E.B. Du Bois and the Universal Races Congress of 1911." *The Phylon Quarterly* 20, no. 4 (1959): 372–378.

———. "W.E.B. Du Bois in the Role of Crisis Editor." *The Journal of Negro History* 43, no. 3 (1958): 214–240.

Sahoo, Sanghamitra. "A Prehistory of Indian Y Chromosomes: Evaluating Demic Diffusion Scenarios." *Proceedings of the National Academy of Sciences of the United States of America* 103, no. 4 (2006): 843–848.

Shachar C., T. Wise, G. Katznelson, and A. L. Campbell. "Criminal Justice or Public Health: A Comparison of the Representation of the Crack Cocaine and Opioid Epidemics in the Media." *Journal of Health Politics, Policy and Law* 45, no. 2 (2020): 211–239.

Sharma, Arvind. "Dr. B.R. Ambedkar on the Aryan Invasion and the Emergence of the Caste System in India." *Journal of the American Academy of Religion* 73, no.3 (2005): 843–870.

Sheth, D. L. "Reservations Policy Revisited." *Economic and Political Weekly* 22, no. 46 (1987): 1957–1962.

Sinha, Babli. "Dissensus, Education and Lala Lajpat Rai's Encounter with W.E.B. Du Bois." *South Asian History and Culture* 6, no. 4 (2015): 462–476.

Slate, Nico. "Translating Race and Caste." *Journal of Historical Sociology* 24, no. 1 (March 2011): 62–79.

Sohi, Seema. "Immigration Act of 1917 and the 'Barred Zone.'" In *Asian Americans: An Encyclopedia of Social, Cultural, Economic, and Political History [3 volumes]: An Encyclopedia of Social, Cultural, Economic, and Political History*, edited by Xiaojian Zhao and Edward J.W. Park, 534–535. Santa Barbara, CA: ABC-CLIO, 2013.

———. "Repressing the 'Hindu Menace': Race, Anarchy, and Indian Anticolonialism." In *The Sun Never Sets: South Asian Migrants in an Age of U.S. Power*, edited by Vivek Bald, Miabi Chatterji, Sujani Reddy, and Manu Vimalassery, 50–74. New York: New York University Press, 2013.

"Some Facts of Constituent Assembly." *Parliament of India*, National Informatics Centre, accessed September 18, 2020. https://web.archive.org/web/20110511104514/http://parliamentofindia.nic.in/ls/debates/facts.htm. Accessed September 18, 2020.

Teed, Paul E. "Race Against Memory: Katherine Mayo, Jabez Sunderland, and Indian Independence." *American Studies* 44, no. 1/2 (2003): 35–57.

The Library at University of Washington, Special Collections. "Taraknath Das." https://www.lib.washington.edu/specialcollections/collections/exhibits/southasianstudents/das. Accessed May 1, 2021.

Tikkanen, Amy. "*The Crisis* American Magazine." In *Encyclopedia Britannica*. https://www.britannica.com/topic/The-Crisis-American-magazine. Accessed September 27, 2019.

Tolen, Rachel J. "Colonizing and Transforming the Criminal Tribesman." In *Deviant Bodies: Critical Perspectives on Difference in Science and Popular*

Culture, edited by Jennifer Terry and Jacqueline Urla. Bloomington: Indiana University Press, 1995.

———. "Colonizing and Transforming the Criminal Tribesman: The Salvation Army in British India." *American Ethnologist* 18, no. 1 (1991): 106–125.

Underhill, Peter A. "The Phylogenetic and Geographic Structure of Y-chromosome Haplogroup R1a." *European Journal of Human Genetics* 23, no. 1 (2015): 124–131.

Upadhyay, Nishant. "Ghadar Movement: A Living Legacy." *Sikh Formations* 10, no. 1 (2014): 1–3.

Vargas, João H. Costa. "Genocide in the African Diaspora: United States, Brazil, and the Need for a Holistic Research and Political Method." *Cultural Dynamics* 17, no. 3 (November 2005): 267–290.

Vithayathil, Trina. "Counting Caste: Censuses, Politics, and Castelessness in India." *Politics and Society* 46, no. 4 (December 2018): 455–484.

Warner, W. Lloyd. "American Caste and Class." *American Journal of Sociology* 42, no. 2 (1936): 234–237.

West, Cornel, and Suraj Yengde. "A Shared History of Struggle Should Unite India's Dalits and African Americans in the Shared Struggle for Equality." *The Root* (June 12, 2017).

Witzel, Michael. "Indocentrism: Autochthonous Visions of Ancient India." In *The Indo-Aryan Controversy. Evidence and Inference in Indian History*, edited by Edwin Bryant and Laurie L. Patton, 341–404. London: Routledge, 2005.

Wolgemuth, Kathleen L. "Woodrow Wilson and Federal Segregation." *The Journal of Negro History* 44, no. 2 (1959): 158–173.

Wynne, Robert E. "American Labor Leaders and the Vancouver Anti-Oriental Riot." *Pacific Northwest Quarterly* 57, no. 4 (1966): 172–179.

Yengde, Suraj. "Castes of Mind: On the Intersection of Race and Caste." Review of *Caste: The Origins of our Discontents*, by Isabel Wilkerson. *The Baffler* no. 56, March 24, 2021.

———."Charge of Dalit Patriarchy Is Now Being Used to Put Down Any Assertion of Being Dalit." *Indian Express*, December 13, 2020. Accessed March 1, 2022.

Zarchin, Tomer. "Israeli Arabs More Likely to Be Convicted for Crimes Than Their Jewish Counterparts, Study Shows." *Haaretz*, August 2, 2011. https://www.haaretz.com/1.5039052. Accessed May 26, 2020.

Books and Papers Presented at Conferences

Mukherjee, Pritam. "William Wilson Hunter and Colonial Bengal Historiography Literature Modernity." PhD diss., Jadavpur University, 2015.

Sen, Dwaipayan. "Uncanny Juxtapositions: Conditions of Possibility for the Comparison of Race and Caste." Lecture, *Race and Racism in the Global South* from King's College London, June 1, 2021.

Zelliot, Eleanor. "Dr. Ambedkar and America." Paper presented at the Columbia University Ambedkar Centenary, 1991. http://www.columbia.edu/itc/mealac/pritchett/00ambedkar/timeline/graphics/txt_zelliot1991.html. Accessed September 30, 2020.

Index